NO-FAULT INSURANCE

NO-FAULT INSURANCE

by
WILLIS PARK ROKES
J.D., Ph.D., C.L.U., C.P.C.U.

Professor, College of Business Administration
Chairman, Department of Insurance
The University of Nebraska at Omaha

Member, Nebraska and Utah Bars

1971
INSURORS PRESS, INC.
Santa Monica, California

First Printing, November, 1971

Library of Congress Catalog No. 72-173308

Printed and bound in the United States of America

TO

GOTTLIEB DAIMLER
of Germany, who in 1886 patented his high-speed internal-combustion engine, creating the impetus for development of the highly destructive and polluting motor vehicle, a nevertheless eminently useful contrivance of 20th Century transportation.

PUBLICATIONS IN THE
INSURORS PRESS
INSURANCE MANAGEMENT AND EDUCATION SERIES

Adams	*Insurance Salesense*
Morrison & Bakst	*Insurance Agency Purchases and Mergers*
Nordhaus	*Insurance Agency Advertising and Public Relations*
Rokes	*No-Fault Insurance*
Webb	*Mass Merchandising of Automobile Insurance*

Publishers of the complete series of study guides for the Insurance Institute of America programs in IIA, CPCU, and ADJ.

Publishers of study manuals for numerous state licensing examinations.

INSURORS PRESS, INC.
1661 9th Street, Santa Monica, Calif. 90404

FOREWORD

The author's interest in automobile indemnification proposals dates back over two decades. Beginning as a multiple lines insurance claims adjuster, recently graduated from law school, he had occasion to handle thousands of automobile insurance claims over a period of some six years. In the process, he became intimately acquainted with the practical problems of ambiguity of establishing valuation on bodily injury liability claims and the difficulties of ascertaining the liability of the parties to automobile accidents which generate insurance claims.

In addition, the author handled automobile insurance matters both as defense and subrogation attorney for automobile insurance companies and also as attorney for personal injury claimants. The phantom quality of liability determination—the fixing of blame—always fascinated him.

Returning to graduate school in 1957, the author obtained a masters degree and the Ph.D. degree, the latter received in 1959 from Ohio State University with a major in insurance. His dissertation topic was selected from a subject matter relating to automobile insurance, AUTOMOBILE PHYSICAL DAMAGE INSURANCE AFFILIATES OF SALES FINANCE COMPANIES.

In 1961 the author spent a week in Regina, Saskatchewan, visiting the offices of the Saskatchewan Government Insurance Office and studying the Saskatchewan Automobile Accident Insurance Act, the only automobile compensation plan on the North American Continent at that time. The results of this study were presented at the annual meeting of the American Risk and Insurance Association in New York City in December of 1961 and were subsequently published in the September 1962 issue of the *Journal of Risk and Insurance.*

Much of the material contained herein was prepared for discussion purposes in connection with a CPCU clinic held at York, Nebraska, on May 15, 1968. The material presented in this book is taken from a wide variety of literature on the subject of automobile indemnification proposals and represents, as much as possible, a balance in the diversity of opinion on this vital and controversial topic. Many of the opinions expressed were taken from the literature listed in the extensive bibliography cited at the conclusion of the material.

A comprehensive survey of the literature of automobile insurance reform indicates that there has been heavy insurance industry reaction to the Keeton and O'Connell proposal which was introduced several years ago. For that reason, and because alternative proposals have been recommended from the insurance industry itself, it is natural to expect a heavy weighting of trade press and insurance publication response to the concept of automobile insurance reform. Nonetheless, the bibliography is representative of the great body of commentary emanating from the nation's presses on automobile indemnification proposals. Many of the entries are shallow commentaries from trade news magazines. However, it is from such source materials that some of the most imaginative and innovative automobile insurance reform proposals have been best reported. Further, constructive discussion and criticism have been reported in this material.

The automobile insurance reform problem was discussed in May of 1968 in the author's monograph entitled AUTOMOBILE INDEMNIFICATION PROPOSALS—A COMPENDIUM, compiling a large number of the various plans that had been submitted by a variety of sources. The material was reprinted and updated in November of 1968 to accommodate the heavy damand for the original printing and to reflect the addition of newer materials relating to automobile indemnification proposals.

Since the compendium was printed, increased national attention has been devoted to the subject of "no-fault" plans on the federal level and in the state legislatures. The author himself participated in some of the deliberations which culminated in the Illinois proposal. The President of the United States has called upon the states to remedy the national automobile insurance problem before it becomes incumbent upon the federal government to do so.

In the months and years to come, thousands of state and federal legislators will be called upon to judge the merits of a variety of automobile indemnification reform proposals. Attorneys, insurance companies, agents and many others will require an understanding of the myriad of complexities surrounding the automobile insurance problem.

It is to serve the needs of these people that the book was written, not to furnish an intensive study of individual proposals, but to present an extensive overview of automobile insurance reform. The author believed this could best be accomplished by presenting an explanation of the issues of the controversy, a history and explanation of the "no-fault" concept, brief expositions of the proposals, and arguments for and against change to "no-fault". No-fault legislation already passed in some states is contained in the appendix as an aid for other states' legislators and for federal legislators. An easily-read reference book on what has become a rather complex and cluttered subject is the objective of the author.

Thus, the present material is an attempt to present a helpful reference guide to the many plans which have been introduced on the critical matter of automobile indemnification over the past four decades, and the author acknowledges a debt of gratitude to the many individuals who have contributed to the literature on the subject. The vast majority of the views expressed herein are those of other people. The author, however, has in many cases assumed the role of "devil's advocate" in attempting to afford balance in presenting arguments for and against change to a no-fault system. In addition, he has drawn materials from literature authored by him. Further, in his editing of materials and in his selection and organization of controversial matter, there is obviously reflected his value judgments and bias of what is or is not significant.

Any errors contained herein are the sole responsibility of the author, and, anticipating the existence of some, he attributes them to the exigencies of deadlines met to assure production of a timely book on a rapidly-developing subject.

The author expresses gratitude for the research grant from the Senate Research Committee of the University of Nebraska at Omaha which financed the manuscript preparation and related expenses. He is grateful to Dean William T. Utley of the University of Nebraska at Omaha College of Continuing Studies under whose auspices the original monograph was prepared and who encouraged the present publication.

Special appreciation is expressed to Mrs. Karen Rozgall Hanna and Miss Carol Mayhan for their assistance in preparing the manuscript.

Willis Park Rokes
Omaha, Nebraska
October, 1971

TABLE OF CONTENTS

PART I
INTRODUCTION

CHAPTER I

NO-FAULT

In the year 1970 an estimated 109 million motor vehicles traveled the streets and highways of the United States. According to the Secretary of the Department of Transportation, "The population growth rate is about 6,000 persons daily while motor vehicles are increasing at a rate of nearly 12,000 per day." The number of vehicles in the U.S. will increase by another 30 million in the next decade.

Watching the endless stream of cars and trucks whizzing by on a busy freeway—or, more typically, lurching and stopping—it almost seems as if Aldous Huxley's *Brave New World* has arrived, as if all anyone really is doing is consuming transport without purpose or destination.

In the process of all of this vehicular movement, people are getting killed and injured at a monumental rate. The carnage on the nation's highways and the staggering economic loss to the nation mount as we depend on this highly personal, individualized mode of transportation—the motor vehicle. U.S. traffic accidents in 1969 killed 56,000 people and injured 4,600,000 others. In addition to the human suffering, the economic loss amounted to $16.5 billion in the form of medical costs, lost income, and property damage. How to compensate victims of this unprecedented man-made destruction is one of the greatest dilemmas confronting a civilized people. We have traditionally relied upon the fault system and have administered automobile accident reparations through the insurance industry.

EMERGENCE OF THE FAULT SYSTEM

In the earlier days of the automobile, the assignation of the responsibility for motor vehicle damage seemed simple. If your motor car upset the neighbor's horse, driving his carriage into a ditch, or if you inadvertently ran into his buggy, your culpability seemed clear enough. Because of your negligent conduct, you were expected to make restitution for the damages you caused.

The negligence concept had received public acceptance in the United States in the 19th century when the doctrine of strict liability made way for the more conservative concept of negligence—liability

1

for fault or antisocial conduct. Adopted to meet the realities of a
rapidly expanding industrial economy and at the same time to satisfy
a basic moral belief in individual accountability, the fault system
stressed "the injustice of visiting burdensome liability upon an individual who has done no wrong—whose conduct was neither morally
blameworthy nor anti-social." (See Fleming James, Bibliography entry No. 132).

Automobile Insurance

Because of the individual accountability and the duty of care
imposed on motor vehicle operators by society, motorists faced the
peril of liability claims—or what is called *third-party claims* (claims
made by victims).

A special liability insurance coverage was made available to a
motorist so that third-party claim payments could be made on behalf
of the motorist-policyholder, in the event that through his fault he
caused injury to the third party.

Further, the insurance industry supplemented the third-party liability system with contractual coverage for the motorist (insured) himself. This provided the motorist-insured (*first-party*) a variety of coverage to cover his (the motorist-insured-first-party) losses. His insurance company (*second-party*) reimbursed the insured for medical and
funeral expenses and damages to his automobile. All the insured needed to do was to prove that he suffered personal injury or damage to
his automobile in order to collect under his *first-party coverage.*

The *third-party system*, or legal liability system under which
fault must be established, has been the backbone of the automobile
accident reparations system in the United States. In order to recover
large amounts for bodily injuries, disability, or death, fault typically
must be established and recovery made against a negligent motorist.
This is so, because *first-party* automobile coverage typically is paid
only for medical and funeral expenses, and then only to a maximum
of $5,000 (under medical payments coverage). Death and disability
benefits for a first-party usually had to be obtained from insurance
other than automobile coverage.

Likewise, the third-party's source of recovery for *any* reimbursement depended upon other insurance coverages, if he failed to establish a liability claim. Failure to obtain such other coverages frequently left both the first party and the third party ill-compensated for
automobile accident personal injury losses.

Assault on the Fault System

As more and more motor vehicles clogged the nation's highways, traveling at higher and higher speeds, accident frequency and severity have increased over the decades. More and more of the third-party claims have been presented to insurance companies for payment. In every case, the issue of liability must be resolved, by informal settlement if the fault is clear, by possible compromise if fault is in dispute, or by resolution by the courts if the issues cannot be resolved in pretrial disposition.

The rationale of committing to the tort liability system the function of compensating automobile accident victims has been under attack for some years now. But the glare of public scrutiny and an inquiry into the logic of using the fault system as the basis for automobile accident reparations has come under increasing attack and is the subject of intense controversy today.

The controversy rages, and the reformation, the partial modification, or the complete abandonment of the tort liability system in compensating the motor vehicle victim awaits the judgment of the American public.

Basic to partial or complete abandonment of the traditional fault system is the selection of a substitute method of compensating accident victims. The suggested substitute is the "no-fault" system.

WHAT IS "NO-FAULT"?

The fundamental basis for a no-fault system is the abolishment of tort liability in automobile accidents, with each driver or owner accepting responsibility for some or all losses sustained by pedestrians and by occupants of his own vehicle in return for which he would enjoy immunity from liability for those losses. Basic to partial or complete abandonment of the traditional fault system is the selection of a substitute method of compensating accident victims—handling the social problem. Consequently, embodied in the "no-fault" concept is the requirement for a means to make such reimbursement. It is here that the so-called "no-fault" automobile insurance system enters the picture.

Under a no-fault system, first-party insurance coverage would take care of all those cases now reimbursed under the fault system. This coverage would include such insurance as medical payments, accidental death, disability income, and property damage coverages paid to the automobile accident victim as a contractual obligation of an insurance company or as a mandatory payment imposed by statute.

From the standpoint of the insured, a no-fault system would protect the insured from being sued for his negligent operation of an automobile, but only to the extent that the no-fault principle was adopted in a given state. The typical no-fault proposals apply only to bodily injury liability and then only up to a certain amount. (For example, the Puerto Rico law provides that the injured victim may sue for claims over $1,000). Unless the no-fault concept is carried all the way, there would still be the residual tort liability for negligent operation of a motor vehicle resulting in property damage or for a claimant's medical expenses exceeding a certain dollar amount and for catastrophic personal injuries or death.

Of interest is the application of no-fault to the right of guest passengers to collect for damages. Whereas under the present liability insurance system, gross negligence by the driver of the motor vehicle must be proved before guest passengers are able to recover, proponents argue that the no-fault system provides them with immediate compensation for personal injury damages.

Actually, the medical payments coverage now available under the tort liability system provides guest passengers with immediate payment for medical expenses. Adoption of the no-fault concept would merely be an extension of medical payments coverage for the guest passenger with one important stipulation—the right to bring a liability claim would be forfeited. Medical payments, like other first-party coverage—life, accident and health, home-owners, and other types of insurance, provides coverage without having to go through the tort liability system.

Pseudo "No-Fault" Proposals

There have been a considerable number of proposals advanced by insurance companies and others which have been erroneously labeled as "no-fault" proposals. These plans, capitalizing upon the "no-fault" controversy, purport to provide features inherent in a true no-fault plan. The latter would substitute automobile insurance compensation in the place of the tort liability system. The pseudo "no-fault" proposals merely provide an extension of the medical payments, disability, accidental death, uninsured motorists, and/or property damage coverage without altering the basic tort liability system.

Requisites of No-Fault

Although it appears reasonable to say that first-party coverage is paid "regardless of fault" and is, therefore, no-fault insurance, considerable confusion is generated when the "no-fault" label is applied to the simple extension of first-party benefits without an alteration of tort liability rights. Merely offering more medical payments coverage and adding disability and accidental death coverage under an insured's policy is not "no-fault" coverage. It is a modification of a two-party contract and in no sense alters legal relationships to a no-fault system. The right to recover for negligence under the tort liability system remains unchanged, irrespective of expanded two-party (insured and insurer) coverage.

If, however, two party insurance coverage is expanded concurrently with the reduction of rights under the tort liability system, the element of "no-fault" coverage enters in. Thus, if the insured receives increased medical payments, disability, property damage, and accidental death coverage as a *mandatory substitute* for the liability chose in action (legal right of action) which he would otherwise have under the tort liability system, there is a definite "no-fault" program created.

Mis-labelling as "no-fault" coverage the mere extension of first-party contractual coverage, without a simultaneous alteration of rights under tort liability, compounds the confusion inherent in understanding the "no-fault" controversy and renders a disservice to public understanding.

Basic requirements of a true "no-fault" plan are:

1)   Alteration or complete elimination of the tort liability system in the handling of automobile accident reparations.

2)   Whole or partial substitution of a compensation system in the place of tort liability to handle automobile accident reparations.

3)   A system, probably made compulsory by legislation, assuring that there would be universal application of the substitute system.

A pure "no-fault" system would completely eliminate tort liability (negligence) claims arising out of automobile accidents. It would apply to both bodily injury and property damage claims. Most "no-fault" plans thus far proposed apply only to bodily injury claims, leaving property damage claims to be handled under the conventional tort liability system. In addition, most plans provide only partial substitution of first-party compensation for tort liability rights of action.

Examples of Pseudo No-Fault Plans

Typical of the pseudo no-fault plans is one offered by the Preferred Risk Mutual Insurance Company of Des Moines, Iowa, which beginning July 1, 1969, provided a "new kind of automobile insurance" that pays for accident injuries "regardless of who is at fault." The proposal was approved by the Iowa Insurance Commissioner.

The so-called "no-fault" plan offered by Preferred Risk Mutual Insurance Company provided basic $10,000 personal injury coverage which would pay out-of-pocket costs—medical bills and loss of income—for injuries sustained in an accident. The insurance company and the injured persons would still be able to sue for damages if the other driver in the accident was at fault. (See Bibliography entry

No. 224). Since no alteration of the tort liability system is incorporated into the plan, it is not a "no-fault" system.

Other proposals in the same category are the Miley Plan (See Miley, No. 309), the Cooperators Plan (offered by Cooperators Insurance Association, a Canadian insurer writing in Ontario), and a number of other similar proposals. The Cooperators Plan, called the "extended medical payment and accidental death and impairment policy," resembles a restricted travel-accident policy. (See Dammann, No. 97). Most of the Canadian plans merely extend first-party coverage to provide for expanded medical payments coverage, disability income and accidental death benefits. They in no way affect an individual's right to sue under the traditional tort liability system. However, under the Canadian plans, a tort liability recovery would be reduced by the amount paid as accident benefits.

Typifying the confusion created when expansion of first-party coverage is mis-labelled "no-fault coverage" is an article which appeared in *U.S. News & World Report* ("Drive for Cheaper Auto Insurance," July 26, 1971, p. 22). In the article, the magazine outlines features of various "no-fault" plans in a number of states, including Oregon and South Dakota. The writer of the article details in cursory fashion the provisions of the legislation passed by the two states. Inclusion of Oregon and South Dakota confuses even the reader who is aware of the distinction between a true no-fault system and a pseudo no-fault system. The author of this book was skeptical that the two states had passed no-fault laws, and upon examination of the recently-enacted legislation of both states, he soon ascertained that the magazine article was helping to perpetuate the confusion surrounding the "no-fault" label. Neither state had a no-fault law as of August, 1971.

Oregon in June of 1971 passed legislation hailed as "no-fault", providing for mandatory extension of first-party coverage. It limited rights of insurers to cancel automobile property and casualty insurance policies. In addition, it provided for contribution between joint tortfeasors in negligence actions in proportion to the negligence attributable to each and provided for joinder of actions and parties in the same court proceeding. It also set up legal rules for the use of advance payments techniques (described in a subsequent chapter in this book). Further, the recently enacted bundle of legislative bills in the state included one which changed Oregon from the "contributory negligence" doctrine to that of "comparative negligence." The legislation did not substitute first-party compensation benefits in the place of tort liability rights to recover for negligence.

South Dakota, similarly, did nothing to alter the basic system of "liability for fault." The South Dakota statute specified that policies could not be offered to the public unless certain "supplemental coverages" are offered to the insured. The insured was given the right to reject the coverages. The supplemental coverages included accidental death coverage of at least $10,000, disability income benefits, and at least $2,000 medical payments insurance "to the named insured and to any other insured." Both Oregon and South Dakota afford excellent examples of pseudo no-fault approaches to the automobile reparations problem.

Other pseudo "no-fault" proposals offer expanded or "extended protection" against the uninsured motorist. These proposals, offering strictly first-party coverage, do nothing to modify the tort liability system. An example of the expanded uninsured motorist coverage proposal was that afforded by the American Family Mutual of Madison, Wisconsin, which offered higher limits on uninsured motorist coverage under "The American Family Plan." (See Dammann, No. 97).

Since under a true "no-fault" scheme the machinery for recovery would be eliminated if the tort liability system were abolished in whole or in part, a substitute reparations system would be needed. That substitute system would be a two-party compensation program wherein automobile accident victims would recover, regardless of fault, from an insurer. The insurer would be either an insurance company or the government.

STATE V. FEDERAL PLAN?

A great concern has been expressed over the exact form that the no-fault automobile insurance plan would take in regard to the governmental unit which would be responsible for the administration of the plan. For example, the proposal is made that a federally regulated plan is imperative in order to provide for the uniformity and the simultaneous requirement throughout all 50 states of a no-fault plan. Advocates of the federal plan argue convincingly that if it is left up to the individual states to decide when and whether to pass no-fault legislation, the nation will experience the same situation as it did in the case of workmen's compensation, where it took some 50 years for all of the states to enact laws. The conflict-of-laws difficulties and the wide variations in coverage provided under the several state workmen's compensation statutes have produced considerable problems in the administration of the workmen's compensation schemes. Workmen's compensation, moreover, lends itself more to a local solution than would the automobile insurance situation, because motor vehicles are so mobile that they are constantly in states other than their own state of registration.

The argument for a standard, uniform, simultaneously effective plan is compelling. It would go into effect in all of the states at the same time, providing for a strong, centralized program which would bring the otherwise weak individual state plans up to a common level.

Criticism of State Approach

It is recognized that a serious drawback to the state approach to automobile insurance reform is the distinct probability that there would be a pattern of diversified legislation which would be inefficient and expensive to operate. Robert N. Gilmore, Jr., general counsel for the American Insurance Association, has observed, however, that "we do not believe that it should be assumed that we will have a hopelessly disjointed pattern of state laws, as this did not occur when state financial responsibility laws were enacted. While differing in some important respects, they are compatible and in fact conspicuous for their high degree of uniformity." (See Jennings, No. 506).

It is charged by some no-fault advocates that leaving the decision of legislation up to the state governments is tantamount to saying that the American public should be denied the full potential benefit of the no-fault concept. Federal advocates argue forcefully that no-fault must be legislated on a national rather than a state-by-state basis for several reasons. They point out that many state legislatures include members who are more responsive to the interests of negligence lawyers and insurance companies than they are to the interest of consumers. By contrast, Congress, according to these critics, is more independent of special interests and has demonstrated more meaningful and concentrated concern for the problems of the consumer. The advocates are concerned that if, despite the formidable lobbying power of the special interests, a state in fact enacts a no-fault law, it will probably be a weak and limited thing. They point to the Massachusetts law as an example.

Critics of the state approach also point to the record of the 1971 state legislative sessions in which an amazing number of different automobile insurance bills (all called "no-fault") were considered by a large number of state legislatures. They also argue that there is enormous profit potential for companies in no-fault automobile insurance, and that the Federal government has a greater capacity than the state governments to protect the consumer against special interests, so that reasonable, rather than excessive, profits are earned by insurance companies. (See Robert H. Joost, a Massachusetts attorney, formerly Assistant to the Legislative Chairman of the American Trial Lawyers Association, entry No. 508).

Opponents of Federal Administration

There are compelling arguments for preservation of a state approach to the automobile insurance reform problem. Opponents of federal administration fear the "undue concentration of power in Washington." The National Association of Insurance Commissioners particularly is concerned with the spectre of federal regulation destroying the historic state regulation pattern. Spokesmen argue that "an important guardian of the public interest is the dispersion of power between state and Federal government, so each can discipline the other and compete in the public interest. Undisciplined power tends to become unresponsive at best and corrupt at worst, and one of the most effective ways of disciplining power is the split of power in the Federal system." (Commissioner Herbert Denenberg, State of Pennsylvania).

There is a further argument that a variety of plans can reflect the variety of conditions and public attitudes in the various parts of the country. Further, a variety of plans will permit experimentation, and will at least give a chance for reform more fundamental than would be included in any national program. There are persuasive arguments that the use of several states as laboratories to test some of the reasonable reform concepts would have considerable value.

The proponents of federal regulation and uniform federal legislation discount the alleged differences existing in the several states. They cite a report of the Federal Judicial Center to the Department of Transportation, which stated:

"In summary, the factors influencing automobile accident litigation—population, vehicle ownership, accident rates, ratio of suits filed to injuries and damage, the resources allocated to processing cases once they have entered the system, and the manner in which urbanization affects the legal process—these factors are simple, straightforward, relatively uniform across the United States . . . commonly held views about factors influencing accident litigation have been tested, and the majority have been rejected as false." (See Bibliography entry No. 118).

Nevertheless, advocates of the state approach maintain that if states retain the power to change the auto accident compensation system in the future, the possibilities for further reform are greatly enhanced. In their view, there will be two ways to change the system, by state action or Federal action. The possibility of Federal intervention will be a goad to reform by the states and will still be available if state activity fails. However, according to the state approach advocates, once a national system is adopted, the chances for further reform are severely limited.

State advocates inquire: "Is there a way to reconcile the need for prompt reform with the undesirability of a uniform national system?" United States Secretary of Transportation, John A. Volpe, has suggested that Congress might establish "broad outlines at the Federal level" and provide incentives or penalties to encourage state action in line with the guidelines. There is considerable precedent for using this approach to obtain "voluntary" action on the part of the states.

States have cooperated remarkably in adopting uniform legislation in some areas of activity (*i.e.*, uniform acts on commercial transactions), but the states have stoutly resisted many other types of uniform legislation. An example of the latter is unemployment compensation, where the Federal government obtained universal compliance by withholding millions of dollars in the new unemployment compensation taxes from the states until they complied with federal standards. Likewise, the financial incentive is used by the federal government to effect compliance by the states in highway building, highway safety, removal of billboards along federal-aid highways, hospital construction, and in other areas. The same "Federal carrot" can be offered or withheld in obtaining uniform acceptance of a change in the automobile reparations system.

Economics in Federal Approach — Group Automobile

Advocates of the federal approach point to the considerable economies which, in their opinion, could be realized if federal legislation also make it possible to market automobile insurance under the group approach. Group life and health insurance, for example, has produced considerable economies for the American public over the cost of individual policies. A conservative estimate is that group purchasing of automobile insurance would bring premium costs down by at least 15 percent.

Federal mandates could eliminate the present obstacles to group merchandising which have been thrown up by special interests in the states. There are now some three dozen states which prohibit the sale of automobile insurance under the group approach. Such laws were enacted and continue to be on the books because of the pressures brought by insurance agents throughout the United States. They fear, and understandably so, the loss of income which would result if the group approach were adopted in the United States.

Agents are also concerned with the underwriting problems of including bad risks along with the good risks in the group. They would prefer to insure only the better drivers. However, the group approach in automobile insurance would be no different than in marketing group coverage in life and health insurance. There, too, bad risks, average risks, and good risks are all insured together with the result that the average risk in the group is indeed average.

Opponents of the group approach in automobile insurance argue, however, that the safeguards against adverse selection inherent in marketing group life and health insurance are not available in the case of group automobile insurance. For example, it is easy to weed out the impaired lives in group life and health insurance by requiring that participants under the group plan be full-time workers who have been employed for a certain period of time before they are eligible for coverage. This rules out many of the unhealthy, substandard risks. The question in marketing group automobile insurance is how to guard against adverse selection by ruling out the bad drivers from coverage.

Nevertheless, there are strong arguments for the enactment of federal legislation to overrule the restrictive statutes which exist in the three dozen states which deprive the American public from obtaining the economies of group marketing of automobile insurance. A proponent of the group approach, Senator Philip A. Hart, on February 24, 1971, introduced S. 946, the "Motor Vehicle Group Insurance Act" providing that "no state shall prohibit, inhibit, restrict, or condition, by means of fictitious group statutes or regulations, agency licensing requirements, application or prohibitions of unfair discrimination, eligibility; or penalize or deny authority to an insurer because of its engagement or intention to engage in the marketing and issuance of group insurance." (For an interesting discussion of the group automobile approach, see Chastain, Nos. 476 & 477; Webb, No. 555).

An interesting corollary of the group automobile insurance concept is the fact that not only would its implementation allegedly bring about savings to individual insureds, but it would open the way for labor groups to bargain for group automobile insurance contributions as a fringe benefit, which would directly lower consumer costs for this insurance further. To make such a proposal palatable to employers, Senator Philip A. Hart introduced S. 947 into the United States Senate on February 24, 1971, to provide that contributions by an employer to a group automobile insurance plan would be deductible as a business expense.

The bill provides: "gross income does not include contributions by an employer to or under motor vehicle insurance plans which provide motor vehicle insurance coverage for his employees." Senator

Hart, by virtue of S. 948, a bill introduced the same date to amend the Labor Management Relations Act of 1947, would provide for collective bargaining in the case of "automobile, fire, homeowners multiple peril, or other insurance benefits, or legal services, or recreation benefits, or defraying the cost of counseling or other community service programs." (See Bibliography entry No. 449).

Conclusions

Since the compelling reason advanced for proposed change to a "no-fault" system is the alleged inadequacy of the present tort liability system for reimbursing the injured victims in automobile accidents, there necessarily must be some substitute method for reimbursement of those victims. Consequently, an abandonment of the tort liability system carries the concomitant responsibility to substitute a new method of reimbursement. The substitute would be a mandatory basic insurance coverage which would provide partial or total reimbursement of all special and general damages sustained by the automobile accident victim, depending upon the extent to which state and/or federal lawmakers would be willing to provide for such substitute compensation.

The "no-fault" concept entails a rather dramatic change from what historically has been the method for providing compensation for victims of automobile accidents. The enormity of that "revolutionary" change can best be judged by examining the tort liability system which would be replaced by the "no-fault" system.

CHAPTER II

THE "FAULT PRINCIPLE"—NEGLIGENCE

From the controversy which has raged around the "no-fault" proposals has come the widespread notion that "negligence," or the idea that man should be responsible for his failure to exercise reasonable care, has legal roots stretching back into antiquity. This notion has been the basis for the moral indignation which is expressed by opponents of change to no-fault in a repetitious reiteration that the Divinity has from time immemorial dictated that man should be responsible for his transgressions, particularly in the handling of motor vehicles.

The notion that negligence has such deep roots is in error. Legal scholars are well agreed that "negligence" constitutes a relatively recent development in Anglo-American law. Superseding a strict liability regime, the ascendancy of the negligence principle can be traced to the Industrial Revolution. Its rationale was that the needs of society demanded that the growth of industry and the expansion of commerce should not be impeded by the onerous financial liabilities inherent in a strict liability regime. As Professor Fleming James states:

> "While the basing of liability on fault is no new thing, the concept of negligence as an independent ground of liability is quite modern, and it succeeded a period in which liability for accidental harm was dominated by the trespass or strict liability principle. This was a development largely of the 19th century; it coincided with the transportation and industrial revolution and with the climate of opinion that has been called social Darwinism with its individualism and its acceptance of laissez faire. During this period the notion that liability should be based on fault did indeed become dominant." (See Bibliography, entry No. 132).

The great emphasis upon laissez faire and the materialistic flavor of the latter part of the 19th century and the first half of the 20th century in the United States dictated the judicial philosophy that the concept of strict liability would have to give way in order to promote the socially useful activities generated by the American Industrial Revolution. Fault became a morally flavored compromise between earlier strict liability concepts and the total abnegation of responsibility for

harm flowing from socially desirable activities. It was felt that liability should be predicated upon fault, and it was better for the victim of an accident not provably the "fault" of some other individual
to bear the financial consequences of his injury than to deter others
from engaging in socially useful activities because of the risk of having to bear the costs of accidents that might occur.

The "Reasonable Man" Standard

The concept of "fault" embodied in negligence carries no con-
notation of intent or evil motivation. It concerns itself solely with a
breach of legal duty which the law imposes upon every individual to
act as a "reasonable man" would act. Negligence is a consequence of
failing to act in a reasonable manner or the omission to act when there
is a duty to act in a reasonable manner under the circumstances. Negligence is concerned solely with a breach of legal duty resulting from
a failure to exercise that care which "a reasonable man of ordinary pru-
dence in like circumstances" would exercise.

The "reasonable man" standard is a fiction—he is an abstract ideal.
Embodying the normal standard of community behavior, there is, unfortunately, no latitude within the interpretation of the standard for
that "reasonable man" to be guilty of any error or lapses in his conduct. Unlike the ordinary individual who might occasionally do un-
reasonable things, the "reasonable man" is a "prudent and careful man
who is always up to the standard." (William Prosser, *Torts*, 3d ed.,
1964, p. 154).

Under the strict liability principle, the focus of concern was the
activity giving rise to the injury or damage; under the negligence principle, the focus shifted to the conduct of the actor and whether or not
his conduct deviated from the standard of the ordinary, prudent and
reasonable man. In noting that the mood of the times called for a scrutiny of the actor's conduct rather than the consideration of the victim's plight, Professor James has written: "In the climate of opinion
prevailing in the 19th century, it is not at all surprising that the fault
concept. . . emerged as dominant." (See Bibliography entry No. 132).

The same era which gave birth to the philosophy that social progress should not be stifled by fastening the costs of injuries and losses
upon useful activities also gave birth to the automobile, and the same
deference to progress militated against holding the vehicle's owner or
operator strictly accountable for any and all injury or damage which
it might cause. In general, the contention that the automobile was inherently dangerous, and therefore that principles of strict liability
should apply, was rejected.

Elements of Negligence

The tort of negligence requires as a precondition to the fixing of responsibility onto the wrongdoer, the following elements:

1.   A standard of care—the "ordinary, prudent and reasonable man" standard established by community moral values.

2.   A failure to meet that standard, through an act or omission.

3.   Damages (injuries and/or property damage) proximately caused by the failure or breach of the standard.

Thus the tort system requires that the injured party affirmatively establish that the alleged wrongdoer was negligent as a condition precedent to the recovery of money damages. As a consequence, negligence claims under automobile liability insurance resolve themselves into adversary relationships and proceedings which are characterized by "arms length" negotiating and the other features of the adversary forum. The factual and legal hurdles that the accident victim must surmount if he is to achieve economic recovery generate adversary proceedings which alone can resolve the disputed issues if the parties are unable or unwilling to resolve them by agreement. If the injured accident victim fails to prove that the alleged wrongdoer was negligent or that such negligence was the proximate cause of the accident, or fails to prove any other essential element of his case, he cannot shift his loss to the wrongdoer.

Doctrine of Contributory Negligence

The doctrine of contributory negligence has been an inherent part of the functioning of the negligence system in most of the states. It has also produced an even more severe application of negligence law to motor vehicle accident situations. Under the doctrine, a plaintiff in a negligence action is not entitled to recover if his own negligence contributes in even the slightest degree to the proximate cause of the accident.

The rationale for the application of the doctrine of contributory negligence again traditionally rested upon the societal consideration that the public interest stood to benefit from the workings of an industrial economy, and as a general proposition it would not be right to hamper the development of that industrial economy by burdening itself with compensating individuals who were in some way authors of their own misfortune. The courts have applied the doctrine of contributory negligence upon the rationale that the law will not settle disputes between wrongdoers and that it has no scales with which to measure the relative fault of the negligent parties.

The consequences of the application of the doctrine have been severe. An injured party, even if hypothetically only 1 percent at fault for an accident resulting in his injuries, could not recover from the other party who hypothetically was 99 percent at fault for the accident. The harshness of the application of the doctrine is patently clear; however, its application is also eminently practical from the standpoint of the insurance claim adjuster, the attorney, the judge, or the juries who are called upon to apportion fault into relative percentages in those jurisdictions which apply the comparative negligence doctrine.

Comparative Negligence Doctrine

The comparative negligence doctrine was adopted as an attempt to soften the harsh results of the application of the contributory negligence doctrine. Under the comparative negligence rule, the plaintiff may recover so long as his negligence was less than that of the other party, with his recovery being diminished proportionate to his negligence. The practical difficulty in applying the comparative negligence doctrine is the obvious lack of scales with which to measure the relative fault of the negligent parties. For example, if two vehicles collide in an open intersection, and Driver "A" is traveling too fast for existing conditions, while Driver "B" failed to keep a proper lookout, how does one go about deciding the relative percentile fault to be assigned to each driver? Claim adjusters, attorneys, judges, and juries have not been able to come up with a scientific method for apportioning fault in these situations, and, as a consequence, the apportionment of fault in comparative negligence cases is usually wildly erratic and arbitrary.

Trend Away from the Negligence Concept

The development of negligence law reached its crest in the early years of the present century. Since then there has been a decided shift back toward strict liability through statutory change and judicial decision. Case law favoring strict liability has become increasingly vigorous since the Second World War. A 1681 English case expresses the philosophy of strict liability: "In all civil acts the law doth not so much regard the intent of the actor, as the loss and damage of the party suffering. . ." (Lambert v. Bessey, 83 Eng. Rep. 220, K.B. 1681).

This concern for the victim, innocent or not, under strict liability is contrasted to the law of negligence, on the other hand, which stresses the importance of *not* putting burdensome liability upon dangerous but useful activity. The negative objective of negligence law was well suited "to serve the interest of an expanding industry and the rising middle class, by relieving them from the hampering burden of strict liability and by conducting to that 'freedom of the individual will' which was at the forefront of all contemporary aspiration." (L. Green, *Traffic Victims—Tort Law and Insurance*, chs. 1-3, 1958).

The strong influence of the Puritan ethic stressed individual responsibility and accountability for one's own actions. The harshness of Calvinistic doctrine dictated that man would be punished for his transgressions—negligence law was completely consistent with contemporary moral values. The fault system stressed the injustice of visiting burdensome liability upon an individual who had done no wrong—whose conduct was neither morally blameworthy or antisocial.

Strict liability in the U.S. system of jurisprudence never disappeared entirely from the scene, and with the provision for certain human needs under various systems of social insurance, increased emphasis was placed upon the concept of strict liability. In addition, procedural devices which shift the burden of proof to the plaintiff to prove absence of fault have made it easier for plaintiffs to show negligence. An example is afforded by the *doctrine of res ipsa loquitur* where a presumption of negligence arises when certain conditions are present. The erosion of governmental and charitable immunity, the dramatic reversal of restrictive rules for products liability, and case and statutory adoption of strict liability in many instances has revealed the marked shift of public attitudes toward the concept of negligence law.

Conclusions

The evidence is compelling that social attitudes in the United States are focusing more upon the loss of the injured than upon his moral shortcomings. The implications toward the survival of the tort liability system for the operation of motor vehicles is clear. Strong pressures are at work to adopt the "no-fault" principle in the handling of damages sustained by victims in automobile accidents, irrespective of fault. (For an excellent discussion, see Fleming James, Bibliography entry No. 132).

CHAPTER III

HISTORY OF THE NO-FAULT CONCEPT
IN AUTOMOBILE INSURANCE

The history of the "no-fault" concept in automobile accident insurance dates from the philosophy which prompted the passage of the workmen's compensation statutes in the United States, and the early recommendations for the adoption of an automobile compensation plan extend back over 50 years. In 1919 Rollins and Carman, in two unrelated articles, suggested that the workmen's compensation no-fault principle be adapted to the problem of automobile accident compensation. A more detailed proposal was advanced by Judge Robert Marx of Cincinnati during the 1920's.

Columbia University Committee Study

An automobile compensation system was advocated in the *Report by the Committee to Study Compensation for Automobile Accidents* at Columbia University in 1932. Nothing much came of the proposal until 1946 when the Cooperative Commonwealth Federation, a socialistic political party made up of farm and labor leaders in Saskatchewan, adopted what became for many years the only example of an automobile accident compensation scheme in North America. (See Rokes, Bibliography entry No. 413).

The issue was revitalized in the early 1950's by Professor Albert E. Ehrenzweig through his "Full Aid" Insurance Plan, and also by Professor Leon Green's proposal and Professor Fleming James' legal writings.

The Keeton–O'Connell Plan

Although the Saskatchewan Plan and other proposals were widely studied, there was little concern that any of the states in the United States would adopt the no-fault or compensation system until Keeton and O'Connell unveiled their "Basic Protection" Plan several years ago. Although there was nothing strikingly novel about the Keeton & O'Connell proposal, several factors have been responsible for focusing public attention on the "Basic Protection" Plan and have given impetus to the movement to adopt an automobile compensation system:

1. Keeton & O'Connell are highly literate and articulate salesmen for their proposal, writing books and articles and stumping the

nation in speaking engagements;

 2. They offer their plan in an easily-read format for popular consumption;

 3. They provide a ready-made statute for adoption by legislatures;

 4. The attention of the American public has turned increasingly to the automobile's poor safety record and its polluting qualities;

 5. The public's attention is directed to the ever-increasing costs of automobile insurance, and lack of availability of coverage; and

 6. A strong trend is apparent in tort law to impose liability irrespective of fault—much of the public seems to be more concerned with the plight of the injured accident victim than it is in punishing him for negligence. (See Rokes, No. 412).

Puerto Rico and Massachusetts Laws

The combination of the above factors culminated in the passage of a compensation law in Puerto Rico in 1968 (effective in 1970), a Massachusetts program passed in 1970, and similar proposals introduced in a number of other states at the same time. There was also considerable interest directed by the federal government to the subject of automobile reparations systems.

Particularly disturbing to the insurance industry was a proposal made in 1967 by Daniel Patrick Moynihan, then Director of the Joint Center for Urban Studies of M.I.T. and Harvard and chairman of a federal advisory committee on traffic safety research during the Johnson Administration. Moynihan, who later served as architect of President Nixon's "family assistance" plan and in 1971 resigned as Nixon's counselor to return to teaching, challenged the Bar and the insurance industry to reform or to get out of the "traffic accident business" and let the government take over. He suggested the creation of a national system of automobile accident compensation, modeled perhaps on the existing accident compensation system for Federal employees. He would finance the plan with interstate highway money and an extra "penny or so" on the gasoline tax.

Department of Transportation Study

The widespread national interest in the subject prompted Congress to enact a law late in the Johnson Administration, directing the Department of Transportation to conduct a $2 million, two-year automobile insurance study. The deadline set by Congress for completion of the study was May of 1970, and Senator Warren G. Magnuson, chairman of the Senate Commerce Committee, asked Secretary of Transportation, John A. Volpe, to no avail, to make his report on the study to the committee by mid-September.

Volpe attributed his delay to the complexity of the problem studied, and he denied that political considerations had influenced postponement of the long-awaited final report and recommendations until after the November elections. He acknowledged, however, that automobile insurance reform was a politically sensitive subject and particularly so in an election year.

The recommendations of the Department of Transportation to Congress were delivered in March of 1971, although the two dozen or so volumes of the report itself had been available at the United States Government Printing Office for a number of months. The actual report was presented by Secretary John A. Volpe to the Congress on March 18, 1971, and is entitled *Motor Vehicle Crash Losses and Their Compensation in the United States.* (See Bibliography entry No. 131). The publication represented the findings, conclusions and recommendations of the Department of Transportation about the automobile insurance and compensation system.

President Richard Nixon had indicated for some time that he was opposed to direct federal intervention in the matter of automobile insurance reform. He also expressed the conviction that effective action should be taken voluntarily on the part of the states. Secretary Volpe had stated that the Department of Transportation report indicated a need for "a more effective, more efficient way" to compensate the losses of victims of automobile accidents. Volpe had suggested that Congress might establish "broad outlines at the Federal level" and provide incentives or penalties to encourage state action in line with the guidelines.

Criticism of Volpe's Report

When the report was finally submitted to Congress, there was widespread disappointment in its contents. Specific recommendations contained in many of the individual reports were not included in Secretary Volpe's report to Congress. The Secretary's report recommended virtually no definite solutions, nor did it even strongly support any possible solutions. The only concrete suggestion to come from the report, according to the critics, was that some form of no-fault insurance should be provided and that the states should be required to begin experimenting to find out exactly what form is best.

Rather than proposing a no-fault model bill to guide the states in their efforts, the report set forth the "principles of reparations systems toward which the states should strive." Instead of calling for a national program, Volpe asked Congress to encourage states to devise their own no-fault plans. He proposed no timetable or standards for state action.

Within the Administration's councils, Volpe had fought privately for stronger measures, urging that states be given a deadline to adopt no-fault insurance or face imposition of a federal plan. The general feeling throughout Washington insurance circles was that the Department of Transportation's rather innocuous stand on auto insurance reform came straight from the White House and that Secretary Volpe was unhappy about the whole situation. Proposed stronger recommendations from the Department were reportedly watered down by direct White House intervention.

"The Department was forced not to retreat but into a near rout," complained Richard J. Barber, a former Deputy Assistant Transportation Secretary and Johnson Administration appointee. Barber, who resigned late in 1970, directed the two-and-a-half year, two million dollar study that was supposed to form the basis for the Administration's recommendations. Barber called the Administration's proposals "a disgraceful sham."

Senator Hart's Proposals

It was apparent for some time that President Richard Nixon would not elect to take the initiative in effecting a change, but the Democratic Congress sought to bring the matter to a head. Senator Philip A. Hart (Dem., Michigan) pushed for "direct" and "pre-emptive" Federal action in 1970 by introducing in the Senate a series of bills for remodeling the automobile liability insurance system. His key bill, S. 4339, The Uniform Motor Vehicle Insurance Act, sought to establish a "no-fault" system. The bill was reintroduced in slightly modified form on February 24, 1971, as S. 945, with Senator Warren Magnuson (Dem., Washington), a strong consumer advocate, as co-sponsor.

Senator Hart, chairman of the Antitrust and Monopoly Subcommittee of the Senate, had been a severe critic of the insurance industry prior to introduction of the bills. In addition, there was deep distrust of the commercial insurance industry among some of the staff of the subcommittee, and the conviction was openly expressed that the industry's alleged failure to serve the public interest was an open challenge to government leaders to supplant the insurance industry with government insurance operation—this referred not to automobile insurance alone but to other lines as well.

Dozens of Plans Emerge

Several dozen automobile indemnification proposals have been aired during the past several years, and with concentrated attention being devoted to the subject both by government and industry, change is inevitable. Action on the part of the states has been slow, but the impetus is there and will accelerate as the nation's attention, and particularly that of the federal government, is focused on the subject of automobile insurance reform.

Action by the States

   Bills to put "no-fault" automobile insurance into effect were introduced in 28 state legislatures in the early part of 1971, and at the time of this writing, the Delaware, Florida, and Illinois legislatures had passed no-fault automobile insurance laws. Governor Russell W. Peterson signed a bill on May 27, 1971, that made Delaware the second state in the United States with a no-fault automobile insurance law. In June the Florida legislature passed (against bitter opposition by lawyers) a modified no-fault system, reserving the rights of the seriously injured to seek redress from wrongdoers in automobile accidents. Later in the month the state of Illinois passed a no-fault law.

   The Nixon Administration in 1971 expressed the desire to give the states two years to show substantial progress in developing a national no-fault system. However, Congressional sentiment appears to be increasing for a uniform Federal law, or at least a Federal mandate for the states to enact uniform laws within a specified time.

   President Nixon's admonition to the states to enact their own no-fault legislation, with the tacit specter in the background that if the states did not act the Federal government would, had by May of 1971 produced little consensus among the state insurance departments of several of the key states. A survey conducted by *Business Insurance* indicated highly divergent views on the subject of no-fault automobile insurance among the state insurance regulators. Understandably, insurance commissioners, as political appointees of governors in many of the states, hold to the states rights doctrine. Some regulators indicated that they already had no-fault plans ready for submission, and others were working on such plans. The Commissioners of other states, however, indicated that they were not convinced that no-fault automobile insurance was the answer to the problem.

   By mid-1971, nine of the states had set aside no-fault bills; the legislatures substituted resolutions calling for studies, with reports to be submitted to the next session. In Minnesota, the third such study was ordered. Studies were also ordered in Connecticut, Colorado, Hawaii, Maryland, Montana, New Mexico, North Dakota, and Washington. Some of the studies, notably Minnesota's, Connecticut's and Maryland's, were widely regarded as a delaying tactic of no-fault opponents. Connecticut postponed consideration of automobile insurance reform "pending a complete, in-depth study of the entire situation" (a recommendation of the Connecticut Bar Association).

No-fault bills died in Alaska, Indiana, Kansas, New Jersey, Nevada, New York, Oklahoma and West Virginia, and appeared to be languishing in other state legislatures. Despite the obvious delay by some states, there is a strong belief on the basis of country-wide evidence that many legislatures are concerned about the problem and are inclined to effect changes in the automobile insurance system.

Supreme Court Pressure for "No-Fault" Legislation

The United States Supreme Court on May 24, 1971 issued an interesting ruling regarding state "financial responsibility" laws, which has been interpreted by some writers to be a boost for no-fault legislation. (See Bibliography entry No. 486). The Supreme Court ruled that before a license can be revoked under a state "financial responsibility" law, the uninsured motorist must be given a hearing, at which there must be proof of "a reasonable possibility" that a court would hold him liable for damages. By virtue of the court's ruling, the laws of 37 states are affected. The laws of these states made it possible to revoke the driver's license and automobile registration of uninsured motorists who were involved, regardless of whether they were at fault.

With no consideration given to whether the driver is at fault, the state laws have served as a strong inducement to pressure motorists into carrying adequate liability insurance.

The federal court said that such "financial responsibility" schemes violate the Constitution's due process clause, because motorists, who are liable for damages only if they negligently cause injuries, are stripped of their licenses without an opportunity to show that they were not negligent. The opinion of insurance industry spokesmen is that the ruling will "take some of the teeth out of the present financial responsibility laws," and will place more pressure upon authorities to enact compulsory-type legislation.

Conclusions

Automobile insurance, long defended as an institution whereby man's faults could be judged in terms of right and wrong, weighed on the scales of a God-made justice, appears to its critics as an anachronism inapplicable to the humanitarian standards of today. Indeed, the industry is being accused of selling the wrong product. The critics of the fault system argue forcefully that society is more concerned with taking care of the plight of the person injured by the motor vehicle than it is to punish the wrongdoing motorist. There is little logic in arguing that such critics are wrong, considering the fact that the punishment meted out to the wrongdoing motorist is a fiction—the shift of the financial burden to an insurance company—while the real punishment—revocation of driving privileges or "driver removal"—is winked at by a condescending public.

It is appropriate to study automobile insurance and its evolution in the United States. Such a study is presented in the following chapter and should provide a useful insight for analysis of the issues raging around automobile insurance reform today.

CHAPTER IV

AUTOMOBILE INSURANCE IN THE UNITED STATES

The end of the 19th century ushered in a new invention which would in a few years create the nation's number one industry. This invention was the automobile. Its early development came during an era of engineering miracles in the United States—miracles which launched the Industrial Revolution. Fomenting sweeping economic and social changes, the massive industrialization would ultimately give the United States the world's highest standard of living. The automobile was to play an important role in effecting these changes.

The automobile, a complicated mechanical contrivance, presented a myriad of business problems. Manufacturing difficulties were many. Its production necessitated the expenditure of a great amount of time and money. This, in turn, brought about the need for methods of financing the new product. Where financing facilities were lacking, new institutions sprang up to provide the required services. As public awareness of the new product grew, channels of distribution were established, and finance facilities were extended to the consumer as well as to the manufacturer.

The Need for Insurance

Soon it became apparent that here was a form of personal property which was subject to a number of perils because of its value, mobility, and destructibility. The automobile, a highly mobile personal chattel, careened about the countryside at relatively unheard-of speeds. Characterized by a comparatively high original cost and inordinate maintenance expenses, the automobile was always breaking down; it was unreliable, uncomfortable, and costly to operate. Repairs were expensive and difficult to make.

To protect the public against insurable economic losses, new insurance coverages evolved. The threat of fire, collision and other perils caused insureds—particularly the specialized sales finance companies emerging to handle the new automobile finance paper—to seek physical damage coverage. This coverage was first written as marine insurance written on automobiles carried on coastwise steamers. In addition, the new mechanical contraptions were running into each other and into people, horses, cows, carriages and other property. Liability insurance was needed.

25

The first automobile bodily injury liability insurance policy was issued in 1898. The policy was a team's form used to give liability protection to owners of horse-drawn vehicles. Since then three other coverages have been developed which are commonly sold in conjunction with liability coverage—medical payments and death and disability coverage, which pay regardless of fault, and uninsured motorist coverage, which provides protection for the insured if he is unable to collect against the uninsured or hit-and-run motorist. (See Wallace, No. 461).

Parallel physical damage coverage on the automobile developed slowly during the early years of automobile manufacturing. By 1912 there were engaged in the automobile insurance business in this country about 18 regular marine companies and some 15 fire companies whose charters permitted the assumption of the automobile risk. Some mutual companies offered automobile contracts of one form or another, and there were about 25 casualty companies engaged in insuring against the hazards incident to the operation of automobiles. (See Charles D. Dunlop, "Automobile Insurance", *The Business of Insurance*. Edited by Howard P. Dunham in three volumes. New York: The Ronald Press Company, 1912, vol. II, p. 399. Further discussion is found in Rokes, *Automobile Physical Damage Insurance Affiliates of Sales Finance Companies*. Ann Arbor: University Microfilms, Inc., dissertation, The Ohio State University, December, 1959).

Emergence of Financial Responsibility Laws

By the 1920's, considerable discussion had appeared in the nation's press concerning the enormity of the automobile hazard in terms of deaths, personal injuries, and other damages. Financial responsibility laws began to emerge, providing various degrees of compulsion to motivate the motoring public to obtain automobile liability insurance. The liability coverage contemplated was that predicated upon the responsibility for fault concept embodied in the tort liability system.

Financial responsibility measures sprang from a public recognition that the claimant's theoretical right of tort recovery in a motor vehicle accident was illusory unless the judgment obtained was actually paid, and that this was quite unlikely to happen unless the judgment became the obligation of an insurer. Except for Massachusetts, which enacted a compulsory automobile liability insurance law as far back as 1927, early financial responsibility measures generally were loose and persuasive in character rather than obligatory. Recognition of their inadequacy grew with mounting numbers of automobile accident victims and led to the strengthening of automobile financial responsibility laws in the late 1940's and early 1950's.

In 1971, every state had a financial responsibility law ranging from outright compulsion, such as those in Massachusetts, New York and North Carolina, to the security deposit type of law which, while not actually compelling the purchase of liability insurance, did exert a powerful pressure for its purchase. The security deposit law requires that a motorist involved in an automobile accident and unable to establish evidence of liability insurance must deposit security sufficient to cover the amount of any claim or suit against him or lose his driving privileges and registration certificate.

By 1971 some 37 states had laws requiring the deposit of security without regard to whether the motorist involved in the accident was at fault. The purpose of these laws was to pressure motorists into carrying adequate liability insurance. Arizona, California, Colorado, Maine, Minnesota, New Hampshire, New Jersey, Utah, Vermont and Virginia have laws or court decisions that require proof of fault before revocation of driver's license and registration certificate.

The Supreme Court Ruling - License Revocation

Previously discussed in some detail was the United States Supreme Court ruling on financial responsibility laws. On May 24, 1971, the Court declared unconstitutional the provisions of state financial responsibility laws that revoked drivers' licenses of uninsured motorists involved in accidents, regardless of whether they were at fault. In unanimously striking down the State of Georgia's financial responsibility law, the Supreme Court ruled that, before a license can be revoked, the uninsured motorist must be given a hearing, at which there must be proof of "a reasonable possibility" that a court would hold him liable for damages. Additionally, where courts in civil actions found uninsured motorists liable for damages, there would naturally be grounds for revocation of driving privileges.

The rationale of the Supreme Court decision was that the Georgia type of financial responsibility scheme violated the Constitution's due process clause, because motorists were stripped of their licenses without an opportunity to show that they were not negligent. The ruling is consistent with the fact that under tort liability only a motorist that negligently causes injuries is liable for damages.

A Change in Emphasis

Originally, the sole purpose of automobile liability insurance was to defend insured motorists against claims by others and to protect their assets from being depleted by adverse judgments. No consideration of the adequacy, the timeliness or the assurance of compensation for the injured party played any part in the matter. Indeed, the entire avoidance of compensation of the accident victim was calculated to further the interest of the contracting parties, since the insurer stood to gain from the maximization of its profits and the insured stood to gain from the minimization of his rates.

Moreover, the insured and his insurer were free to circumscribe their mutual obligation however they desired with respect to the scope of the risk insured and the amount of premium to be paid. These were matters in which the potential accident victim had no rights, since he was neither a party to the contract nor an intended third-party beneficiary. The theoretical right of the accident victim to recover in a tort action was, of course, not jeopardized in any way by the insurance contract. Under such circumstances, the liability insurer's right to require the insured to observe the terms of the contract meticulously and to condition its own obligations upon such observance was beyond question, either in law or in morals. It was time-honored business practice. (See Bibliography entry No. 131).

However, the courts over the years have discerned in the financial responsibility measures a pervasive public policy to imbue the automobile accident reparations system with a fundamental concern for the accident victim. For example, the California Supreme Court has ruled:

> "The entire financial responsibility law must be liber-
> ally construed to foster its main objective of giving
> monetary protection to that ever changing and tragi-
> cally large group of persons who, while lawfully using
> the highways themselves, suffer grave injury through
> the negligent use of those highways by others." *(In-
> ter Insurance Exchange of Automobile Club of South-
> ern California v. Ohio Casualty Insurance Co.*, 58 Cal.
> 2d 142, 373 P. 2d 640).

In recognition of the importance of insurance to the compensation of the victim, the courts have often refused to recognize any forfeiture of the insured's coverage because of breach of policy conditions (*e.g.*, such as those requiring immediate notice of accident or the provisions requiring the insured's cooperation) in the absence of a clear showing by the insurer that its rights have been actually and substantially prejudiced. A New York appellate court in 1969, commenting upon the necessity for the insurer to prove prejudice in order to be relieved of obligation through the insured's failure to give notice, stated:

> ". . . it becomes unreasonable to read the provisions un-
> realistically or to find that the carrier may forfeit the
> coverage, even though there is no likelihood that it was

prejudiced by the breach. It would also disservice the public interest, for insurance is an instrument of social policy that the victims of negligence be compensated." (*Allstate Insurance Co. v. Grillon*, 251 A. 2d 256).

Since the accomplishment of the objectives of the financial responsibility statutes demands that the motorist required to obtain automobile liability insurance be able to do so, it is understandable that the adoption of assigned risk plans and their rapid growth in size followed hard upon the heels of the strengthening of the financial responsibility laws. (See Bibliography entry No. 128).

The Uninsured Motorist Problem

Despite the legal pressures imposed upon motorists to possess liability insurance and the pressures upon insurance companies to make that coverage available through assigned risk plans and through restrictive court decisions, the problem presented by the uninsured motorist has remained. It is conservatively estimated that 15 to 20 percent of the nation's automobiles in 1967 were not even nominally insured with respect to liability. (See Bibliography entry No. 124). Aggravating the situation is the fact that the owners and drivers of uninsured automobiles contribute more than their proportional share of automobile accidents than do insured owners and drivers. The uninsured motorists are typically poor risks, and insurance companies, understandably, don't appreciate their business.

Failure of the financial responsibility laws to compensate innocent victims of automobile accidents has led to legislative solutions along the lines of compulsory insurance. The compulsory laws, already mentioned, of Massachusetts, North Carolina, and New York, require that motorists obtain liability insurance as a condition precedent to driving. Unsatisfied judgment laws have been passed to provide funds from which automobile accident victims could draw in the event that an uninsured motorist could not respond to judgment. The uninsured motorist coverage has been hailed as a solution to the problems presented by the financially irresponsible motorist, and states have enacted laws requiring that such coverage be provided with every liability insurance policy issued or delivered within their jurisdiction. By March of 1971 only the District of Columbia, Maryland and North Dakota were without legislation mandating that such coverage be offered, although in a majority of states the insured was permitted to reject the coverage. The purpose of the uninsured motorist coverage was to provide the insured with essentially a first-party coverage, enabling him to collect from his own insurance company if he was unable to recover from an uninsured motorist legally responsible for his damages.

The scope of the uninsured motorist coverage, at least as interpreted by the courts, is considerably broader than originally formulated by the insurance industry. For instance, it is generally held that when a motorist was nominally insured at the time of the accident but somehow breached his policy's conditions, or suffered a rescission because he misinterpreted certain material facts in his insurance application, the victim's uninsured motorist insurance covers the loss. Again, where the wrongdoer's insurance company becomes insolvent subsequent to an accident, the wrongdoer is often considered an uninsured motorists, and the victim can collect under his uninsured motorist coverage.

Conclusions

In reviewing the evolution of automobile liability insurance coverage, it is apparent that coverage originally was adopted to complement the public's attitude that each person should be responsible for his own transgressions. This was the essence of personal responsibility under the Puritan Ethic.

Needless to say, the increasing emphasis upon the plight of the victim of the automobile accident, particularly when struck by an uninsured vehicle, has marked a shift in attitudes. The public's disenchantment with the inequity of a tort liability system which provides for collection from an insured wrongdoer, but for all practical purposes exempts the uninsured wrongdoer from responsibility, has hastened the breakdown.

The basic weakness of such a system of inequities and socially undesirable consequences has destroyed the entire rationale for the tort liability concept. This disenchantment with tort liability, combined with an increasing feeling that fault is unascertainable in a majority of situations, plus the social concern with the automobile accident victim, irrespective of fault, has produced the present impetus toward supplanting the tort liability system with a no-fault concept.

PART II
THE NO-FAULT PLAN

CHAPTER V

THE NO-FAULT LAWS ADOPTED

The no-fault laws in existence provide an important laboratory setting, for it is only through the experience of actual plans in existence that changes and innovations in the automobile reparations proposals can be tested in terms of public acceptability, equity achieved, efficiency, and other results.

For many years the Saskatchewan Plan was the only automobile no-fault plan in existence on the North American continent, and it served as a point of reference for a number of studies which were conducted by various states in the determination of the plans which they subsequently adopted. For example, the state of North Dakota in the 1950's studied the Saskatchewan Plan as a possible solution to its automobile accident problems. At that time it rejected the compensation concept.

Another study made a cost analysis of the Saskatchewan Plan and the conditions existing in that province and compared them with the automobile accident problem in the state of New Jersey (study conducted at Temple University). Such studies usually concluded that conditions were highly dissimilar between the United States and the little-populated province of Saskatchewan, and a no-fault principle did not catch on in the states for some time.

However, with the passage of the Puerto Rico law in 1968, the Massachusetts law in 1970, and the Delaware, Florida, and Illinois laws in 1971, a compelling precedent has been established for the remainder of the states.

It will be helpful for the reader to acquaint himself with the provisions of the no-fault laws which have been enacted. The background and principal features of those laws follow. Complete texts of several of the "no-fault" laws appear in the appendix.

THE SASKATCHEWAN PLAN
"Automobile Accident Insurance Act"

The Saskatchewan Plan was created by statute in 1946 in the Canadian province of Saskatchewan. The impetus behind the passage of the Plan was the 1944 political victory of the Cooperative Commonwealth Federation, a socialistic political party made up of farm and labor leaders. The Plan is designed not to produce "absolute justice" in individual cases, but rather to provide a type of "average justice" for all motorists.

Features of the Plan

Under the Plan benefits are paid to almost all victims of automobile accidents, irrespective of fault. Compensation is denied in some cases if the automobile is being driven in breach of conditions specified by the statute.

A schedule of benefits provides the following:

1.   A $10,000 accidental death benefit (with graded benefits for minors).

2.   Four thousand dollars ($4,000) maximum for dismemberment or loss of function.

3.   Two thousand dollars ($2,000) coverage for medical payments not covered under Saskatchewan's compulsory hospital expense plan.

4.   For total disability, a weekly indemnity of $25 is payable for a period of not more than 104 consecutive weeks. In case of partial disability preventing an injured person from carrying out an essential part of his occupation, weekly indemnity of $12.50 may be paid up to 104 consecutive weeks, less any period during which total disability payment has been made.

5.   A sum of $300 is paid for funeral expenses.

In addition, third-party liability coverage for bodily injury and property damage over and above the basic compensation coverage is compulsory in the amount of $35,000, inclusive limits. Also required is physical damage coverage on the insured vehicle covering both collision and comprehensive risks, subject to a $200 deductible.

The plan is popularly called "Drivers License Insurance", for no policy is issued. Coverage is effective when drivers and automobile owners obtain licenses or register their automobiles; the premium is paid at that time. A very small fee is paid license agents who handle the combined licensing and insurance issuance.

Excess Liability Is Retained

Liability for fault is retained for claims in excess of the basic coverage provided by the statute. An "extension policy" may be purchased to provide liability coverage up to $300,000 and to reduce the deductible under the physical damage basic coverage. The Saskatchewan Government Insurance Office writes roughly 50 percent of these "extension policies" in competition with some 145 insurers in the province.

The rating system is a model of simplicity. Premiums are pegged largely to the age and size of the automobile.

Legal System Differs from U.S.

The Saskatchewan Plan operates within a legal system which differs somewhat from that prevailing in the United States. Canada does not recognize the contingent fee system; consequently, individuals seeking the services of attorneys must pay whether they win or lose their lawsuit. The loser may be ordered by the court to pay specified charges as a fee for the winner's attorney. This is the English practice. There is, therefore, some hesitation on the part of claimants to go to court to pursue liability claims which may be based somewhat upon shaky premises. However, a litigant can collect under the basic coverage, using the money to finance his legal action. (See Rokes, Nos. 413, 414, and 415; Lyons, No. 287; and Bibliography entries Nos. 424 and 550).

PUERTO RICO
"Social Protection Plan"

Puerto Rico became the first United States jurisdiction to adopt a compensation system for automobile accident victims when in 1968 is passed the "Social Protection Plan." On June 26, 1968, House Bill No. 874, known as "Social Protection Plan for Victims of Automobile Accidents," (Act No. 138) was signed into law by the Governor of Puerto Rico with the plan to go into effect on January 1, 1970. Drafted by Professor Juan B. Aponte and Professor Herbert S. Denenberg (Appointed Insurance Commissioner of Pennsylvania in 1971), the legislation was based on a comprehensive study of the Puerto Rican automobile problem completed by the authors in February 1966 in response to a request from the legislature of Puerto Rico.

Benefits Provided

Benefits provided by the plan, paid on a compensation basis without regard to fault, include medical expense payments, income replacement, dismemberment, and death and funeral benefits.

The plan is compulsory, government-administered, emphasizing socially adequate benefits rather than individual equity, and provides basic protection for all auto accident victims—drivers, passengers, and pedestrians—through benefits prescribed by law. All persons are automatically covered and protected.

Private Enterprise Excluded in Basic Coverage

There are no policies, no underwriting, no billing, no agents, no cancellation, and no commissions. In short, the system is a social security or social insurance system rather than a private enterprise system. Private insurers market excess liability insurance over the basic compensation limits. They also sell automobile physical damage coverage.

Specific Features of Law

The plan provides for the following features:

1. Medical expense benefits under the plan are provided without limit.

2. Wage loss is reimbursed up to 50 percent of salary, but subject to a maximum of $50 per week during the first year and $25 during the second, at which time these benefits cease.

3. Dismemberment benefits are paid in addition to wage loss replacement and run as high as $5000.

4. There is a $500 funeral benefit.

5. Death benefits depend on the age and relationship of the survivors. A surviving wife with two children under 5 years of age, for example, would receive $10,000.

6. The plan includes certain exclusions: intentionally self-inflicted injuries and victims of automobile races and speed tests.

7. An injured party can sue for catastrophic damages only if pain and suffering exceed $1000 in value or if his economic losses exceed $2000.

8. Property damage is not covered under the new program.

9. Private insurers market liability policies to provide excess coverage for liability claims over the basic limits as well as to market automobile physical damage policies.

10. Benefits under the plan are paid from tax revenues by a government insurance fund. The fund contracts with physicians and hospitals to provide the necessary medical care. (See Fournier, Nos. 164 and 165; Bibliography entries Nos. 432 and 524).

Experience under the Puerto Rico Plan

After 17 months of experience with the Puerto Rico Plan, the following results were reported:

1.   Ninety cents of every premium dollar had been paid in benefits.

2.   The Administración de Compensaciones por Accidentes de Automoviles (the government administering agency) was seeking to boost loss-of-income compensation to 75 percent of regular pay up to a maximum benefit of $100 a week. (Per capita income in Puerto Rico is $1426 per year, or less than half the U.S. mainland level.) Frank W. Fournier, Executive Director of the government agency, believed that this increase in loss-of-income benefits, plus an increased death benefit of $25,000, could be accomplished without raising the rates, according to government actuarial reports.

3.   Critics of the Puerto Rico plan had contended that drivers would get careless and push accident rates sharply upward. In 1970 the rate did go up 5 percent—but this was only half the 10 percent rise of the year before. Traffic deaths declined to 451 from 541 in 1970.

4.   Critics predicted a huge rise in "pain and suffering" claims from accident victims demanding more than the medical and economical loss benefits that the no-fault plan provides. No such rise materialized.

5.   One insurer, Cooperativa de Seguros Multiples de Puerto Rico, stated that it had not had to pay a single automobile accident personal injury liability claim in the first 17 months of the new plan. It proposed cutting the rate on the standard personal injury drivers liability policy to $33 a year—a sharp cut from $50 in early 1971 and from $68 before the no-fault program began.

Criticisms of the No-Fault Plan

The Puerto Rican Bar Association contended that benefits are more "phantom" than real. The maximum survivor benefit of $15,000 is paid only if the victim had a large number of dependent relatives, according to the Association.

Attorneys contend that payments for pain and suffering have been almost eliminated, restricting a citizen's freedom under negligence law to sue for reparation, thus depriving citizens of some of their historic due process rights. (See Montgomery, No. 524).

MASSACHUSETTS
"Compulsory Personal Injury Protection"

On August 13, 1970, Massachusetts Governor Francis W. Sargent signed Senate Bill 1580 into law. The bill became effective on January 1, 1971, making Massachusetts the first United States jurisdiction, other than Puerto Rico, to enact a no-fault plan. The law provided for the amendment of the Massachusetts compulsory automobile insurance law to provide certain first-party coverages on a compulsory basis. It also modified existing tort remedies for automobile accidents within the state.

Features of the Law

The law provides for limited first-party no-fault coverage. Provisions are as follows:

1.   Compulsory first-party coverage, with per person limits of $2000, are provided for the named insured, members of his household, any person responsible for the operation of a motor vehicle, any operator or authorized passenger of a vehicle of a corporation, partnership or business association, guest passengers and pedestrians struck by the insured's vehicle. Excluded from this first-party coverage would be the employees of the owner or registrant of the insured vehicle or other persons entitled to workmen's compensation benefits. All reasonable expenses incurred within two years from the date of the accident would be covered for necessary medical, surgical, X-ray, and dental services, including prosthetic devices and necessary ambulance, hospital, professional nursing and funeral services.

2.   Coverage for wages actually lost by reason of an automobile accident and payments in fact made to non-members of the injured person's household for services which the injured person would have performed, if not injured, are covered. In addition to the $2000 per person limit on the first-party coverage, wage loss payments would not exceed 75 percent of the injured person's average weekly wages for the year preceding the accident. Coverage for reasonable medical and wage losses are provided up to a maximum of $2000 for both kinds of loss.

3.   There is no collateral source setoff except that the combination of wage loss payments made under the plan and any other collateral wage continuation program cannot exceed the 75 percent limit.

4.   Insurers could exclude from coverage under the first-party payments provision those whose conduct contributed to cause their injury through operating of a vehicle while under the influence of liquor or narcotics; operating while in the commission of a felony or trying to aviod arrest; or operating a vehicle with the specific intent to cause injury to themselves or others.

5. The injured person may not make a tort claim for those out-of-pocket expenses covered by the first-party provision of the plan, but, as to other damages, the injured person would be free to pursue his normal tort action.

6. The law provides that a person may not seek or recover compensation for pain and suffering in a tort action unless his reasonable and necessary expenses incurred in treating his injury for necessary medical, surgical, X-ray and dental services, including prosthetic devices and necessary ambulance, hospital, professional nursing and funeral expenses are determined to be in excess of $500 or, unless such injury causes death, consists in whole or in part of loss of a body member, permanent and serious disfigurement, loss of sight or hearing, or consists of a fracture.

7. All motorists driving autos covered by the compulsory insurance are granted tort immunity to the extent of first-party benefits payable by the plan and the pain and suffering limitation. Such tort exemption applies only for accidents occurring in Massachusetts where the motorist and the victims are covered by the plan.

8. The law also provides that an insured may elect to have a first-party coverage deductible of $250, $500, $1000, or $2000 applied to the benefits payable to him and members of his household. The fact that there is a deductible would not affect the tort immunity previously discussed and would not be taken into consideration in determining whether the claimant's medical expenses exceed $500. (See Bibliography entry No. 518).

9. Benefits under the plan are payable as loss accrues on receipt of reasonable proof thereof, but the insurer may agree to a lump sum settlement.

10. Subrogation. An insurer paying benefits under the plan is subrogated to the extent of such payments to any rights the payee may have at tort against an offending motorist, if the latter is not exempt from tort liability.

11. A Massachusetts resident who does not own a car and is not a member of a family household or a named insured under the plan would be covered for benefits under the policy of any motorist in whose car he was riding or by whose car he was struck as a pedestrian. If injured in or by an out-of-state car, such person would have no benefits under the plan. To provide for such cases, insurers are required to organize and maintain an Assigned Claims Plan through which the injured persons may obtain the benefits otherwise available under the "Personal Injury Protection" program.

12. Renewability. All Massachusetts policies, whether covering liability (including the Personal Injury Protection coverage) or Physi-

cal damage, shall be automatically renewed for insureds 65 and over and for all other insureds with clean records.

13.   No insurers shall refuse to issue a policy of liability or physical damage insurance because of age, sex, race, or occupation of the applicant or the place of garaging of his car.

14.   Cancellation of a liability insurance policy requires that the insurer provide the cancelled insured with an assigned risk coverage.

15.   Commercial vehicles are treated the same as private passenger vehicles. How to treat commercial motor vehicles has been a prime point of contention in many of the "no-fault" proposals which have been made. (See Gilkenson, No. 173).

More Moderate than 1967 Bill

The new law is a pale image of its progenitor, the Keeton-O'Connell "Basic Protection Insurance" Bill, which was defeated in the Massachusetts Senate in 1967. The "Basic Protection" plan immunized against tort suits up to $10,000 or economic loss and deducted all collateral source recovery. The "Personal Injury Protection" plan (the new law) sets a $2000 cutoff on tort suits and deducts only for wage continuation. The older plan eliminated pain and suffering suits under $5000; the present plan permits such suits where a medical loss exceeds $500.

The Massachusetts plan is a modest move toward the no-fault concept. It is politically palatable because of the exclusion of benefits for certain individuals, such as drivers under the influence of liquor or narcotics—a vestige of the feeling that people at fault should not be permitted to recover. The low barriers to pain and suffering suits permit attorneys considerable scope for tort liability actions.

Mandatory Reduction in Rates

A controversial part of the Massachusetts Plan was the mandatory reduction in automobile insurance rates of 15 percent, which caused a number of companies to threaten to stop writing automobile insurance in the state. (See Bibliography entry No. 301).

The Massachusetts Supreme Judicial Court on November 9 and November 18, 1970, nullified that portion of the Massachusetts "no-fault" law which provided for an across-the-board automobile insurance rate cut of 15 percent. The November 9 decision covered property damage rates for 1971 and the November 18 decision covered fire, theft and collision. The court called both legislatively mandated rate cuts "confiscatory."

The Supreme Court for the third time rejected legislative efforts to impose automobile insurance rate limitations by holding that the "freeze" of compulsory automobile insurance rates for 1970 imposed by the legislature and promulgated by the insurance commissioner was "confiscatory" and "unconstitutional." The Court's opinion sustained the appeal brought by The Travelers and 45 other insurance companies. (See Bibliography entry No. 304).

Experience under the Law

The immediate impact of the Massachusetts Plan as of the first quarter of 1971 indicated that the program was eliminating so-called nuisance claims. First quarter's results indicated that there was a 60 percent drop in total claims under compulsory bodily injury coverage during the first three months of 1971, with a 36 percent reduction in the average paid claim, according to Governor Francis W. Sargent. "The average paid claim cost in the first quarter of 1970 was $205. The average paid claim cost in the first quarter of 1971 was $131," stated Governor Sargent. He predicted a "future premium cost cut of 25 percent for bodily injury insurance." (See Bibliography entry No. 364).

Insurance industry spokesmen expressed the belief that the plan must be in operation for at least six months before meaningful statistics could be compiled and evaluated. They confirmed that the volume of claims had been lower than anticipated, but indicated this could be due to the transition to the new system and also to "normal time lags between the occurrence of an accident and the filing of claims." Some 70 to 80 percent of the bodily injury claims filed in January and February arose from accidents that occurred in the previous December, November, and October before the new law became effective.

Although the law requires payment of benefits within 30 days after receipt of claim, provided it is accompanied by necessary supporting data, companies discovered that there had been no reduction in the average time lag of 21 days before the form was returned. In many cases the form was not accompanied by hospital and medical bills, because the claimant had not yet received them. Thus, an additional delay ensued before payment could be made. (See Bibliography entry No. 67).

Litigation Challenging the New Law

Some critics question the constitutionality of the Massachusetts plan. The lack of an option permitting the insured the right to waive first-party benefits as he may (but rarely does) under workmen's compensation led some to believe that the courts would strike down the law as unconstitutional. An early case resolved the issue.

A postal worker and his wife, Mr. and Mrs. Milton Pinnick, were involved in an accident in Boston January 2, 1971. The couple's claim amounted to less than $2000 and medical expenses were less than $500. Since Massachusetts law provides that, unless losses exceed these amounts, or unless the accident results in death, loss in whole or in part of a body member, permanent and serious disfigurement, loss of sight or hearing, or a fracture, a tort liability suit could not be instituted.

The Pinnicks' demand that the adverse party's insurer pay for lost wages and for "pain and suffering" was denied by the adverse party's insurance company. Under the Massachusetts law, the Pinnicks could collect only actual medical expenses and 75 percent of their lost wages.

The Pinnicks then instituted a legal suit challenging Massachusetts "no-fault" statute. The petition brought by the Pinnicks contended that the law barring compensation for pain and suffering was unconstitutional and abridged the rights of the petitioners contained in the first eight amendments to the Constitution, and, also, that the new law created privileges and immunities from tort liability for some citizens and exempted them from the operation of standing laws. The lawsuit presented an interesting challenge to the heart of the constitutionality issue of "no-fault" automobile compensation statutes. (See Bibliography entries Nos. 441 and 535).

On June 29, 1971, the Massachusetts Supreme Court ruled that the state's no-fault automobile insurance law is constitutional.

Massachusetts Law in Appendix

For the information of the reader and as a guide for the drafting of legislation, the Massachusetts law has been reproduced in the appendix at the end of this book.

This should serve as a helpful guide, particularly since the Massachusetts Plan contains many of the more popular features of the reform plans which are appearing about the nation.

THE DELAWARE LAW

Effective on January 1, 1972, the state of Delaware inaugurates the implementation of its "no-fault" automobile insurance law.
The bill creating the law was signed by Governor Russell W. Peterson on May 27, 1971, making Delaware the second state to enact a "no-fault" automobile insurance law.

Under the law, Delaware drivers are required to have automobile insurance and their companies will pay claims regardless of fault. The victim of an accident will still retain his right to sue for "pain and suffering."

Features of the Law

Under the legislation, no owner of a motor vehicle registered in the state, other than a self-insurer, shall operate or authorize any other person to operate his automobile unless he obtains minimum insurance coverage, including the following:

1. Liability insurance for bodily injury, death, or property damage of at least $25,000 or to the limit of the Delaware Financial Responsibility Law, whichever is greater.

2. Compensation coverage of at least $10,000 for one person and $20,000 for each accident for reasonable and necessary expenses for medical, hospital, dental, surgical, medicine, X-ray, ambulance or prosthetic services, professional nursing and funeral services, and for loss of earnings and reasonable and necessary extra expense for personal services which would have been performed by the injured person had he not been injured. Funeral expenses shall not exceed the sum of $2000 per person.

3. Compensation coverage for property damage, other than to a motor vehicle, with a minimum limit of $5000 for any one accident.

4. Compensation for damage to the insured motor vehicle, including loss of use coverage up to $10 per day, with a maximum payment of $300.

The coverage applies to each person occupying the insured vehicle and to any other person injured in an accident involving the insured vehicle, but excludes occupants of another motor vehicle. There is an option to provide certain deductibles, waiting periods, sublimits, percentage reductions, excess provisions and similar reductions applicable to expenses incurred as a result of injury to the owner of the vehicle or members of his household. Insureds are permitted to obtain coverage more extensive than the minimum coverages required by the law.

Alteration of Tort Liability System

Any person eligible for the compensation coverage for medical, disability, and funeral expenses and for property damage, other than that involving a motor vehicle, is precluded from suing for these damages, for which compensation is available, under the tort liability system.

Subrogation Rights

Insurers providing the compensation benefits under the law shall be subrogated to the rights, including claims under any Workmens' Compensation law, of the person for whom benefits are provided, to the extent of the benefits provided.

Arbitration

All insurance policies are required to provide that insurers must submit to arbitration claims for damages to a motor vehicle, other than the insured motor vehicle, including the loss of use of such vehicle upon the request of the owner of the damaged vehicle. The state insurance commissioner is designated to administer the arbitration system.

Delaware Law in Appendix

For the information of the reader and as a guide for the drafting of legislation, the Delaware law has been reproduced in the appendix at the end of this book.

Inclusion of the statute should be most helpful, particularly since the Delaware Plan incorporates some of the more unusual features of no-fault proposals.

THE FLORIDA PLAN
"Florida Automobile Reparations Reform Act"

In June of 1971 the state of Florida passed its "Florida Automobile Reparations Reform Act" providing that effective January 1, 1972, Florida citizens would come under a "no-fault" automobile insurance law.

Under the law an injured person would collect his economic loss from his own insurer without regard to fault in an accident. Tort liability actions against others, arising from automobile accident injuries and damages, would be eliminated to the extent of the basic coverage.

Features of the Law

The law provides for the following features:

1.   Maximum limit of coverage is $5000, covering all reasonable expenses incurred for necessary medical, surgical, X-ray, dental and rehabilitative services, including prosthetic devices, hospital and nursing services.

2.   Reimbursement of 100 percent of loss of gross income and earning capacity (or 85 percent, if such benefit is found to be not subject to federal income tax).

3.   Funeral benefits to $1000.

4.   Lawsuits (from the first dollar of loss including claims for pain and suffering and other general damages) are still permitted for serious fractures, permanent disfigurement, loss of a body member, "permanent injury within reasonable medical probability," permanent loss of a bodily function, or death.

5.   Insurers must issue, as a package, the no-fault statutory benefits and liability coverage to provide for those situations wherein an insured is still subject to suit.

6.   Deductibles of $250, $500, and $1000 applicable to the no-fault benefits must be offered by insurers.

7.   The law mandates a 15 percent reduction in premiums.

"Thresholds" Which Govern Right to Sue

A "medical threshold" is established where medical and related expenses exceed $1000. When the threshold is exceeded, the injured party may still sue (and meanwhile be collecting his no-fault benefits).

Although the coverage applies only to bodily injury, the law modifies the right to sue for property damage to private passenger automobiles. Here a "property damage threshold" is established—a person incurring less than $550 property damage cannot sue. If the loss is above this threshold, he may sue.

Handling Property Damage

Persons may take one of three courses with regard to property damage to their own private passenger automobiles: (1) Carry the same collision coverage as exists today, providing for indemnity without regard to fault; or (2) carry a new form of collision coverage, which will be offered, providing payment for only those situations wherein the damages were incurred through the fault of another who is subject to the law; or (3) elect not to carry collision coverage (but such a decision has new meaning with statutory removal of the right to sue one who negligently causes damage not exceeding $550).

Mandatory

Florida motorists are required by the law to carry insurance providing the statutory no-fault bodily injury benefits (or post equivalent security).

Failure to comply with the law provides for revocation of drivers license and car registration, although proof of compliance is not required to secure a license tag. Failure to obtain the coverage, nevertheless, carries the full penalties for noncompliance. It is not necessary for the motor vehicle operator to be involved in an accident before the penalties apply, such as is the case in most financial responsibility laws.

Florida Law in Appendix

The Florida statute has been reproduced in the appendix at the end of this book for the information of the reader and as a guide for the drafting of legislation.

The inclusion of the law should be helpful to the reader, particularly since the Florida Plan contains many of the more popular features of the reform proposals which are appearing about the nation.

THE ILLINOIS PLAN

The Illinois Plan was enacted into law in late June of 1971, making Illinois the fourth state in the nation to pass automobile insurance reform legislation purportedly embodying the no-fault concept. Massachusetts, Delaware, and Florida had previously passed automobile reform statutes. The Illinois law goes into effect January 1, 1972.

The Illinois law incorporates little of the "no-fault" concept in its provisions. Tort liability is retained. First-party benefits are expanded. The most significant feature of the new law is the limitation which it makes upon pain and suffering claims under general damages. "Such damages as may be recoverable for pain, suffering, mental anguish and inconvenience may not exceed the total sum equal to 50 percent of the reasonable medical treatment expenses of the claimant if and to the extent that the total of such reasonable expenses is $500 or less, and a sum equal to the amount of such reasonable expenses, if any, in excess of $500." The limitation does not apply to cases involving death, dismemberment, permanent total or permanent partial disability and permanent serious disfigurement.

The Illinois Plan is a proposal developed for private passenger cars by Governor Richard B. Ogilvie and Insurance Director James Baylor. It is a culmination of a seven-month-long study conducted by the Illinois Insurance Study Commission. The report of that study was submitted March 18 to the Illinois General Assembly and was characterized as "a model for 49 other states."

Insurance Industry Approves

Revealed on April 5, 1971, by the Illinois Governor and introduced April 20 in the Illinois legislature as Senate Bill 967, the Plan was backed by major insurance associations and companies, which reportedly offset strong opposition by some attorney groups. Backing the plan were the two largest automobile insurers in the nation—State

Farm Insurance Company and the Allstate Insurance Company, a subsidiary of Sears. The National Association of Independent Insurers and the American Mutual Insurance Alliance have their headquarters in the state. Other insurers, including the giant Chicago-based Continental Casualty Company, a subsidiary of Continental National Financial Corporation, approved of the plan.

One insurer, Allstate, placed full-page advertisements in newspapers around the state urging residents to push for passage of the bill which created the new plan.

Features of the Plan

The major features of the new Illinois Automobile Insurance Plan are as follows:

1. Effective January 1, 1972, the coverage would apply to any private passenger automobile registered or principally garaged in Illinois and would cover the named insured, members of his family residing in his household, and other persons injured while occupying the insured automobile as guests, or while using it with the permission of the named insured, and would cover pedestrians struck by the automobile in accidents occurring within Illinois.

2. The insurance law is applicable only to those policies covering five or fewer private passenger automobiles; therefore, the law exempts commercial vehicles from its provisions.

3. Benefits are payable within 30 days to cover expenses of the parties covered under the new law. If losses are to extend beyond 30 days, partial payments would be made no less than every 30 days.

4. Punitive payments are provided for under the law. Failure to pay within 30 days would penalize insurers by requiring them to triple their payments. In order to avoid arbitrary or capricious denial of claims or delay in their payment, the reform plan requires that the insurer pay the victim triple damages for a willful or a wanton denial or delay in the payment of benefits.

5. Payment of all reasonable and necessary expenses arising from the accident for medical, surgical, X-ray, dental, prosthetic, ambulance, hospital, professional nursing and funeral services, incurred within one year from the date of accident, subject to a limit of $2000 per person.

6. Payment of 85 percent of the income, including but not limited to salary, wages, tips, commissions, fees or other earnings, lost by an income or wage-earner as the result of total disability arising from the accident, subject to a limit of $150 per week for 52 weeks per person.

7. Where the person injured in the accident was not an income

or wage producer at the time of the accident, payments of benefits must be made in reimbursement of necessary and reasonable expenses incurred for essential services ordinarily performed by the injured person for care and maintenance of the family or family household subject to a limit of $12 per day for 365 days per person injured.

8. Monetary awards for "pain and suffering," under the plan, will be limited to half the first $500 of medical expenses, and equal to the medical expense thereafter. There would be no limitations to those cases which involve death, permanent total or partial disability, disfigurement or loss of limb.

9. The plan calls for setting up court-administered, mandatory arbitration of disputes involving less than $3000. Right of appeal to the courts is preserved. Cases involving disputes of over $3000 would be tried under the present tort liability system.

10. The plan calls for the companies to settle the fault issue, generally after first-party payments to the insured already have been made. Companies would be required to settle disputes between themselves out of court.

11. The plan calls for stringent action against doctors, lawyers, and others convicted of fraud in insurance matters.

12. Benefits may be denied in some cases where the injured party's conduct contributed to the injury (intentional injury, while under the influence of liquor or narcotics, while in commission of a felony, *etc.*).

Optional Coverage

In addition to the mandatory coverages, companies will be required to offer additional optional excess coverage to insurance buyers.

The optional coverage would start at $50,000 per person or at $100,000 per accident. It would extend medical benefit limits, pay for lost income or hired services for five years, and give survivors a maximum of $150 a week for lost income for five years.

Advance Payments

The Illinois law provides for an interesting provision relating to advance payments. The law provides that in any claim or action in tort or contract brought against a person or company, the company may make or offer advance payments (partial payment, loan or settlement, predicated upon possible tort liability or under the contractual obligation of the company to the injured party or on his behalf).

Making of advance payments does not interrupt the running of the Statute of Limitations. However, the recipient of advance payments must be notified in writing of the date the applicable Statute of Limitations will expire. Such payments are not admissible in evidence and may not be construed as an admission of liability. In addition, a subsequent award granted to the claimant because of a verdict in his favor will be reduced by the amount of the advance payments made prior to trial.

Other Recommendations of Study Commission

The Commission, when it made its report to the legislature in March, also recommended the creation of an Illinois Insurance Guaranty Fund to curb failures of insurance companies in Illinois and to compensate innocent policyholders. The recommendation arose out of the Commission's allegation that "the Illinois Department of Insurance has been derelict in discovering the impairment of insurance companies for insolvencies. Four hundred thousand persons were innocent victims of the insolvencies in Illinois, and it would seem almost axiomatic that the industry would have long since attempted to provide solid protection for those so cruelly wronged."

The Commission further commented on the danger of federal control and resultant loss of revenue as an inevitable consequence. The Commission therefore recommended the following:

1.   Greater availability of insurance to thousands of individuals who find it difficult to obtain coverage at almost any price.

2.   A detailed survey should be made of the operation of conglomerates and holding companies in Illinois, followed by legislation imposing strict controls.

3.   Mandatory arbitration of small insurance claims is necessary to break a bottleneck in the insurance industry.

4.   The legislature should consider mandatory jail sentences in order to eliminate drunken drivers from highways and reduce the daily death toll.

5.   Upgrade rules and regulations for licensing of insurance brokers and salesmen in order to raise the level of professional competence.

6.   Study the possibility of establishing a state fund to assist institutions of higher learning as well as secondary schools in efforts to obtain insurance coverage through private industry.

7.   Establishment of a licensing law for adjusters.

Insurance Commissioner Appraises Plan

In appraising the Illinois Plan, Illinois Insurance Commissioner, James Baylor, said, "There is ample evidence that motorists are fed up with their present insurance coverage, for which they must pay promptly, only to have to wait sometimes as long as five years to receive payment for the losses. We estimate that nearly three-quarters of the bodily injury lawsuits now being filed can be eliminated, thus alleviating the court backlog, which is most severe and unacceptable in Cook County." (See Donahue, No. 144 and Bibliography entries Nos. 207, 368, 502 and 504).

Criticisms of the New Law

Although characterized as unpalatable to the legal profession, the new law goes to remarkable lengths to preserve the tort liability system and to keep attorneys occupied in arbitration of minor claims. The arbitration process seems unnecessarily complex, providing adversary parties the right to have their cases heard before as many as three attorneys. In addition, a party may appeal the decision of arbitrators by swearing that the appeal "is not for the purpose of delay. . . but because he firmly believes injustice has been done." Since most, if not all, unsuccessful litigants believe that injustice has been done, it would appear that a potentially inordinate number of arbitrated cases could be appealed.

The slight tampering with the tort liability system in the case of pain and suffering, combined with the preservation of the tort liability system otherwise, suggests that the Illinois law is one of the more conservative approaches to the no-fault concept.

Illinois Law in Appendix

For the information of the reader and as a guide for the drafting of legislation, the Illinois Law has been reproduced in the appendix at the end of this book.

This should serve as a helpful guide for legislative drafting, particularly since the Illinois Plan contains many of the more popular features of the reform plans which are appearing about the nation.

CHAPTER VI

KEETON-O'CONNELL AND OTHER PROPOSALS

Various individuals have made noteworthy contributions to our literature of automobile reparations systems by proposing plans. Some of the plans, such as the "Basic Protection Plan" submitted by Robert E. Keeton and Jeffrey O'Connell have been complex, rather complete systems, replete with recommended legislation. Other proposals are sketchy plans suggesting a concept but without many of the details spelled out.

In the following pages the author presents some of the best-known of the automobile accident indemnification schemes which have been aired in the past years by individuals. Starting with the Columbia University Committee plan, but excluding the Saskatchewan Plan (it is included in the chapter dealing with existing systems), the plans follow.

The previous chapter examined the no-fault proposals which have been enacted into legislation. Following chapters examine proposals made by insurance companies, trade associations, U.S. state and federal officials, and Canadian authorities.

THE COLUMBIA UNIVERSITY COMMITTEE PLAN

The Columbia University Committee Plan, initially prepared in 1932, is perhaps the most important pioneering proposal on "no-fault" or automobile compensation. The study figured prominently in the decision taken by the Saskatchewan government when it adopted its no-fault system in 1946. The Columbia Plan would have created limited liability and a schedule of benefits for out-of-pocket losses, both provisions being similar to basic workmen's compensation coverage. Payment would be made without regard to fault. This was an exclusive remedy. There would be no recovery permitted for general pain and suffering allegations.

The plan covered only those accidents involving another vehicle, and it omitted recovery for victims of nonresidents, hit-and-run, insolvent, or uninsured drivers. It did, however, include model legislation that could have been altered to cover excluded losses. No provision was made for payment of automobile physical damage losses.

The automobile accident victim would be paid a periodic scheduled sum without regard to negligence. The plan would be compulsory. It would be administered by a special board. The option was left up to the individual state as to whether the plan would be handled through private insurers or by a state fund. There was also a deductible feature—out-of-pocket losses, other than medical expenses, were eliminated for the first week. (See Columbia University Council for Research in the Social Sciences, *Report by the Committee to Study Compensation for Automobile Accidents* (Columbia University, 1932.

THE COLLINS PLAN

The Collins Plan was given much consideration by the California legislature in 1953. In the form of an assembly bill, the plan was a complete draft modeled after the California workmen's compensation law but with jurisdiction for settling disputes in the courts rather than in the commission. Despite early interest, the proposal received virtually no support.

The proposal was based substantially on the *Report by the Committee to Study Compensation for Automobile Accidents*, Columbia University, 1932. (See Bibliography entry No. 97).

EHRENZWEIG'S "FULL AID" PLAN

In 1954, Professor Albert A. Ehrenzweig, University of California Law School, published a book in which he proposed replacing some common law liability with fixed statutory scheduled benefits without regard to fault. (See Albert A. Ehrenzweig, *"Full Aid" Insurance for the Traffic Victim—A Voluntary Compensation Plan.* Berkeley: University of California Press, 1954).

Not Compulsory

The coverage was to be underwritten by private companies and was not to be compulsory, but there would be some inducements built into the plan to encourage purchase of the coverage. The plan proposed legislation that would relieve purchasers from the liability for ordinary negligence if they obtained the coverage. They could still be required to defend actions brought against them for criminal negligence.

Those persons injured by uninsured automobiles, hit-and-run drivers, or in cases where recovery was not possible because of insolvency or non-liability, would be compensated from a fund administered by private insurers. This would be an "uncompensated injury fund." A motorist, after his first accident, would be required to obtain the insurance.

Features of the Plan

The distinctive features of the plan:
1.   A schedule of benefits would be paid periodically without regard to fault.
2.   There would be no compensation for pain and suffering. Victims could retain their remedies under tort law, including claims for pain and suffering.
3.   There would be no automobile property damage coverage.
4.   All disputed property damage matters would be submitted to arbitration.

Criticisms of the Plan

The plan has been criticized because of its brevity and incompleteness in concept. The voluntary nature of the coverage also rules out its acceptability by its critics. Relieving the motorist from liability for "ordinary negligence" but not for "criminal negligence" is perhaps one of the greatest weaknesses of the Ehrenzweig plan. How do you distinguish between ordinary negligence and criminal negligence? Everyone would still feel that he must carry liability coverage. "Full aid" coverage then becomes a dispensable additional expense upon the public.

Nevertheless, the author believed that there would be a reduction of insurance costs made possible by the plan, attracting the public to buy such coverage.

The plan served in part as a basis for Nationwide's "Family Compensation" coverage. (See Ehrenzweig, No. 157 and MacKay, No. 289).

THE LEON GREEN PLAN
"Compulsory Motor Vehicle Comprehensive Loss Insurance"

In 1958, Professor Leon Green, of the University of Texas Law School, wrote a book called *Traffic Victims—Tort Law and Insurance* (Evanston, Illinois: Northwestern University Press, 1958). He proposed a compulsory motor vehicle comprehensive loss insurance, providing that operating a motor vehicle without insurance would be a felony. The compulsory insurance would be sold by private companies.

Use of Masters

The Green plan would pay on the basis of common law damages (as opposed to scheduled benefits). Since payment would be based upon common law damage valuations and not upon scheduled benefits, suit would be brought on behalf of the injured party in the appropriate court. The presiding judge would then appoint a master to informally hear the case and to report his findings back to the court for review. If a judgment was found for the plaintiff, it is assumed that a lump sum payment would be made. Damages would be measured by the present legal rules relating to damages with any controversies on damages settled without the aid of juries.

Losses would be paid without regard to fault. No compensation would be made for pain and suffering. The plan included a $100 deductible feature.

Weaknesses

The Green plan has many inherent weaknesses, including the absence of model legislation and cost studies. There was no allocation or details in the plan concerning collisions involving more than one vehicle. The plan fails to compensate victims of uninsured motorists, and because of the delay inherent while a master is reviewing the issue of damages, there would be no provision for advance payments, periodic payments, or rehabilitation. (See MacKay, No. 289).

THE CONARD PLAN

The Conard Plan is a proposal by Alfred F. Conard ("The Economic Treatment of Automobile Injuries," 63 Michigan Law Review 279, December 1964).

A National System

Under the Conard Plan, a national system would be established. A fund, operated by the government or by a private monopoly involving participation by insurance companies, would be created. The plan would be funded by a tax on automobile owners or drivers on a basis which considered accident frequency. The Social Security system could be extended to provide subsistence to all victims and their dependents.

Features of the Plan

Rehabilitation, both medical and vocational, would be provided for all victims of automobile accidents. In addition, disability income, at some fraction of wages but not over the national average wage, is granted wage-earner victims on a lifetime basis, if necessary.

Tort damage would be recoverable. Collateral benefits would be excluded. The element of personal detriment to the defendant would be retained by excluding from insurance coverages punitive and "psychic" (non-economic) damages, and by not permitting unconditional discharge in bankruptcy. Also policyholders previously involved in accidents would be required to pay higher premiums.

Litigation costs would be assessed against the party who rejected a reasonable settlement offer. (See Marryott, No. 294).

KEETON AND O'CONNELL PROPOSAL
("Basic Protection")

The Keeton-O'Connell proposal suggests fundamental changes in law and in automobile insurance policies affecting victims of automobile accidents. The proposal has two main features:

1.   Development of a new form of automobile insurance—Basic Protection insurance; and

2.   A change in law which would do away with claims based on negligence, within specified limitations.

Description of the Proposal

Basic Protection insurance, generally, is a combination of coverages already in existence but most closely resembles medical payments insurance. It initiates a two-party claims procedure which compensates victims regardless of fault. The insured, a passenger, or a pedestrian (anyone injured, arising out of the ownership, maintenance or use of insured's vehicle) is compensated under the insured's policy, with exceptions: a person who intentionally injures himself is not compensated, and persons in other automobiles are not covered.

Since the plan is compulsory, all injured parties will collect from the policy applicable to the vehicle involved. Motorists are exempt from legal liability for negligent driving against injured third parties if damages for pain and suffering are not greater than $5000 and other damages (such as for medical expense and wage loss) are not greater than $10,000.

There is no coverage for property damage. It covers only bodily injury.

Payment is made month by month as the expenses occur. Basic Protection is excess insurance—there are no payments made for losses reimbursed from other sources (except life insurance proceeds).

The plan covers "out-of-pocket net loss," which includes medical bills and lost wages. "Reasonable expenses for reasonably necessary products and services" are covered. (Charges in excess of the customary rate for semi-private hospital room are not allowed; maximum charge for funeral expenses is limited to $500). There is a maximum per accident limit of $100,000.

Deductibles

There is a $100 deductible on net loss. If wage losses exceeded $1000, the deduction would be larger—10 percent of the wage loss, instead of $100. Further, there is a wage loss limit of $750 per month. An additional limitation on recovery is the stipulation that only gross pay less income tax is payable—this amounts to 15 percent of gross wages.

It is possible to increase the amount of the deductible as it applies to both general benefits and work loss or both. This is an optional feature.

Partial Replacement of Negligence Liability

Basic Protection establishes two exemptions of liability under tort law: (1) no recovery for pain and suffering up to $5000; and (2) exemption from liability for out-of-pocket expenses (exclusive of property damage) up to $10,000.

Retention of Negligence Liability

Where injuries cause expenses in excess of $10,000 for economic loss or $5000 for pain and suffering, the Basic Protection Plan reverts to the negligence system. But the exemptions of liability ($5000 or $10,000) are excluded from the amount recovered in a tort action.

"Added Protection Coverage" (Optional)

Limited Property Damage Coverage—the original Basic Protection insurance provided no property damage coverage. Keeton and O'Connell have recently revised their plan to give the insured the following choice:

1.   Insured can obtain coverage on his automobile under Basic Protection and at the same time receive exemption of liability for damage to vehicles of others; or

2.   Insured can continue to carry an automobile property damage liability policy.

Under number 1 there is no coverage for loss to property of others except automobiles.

Under number 2 the two insurers covering two colliding vehicles would not be permitted to sue one another.

When a vehicle of a non-Added Protection insured is damaged

by an Added Protection insured, the non-Added Protection insured would make his claim, based on negligence, against his own tort insurer under what might be termed *EXEMPT MOTORIST COVERAGE*. This would be closely analogous to Uninsured Motorist Coverage now in use. When a non-Added Protection insured is in collision with another non-Added Protection insured, each would have his negligence claim against the other, as at present.

Added Pain and Suffering Coverage (Optional)

There is provided under the Keeton-O'Connell Plan an optional Added Pain and Suffering coverage. It provides coverage for pain and inconvenience not recoverable under the Basic Protection Plan. It would cover an insured or a resident relative.

Catastrophe Protection Coverage (Optional)

Written with or without a deductible, the optional Catastrophe Protection Coverage would cover out-of-pocket expenses in excess of the Basic Protection limit of $10,000. Limits may not be lower than $100,000 per person and $300,000 per accident.

Other Options

The plan permits other modifications to increase benefits. Deductibles can be reduced or eliminated; limits can be increased for hospital and funeral charges; and coverage can be afforded for losses which fall within extraterritorial exclusions.

Assigned Claims Plan

The proposed statute drawn by Keeton and O'Connell makes provision for an Assigned Claims Plan which covers claims of those who are unable to collect under Basic Protection:

1. Where Basic Protection is not applicable;
2. Hit-and-run cases;
3. Where Basic Protection is inadequate because of multiple claims or financial inability of insurer to meet claims.

Insurers are required to participate; assignments are made in relation to premium volume of Basic Protection insurance written by each insurer. Non-residents are covered.

Marketing System

It is anticipated that the new coverage would be marketed in the same manner as under the present automobile liability insurance system. (See F.C. & S., No. 40; Keeton & O'Connell, Nos. 252 & 257; entry No. 95; Chapin, No. 70; Keeton, No. 251; and Hodosh, No. 194).

INVERSE LIABILITY
AUTOMOBILE ACCIDENT INSURANCE PLAN

"Inverse Liability" is a proposal presented by J.B.M. Murray, FCII, AIIC, ACAS, Casualty Superintendent of the Prudential Assurance Company, Ltd., at the May 1967 meeting of the Casualty Actuarial Society.

"Inverse Liability" is an extension of medical payments coverage. The coverage applies to all automobile accidents, and the insured is permitted to choose his own amount of insurance.

Benefits of the Proposal

The plan pays benefits to the named insured and to dependent relatives residing with him, arising out of any automobile accident, whether the injured are drivers, passengers, or pedestrians. Pedestrians without automobiles could purchase the coverage.

Medical, surgical, hospital and nursing expenses, disability income, and rehabilitation expenses are paid. Collateral source benefits are excluded.

Retention of Tort Liability System

The insured has the election to pursue his remedies under tort law. If he elects to proceed under tort law, he forfeits all benefits under his Inverse Liability Coverage.

One compulsory policy could be written, containing Inverse Liability Coverage and regular automobile liability coverage. It would be unnecessary to change the law unless the coverage is made compulsory. The policy contains a subrogation clause so that the company could seek recovery from any responsible third party. The insurer can examine the insured as often as necessary. In addition, the application would contain declarations as to the insured's physical health.

In the event of insured's death, the financial loss sustained by his estate for medical bills would be payable. (See Bibliography entry No. 339; Murray, No. 317; and Marryott, No. 294).

THE COTTER PLAN

The Cotter Plan is a legislative package put together by former Connecticut Insurance Commissioner William R. Cotter in January, 1969. Entitled the "Automobile Insurance and Accident Benefits Reform" program, it proposes the preservation of the present tort liability system. It provides quick payments for basic economic loss on a no-fault basis, but also preserves the right of recovery under the fault system. It is designed to respond to public criticism "by streamlining claim settlement procedures, prohibiting unjustified cancellations, and eliminating other inequities, inefficiencies, and sources of dissatisfaction."

Features of the Plan

Characterized as "a sound, evolutionary approach," the program includes the following features:

1.   Automatically includes in every passenger automobile liability policy at least $2000 medical payments coverage and 52 weeks of disability benefits. This would guarantee to every insured motorist—to his family, injured guest passengers, and pedestrians injured by his car—immediate payment for most economic losses. Disability benefits would specify a monthly maximum of $500, making a total possible recovery of $6000.

2.   The creation of a mandatory small claims arbitration system for cases under $3000.

3.   Adoption of a comparative negligence law (Wisconsin-type with a provision for special verdicts).

4.   Adoption of a standard for measuring damages for pain and suffering. The plan allows up to 50 percent of hospital and medical bills totaling up to $500 for such damages and 100 percent of the excess of $500 as an additional pain and suffering allowance. Amounts in excess of these limitations could be awarded in cases of death, dismemberment, disfigurement or permanent impairments.

5.   Regulation of attorneys' contingent fees. The suggestion is made that such fees be limited to a 25 percent maximum, with the right to apply for additional fees where circumstances justify it.

6.   The plan adopts measures to promote advance payments in every meritorious case of all out-of-pocket expenses of the claimant as they accrue.

7.   Provision for an open competition rating law.

8.   The plan defines damages for loss of income in liability cases so as to take income tax savings into account.

9.   Imposes stiff penalties for fraudulent claims and for improperly withheld information necessary to promote a fair settlement.

10.   Limits the reasons for cancellation of private passenger automobile insurance to non-payment of premium or suspension of operators license.

Support for the Plan

On February 18, 1969, the American Mutual Insurance Alliance endorsed the plan. It has also been endorsed by the 24,000-member Connecticut State Grange, The Connecticut Stock and Mutual Agents associations, most of the newspapers of the state, and the Federation of Insurance Counsel, which represents more than one thousand trial lawyers throughout the country. It has received strong support from the National Association of Independent Insurers. The American Insurance Association, which has been advocating a more radical "no-fault" proposal of its own, has indicated it would find the Cotter Plan acceptable as a second choice.

Criticisms of the Cotter Plan

The Cotter Plan was rejected in May of 1969 by the Judiciary Subcommittee of the Connecticut General Assembly. The Subcommittee commented that the Cotter proposals were experimental, untested and undocumented, and that the changes it called for were unwarranted. An open rating law, incidental to the Cotter Plan, was criticized because it was felt that it would not ease markets for those finding it difficult to secure protection, since the companies would make competitive rates available only to the best risks.

The American Insurance Association was quite critical of the Cotter Plan, indicating that it did not go far enough toward the "no-fault" concept. T. Lawrence Jones, president of the American Insurance Association, stated, "While these benefits are payable regardless of fault, there is no immunity from tort liability. Insurers are expected to pass the loss burden on to the insurer of the so-called negligent party. This loss shifting, in our judgment, cannot possibly serve any real social purpose. It involves unnecessary costs which will only be partially minimized by the requirement that these inter-company suits be arbitrated. We believe it is a mistake, and a costly one, to continue the liability concept."

Professor David J. Sargent of Suffolk University Law School commented, "An analysis of this plan will conclusively show that it would not only fail to solve most of the present problems, but would impose on the public an inequitable and grossly unfair and untested method of compensating victims of motor vehicle accidents. I think the plan could be accurately dubbed 'The Insurance Industry's Relief Act.' " His primary objection was the fact that it limits benefits for injured persons and limits attorney's income but does nothing to reform the basic inequities of the tort liability system. (See Bibliography entries Nos. 69, 88 and 485).

NATIONAL COMPENSATION PLAN
FOR AUTOMOBILE ACCIDENT CASES
(Hofstadter and Pesner)

A plan proposed by the Honorable Samuel H. Hofstadter (Justice of the Supreme Court of the State of New York) and Robert Pesner, Esq.

A *federal highway compensation statute*, similar to a workmen's compensation act, would be established under which all victims would be indemnified for all "actual loss." This apparently would cover medical bills and disability payments.

No details of this plan are spelled out. (See Marryott, No. 294).

COMPENSATION BOARDS

The compensation board is a more radical proposal than most defenders of tort liability will support. Under this proposal, all personal-injury litigation in each state would be taken out of the trial courts. Compensation boards in each state would set specific rules on how much could be collected for a particular injury.

Payments would cover medical costs, plus income lost while the claimant was out of work. Anyone injured in an accident would be compensated by his insurance company unless he caused the accident intentionally.

Eliminates "Fault Principle"

It would almost completely eliminate the "fault principle." No blame would be placed, legally, on any of the parties to an accident. Judges and juries would not be called upon to determine if anyone involved had been negligent. Auto accidents would be treated just as industrial accidents were 40 or 50 years ago.

Proponents of a compensation system say it would slash expenses for lawyers as well as the cost of handling claims. Big awards by juries would tend to disappear, though compensation to accident victims would be prompt.

Right to Sue Retained

Such a plan would not necessarily cut down substantially the number of court cases, because it would put a maximum price tag on compensation that could be paid by the board. If a plaintiff felt this compensation to be insufficient, he could still sue in the courts.

This plan provides on a state level what the Hofstadter and Pesner National Compensation Plan provides for on the federal level.

(See Bibliography entries Nos. 8 and 94).

THE WOODROOF-SQUILLANTE PLAN

The focal point of the Woodroof-Squillante Plan is an insurance policy which includes first-party insurance benefits and liability coverage. The proposal will be incorporated in a book bearing the title, *Automobile Liability and the Changing Law*, to be published in late 1971. The authors, M.G. Woodroof, III, and Alphonse M. Squillante, are professors of law at Drake University.

The expanded first-party coverage would become a mandatory part of automobile insurance coverage; however, motorists could elect not to buy automobile insurance at all. The philosophy behind the right of election is that

> "The individual's right and ability" to refuse coverage "is assured a high priority in America. To the extent, therefore, that individuals use this freedom in an irresponsible manner, and refuse to provide for their needs, and to the combined extent that society takes upon itself voluntarily the duty of compensating these people despite their own voluntary refusal to take care of their own needs, these individuals represent not an automobile accident problem, but a social problem. Such a situation must be cured through education, so that these people's value system will be such as to enable them to function better in our complex modern society. At the same time, these individuals will be compensated from general revenue funds, so that the cost of compensating them will be allocated in a morally appropriate manner, equally amongst the entire society which spawned them and which now takes upon itself the duty of meeting the needs for which they voluntarily refuse to provide."

The authors believe that the plan meets the existing needs of our insurance system through "the application of gradual progressive reform."

Features of the Plan

1.   First-party medical payments coverage for all reasonable hospital, surgical, and medical expenses are provided. Coverage is for a period of one year from the date of accident up to a maximum payment of $2000.

2.   Reasonable funeral expenses to an upper limit of $1000

are included.

3.   Wage losses are compensated at the rate of 80 percent of current wages at the time of accident up to a maximum of $750 a month. The percentile figure can be modified to reflect net wage loss figures. Benefits would be payable for a maximum of six months from the date of accident, beginning the first day of wage loss.

4.   Individuals not earning wages or income at the time of accident would be compensated for up to 80 percent of "actual dollars spent" in replacing the services normally rendered by the victim, with a maximum of $12 per day.

5.   Survivorship benefits of up to 80 percent of current wages for a period of one year, subject to a $500 monthly maximum, are provided. In the case of decedents earning no wages at time of death (such as the non-working mother of a child under the age of 18) the benefit would be $12 a day for a one-year period.

6.   The first-party coverage is excess over governmental sources, such as Medicare and Workmen's Compensation.

Alteration of Tort Liability System

The plan contemplates changes in the existing tort liability system. There would be a limitation upon recovery for pain and suffering awards of a maximum of 50 percent recovery based on the first $500 of medical expenses incurred (excluding X-ray costs) and limited to 100 percent of any excess medical expenses over $500. This limitation would not be applicable in cases where the injuries from the accident resulted in death, disfigurement, dismemberment, permament disability, or a permanent loss of a bodily function. In addition to these specific exceptions, a court may in any given tort suit determine that the injuries resulting from the accident were such that the limitation on pain and suffering would be unfair or would shock the conscience of the court. In such cases the court may instruct the jury that the limitation will not apply in the specific case.

Advance Payments

The plan provides that evidence of advance payments will be inadmissible as evidence of liability in any tort suit resulting from a specific claim. Further, such payments will not be construed as a waiver or estoppel against an insurance company.

Other Features

Tort recoveries under the plan would be reduced to the extent of payments made under the basic first-party coverage. In addition, there is a provision for establishment of arbitration of small claims.

It is also proposed that a system of "open competition rating" be adopted by legislation. Either the California system of "no-file" open rate competition, or any of the forms of "file-and-use" or "use-and-file" rating would be acceptable under the plan.

Safeguards against insurance company insolvency would be provided the public under a mandatory Automobile Insurance Industry Solvency Assurance Plan. This would be a contractual plan whereby the obligations of any company becoming insolvent would be assumed (on a proportionate basis) by the other members of the insurance industry.

Those automobile accident victims not owning automobiles and thus not insured under the basic policy would be included under the coverage of the owner of the automobile involved in the accident, provided that the driver was negligent.

In cases where individuals are unable to recover tort claims because of uninsured motorists, provision is made for claiming under an Assigned Liability Claims Plan. The claim of the uninsured motorist would be assigned to a liability insurer, with the distribution of such claims determined proportionately according to volume of business written. The insurer assigned the claim would investigate the claim, settle it appropriately, and recover any outlay and expenses via subrogation against the tort-feasor.

CHAPTER VII

INSURANCE INDUSTRY PLANS

Some of the better automobile accident indemnification proposals have been made by various segments of the insurance industry. Traditionally the institution entrusted by the American public to administer the system, it can be expected that industry spokesmen are highly familiar with the administrative problems involved in any major change in the reparations system.

Indeed, the large majority of the literature which has appeared on the no-fault controversy has been produced within the industry itself. Problems of rating equity, compensation adequacy, loss verification and claims handling, and other aspects of a reform system have been discussed at length within the insurance industry.

As we can expect industry familiarity with the reparations system, we can also anticipate a considerable expression of self-interest designed to assure that the industry's financial stake in the ultimate reform of the automobile accident reparations system is not prejudiced by over-zealous reformers. Proposals supported by the industry are typified by their willingness to effect economies which "gore someone else's ox."

Thus, the Illinois Plan, strongly supported by the industry, effects economies by limiting pain and suffering losses, eliminating "double recovery" in tort actions and effecting other economies. A typical economy in most plans is that of by-passing the courts and attorneys-at-law in the reparations system. Avoidance of the legal machinery, however, is the essence of the "no-fault" movement and is advocated by many government spokesmen, academicians, and others, as well as insurance industry people.

It is a credit to the industry that a wide divergence of opinion within the industry has been generated out of the no-fault controversy. It is out of the industry's extensive examination of the problem that some of the most imaginative proposals have emanated.

It is a further credit to the industry that individual companies and trade associations have experimented over a number of years with a variety of accident reparations programs. Notable among these experiments have been the Nationwide "Family Compensation Plan," offered to third-party claimants between 1956 and 1965—

and the "Illinois Experiment in Guaranteed Benefits," inaugurated in several Illinois counties in 1968 by a number of insurance companies and a trade association, the American Mutual Insurance Alliance.

The various proposals warrant careful study, and they are presented here for the reader.

NATIONWIDE MUTUAL INSURANCE COMPANY "FAMILY COMPENSATION PLAN"

For ten years—1956 through 1965—Nationwide Mutual Insurance Company offered coverage that protected everyone injured in an auto accident, regardless of fault. Nationwide finally was forced to drop its unique third-party protection early in 1966 mainly because it didn't receive the insurance industry support and participation essential for its success. It was considered by the company as an effective supplement to the negligence system. It didn't replace the traditional "fault" system.

Features of the Plan

Third-party victims had the alternative of accepting specific benefits, or they could pursue their claims under the laws of negligence. They were given as much as three months to decide which course to take.

The protection applied to the policyholder and all occupants of his car, as well as to all third parties such as pedestrians, cyclists, and occupants of other cars in the accident. Maximum payment was $7900 per person. The schedule of benefits included:

1. Maximum of $2000 for medical and hospital expenses;
2. Five dollars per day up to 180 days, for continuous house confinement; $2.50 per day for those under 18; and
3. Death benefit of $5000 for those 18 and over; $2000 for those under 18.

Benefits were reduced by the amount of other insurance payments. Third parties who caused the accident through gross negligence or while under the influence of alcohol or narcotics were excluded from coverage. If compensation was accepted, a release was obtained. Payments were made as medical bills were presented.

Experience under the Plan

Coverage was provided in Maryland, Delaware, Connecticut, Florida, Indiana, Michigan, New York, Ohio, Pennsylvania, Rhode Island, South Carolina, Tennessee, Vermont, and West Virginia. The volume of Family Compensation coverage reached a peak of 865,000 policies. This represented nearly half the 1.75 million auto policies Nationwide had in force in the 14 states.

A study showed that from 1959 through 1963, there were 8,682 separate Family Compensation claim payments made to third parties outside Nationwide-insured vehicles. They were paid a total of $4.6 million. In the same period, 32,000 third-party claimants, who conceivably might have chosen the Family Compensation settlement, preferred to file their claims under bodily injury liability. They collected $43.6 million.

A study of 44,000 claims paid in 1963 and 1964 showed that 80 percent of the dollar payments under Family Compensation went to the policyholder, members of his household, or passengers in his car.

At the same time, there were 18,500 third-party claims handled for persons other than occupants of the insured car. Of these, 15 percent accepted payments under Family Compensation while 85 percent took the bodily injury route. The study showed that 5 percent of the dollar payments went to the Family Compensation claimants and 95 percent went to bodily injury liability claimants.

As an alternative to the bodily injury liability coverage, Family Compensation wasn't as effective as had been hoped. It was believed that claimants were wary of the offer of benefits regardless of liability; the general public wasn't familiar with it. This unfamiliarity may have created suspicion, or even mistrust.

"We still believe the third-party feature of the Family Compensation coverage is a realistic and acceptable method of helping to close a serious gap. But participation by the industry as a whole is essential." (See Griffith, No. 181).

INSURANCE COMPANY OF NORTH AMERICA PLAN

The Insurance Company of North America Plan was first publicly presented before the Federation of Insurance Counsel on February 1, 1968. It was designed to permit immediate implementation by the states, without constitutional amendment. The plan proposes compulsory standard coverage as a prerequisite to automobile registration. The standard coverage would provide both two-party and third-party liability coverage.

Features of the Plan

First-party direct benefits would be paid all occupants of the insured vehicle and all persons injured by the vehicle, except occupants of another vehicle. It would cover reasonable hospital and medical expenses, extra expense incurred as a result of accidental injury, and loss of income. Provision could be made for pain and suffering awards in amounts to be established in each case by a medical panel.

The statute should permit deductibles and co-pay features in the first-party coverage applicable to the named insured and members of his family at the option of the insured, with a maximum limit on such deductibles and co-pay amounts.

There would be a minimum limit of $15,000 per person on the first-party coverage, a maximum aggregate annual retention under deductible and co-pay features of $500, and a minimum single limit of $25,000 on the liability coverage.

The statute would permit a reduction in premium for the exclusion of collateral source recoveries.

No-Fault Features

There would be no abrogation of the tort liability system nor of compensation for pain and suffering damages; however, the insured would be precluded from recovering in a suit against a third party the benefits recovered under his policy, including benefits from other sources which he elected to exclude and any deductible which he elected to take. Thus, the plan appears to have true "no-fault" features. There would be no exemption from tort liability, and the insurer would be subrogated to the tort right of its insured to the extent of indemnification.

The INA Plan provides the insured with the benefits of being able to recover from his own insurance company. It appears to tamper with the tort liability system by barring the insured's right to tort recovery for benefits received from his own insurance comapny only if the insured's right were taken away by statute. However, since the insured's company has the right of subrogation, and collateral source benefits are excluded, the appearance of "no-fault" features is illusory.

Legislation would prescribe realistic standards for licensing.

INA also had its MEND Program, under which immediate payment was made in a broad variety of rehabilitation cases connected with automobile accidents. (See Barker, No. 39).

GUARANTEED BENEFITS PLAN

The "Illinois Experiment in Guaranteed Benefits" was started in several counties in Illinois in March, 1968. Participating companies included Allstate, Chubb & Son, Continental Insurance Companies, Continental National American, Country Mutual, Economy Fire & Casualty, Nationwide, Kemper Group, Liberty Mutual, and the American Mutual Insurance Alliance (which originated the plan), a national association of mutual insurers.

Features of the Plan

Payments were made for medical expenses and disability for automobile occupants and pedestrians, up to $12,500 per person ($5000 in medical expenses; plus a maximum of $7500 in other benefits—disability, "loss of service," and "supplemental lump sum payments").

In two-car accidents and in pedestrian cases, claimants were offered Guaranteed Benefits by the other driver's insurer. In one-car accidents, they collected from their own insurance company.

The $5000 limit on medical benefits included up to $1000 for funeral expenses. All reasonable medical expenses incurred within one year of date of accident were recoverable, subject to the $5000 limit. There was no deduction for benefits received from collateral sources.

Medical benefits were paid in all cases, whether the claimant chose to file a liability claim or accept the Guaranteed Benefits option. Amounts paid in medical benefits were deducted from any liability settlement or court award.

Disability benefits were paid only to injured persons who elected to accept them in lieu of whatever recovery they might expect to get under the tort liability system. Pegged at 70 percent of the claimant's wages or income, payments could not exceed 125 percent of the average weekly wage in the victim's state of residence. Total amount payable could not exceed $7500. Disability benefits were paid even if the claimant received a pay check under a wage continuation plan or other arrangement.

Housewives and other persons with no earnings were eligible for Loss of Service Payments. Available for one year, with a limit of $7500, they (loss of service payments) covered up to 70 percent of the expense of replacing the services of the injured person. A minimum payment was made even if the family managed to get along without hiring a housekeeper.

Both housewives and wage earners were offered a lump sum when monthly payments ceased—50 percent of the amount received under either Basic Disability or Loss of Service Benefits, depending upon which was chosen—minimum payment: $35 weekly. This supplemental payment was to compensate for indignity and inconvenience. A lump sum payment up to $7500 was made for permanent disability.

Survivors' loss payments were made if the victim died of injuries within one year of the accident. Forty percent of weekly income loss (maximum of $5000) was payable.

Right of Election

The injured person had time to make his election, plus a chance to reconsider if he had already chosen Guaranteed Benefits and wished to change his mind. Claimants were not asked to sign anything—experience indicated that the vast majority of claimants would not violate an oral agreement.

Those accepting the plan were paid without having to prove fault on the part of the other party. They could elect to press claims under tort law, however. Drivers clearly negligent were not offered the benefits. The plan did not cover property damage. (See Bibliography entries Nos. 360 and 320; Wise, No. 470).

THE AMERICAN INSURANCE ASSOCIATION PLAN
"The Complete Personal Protection Automobile Insurance Plan"

The American Insurance Association in late October of 1968 announced its endorsement of a compulsory, no-fault, first-party automobile accident compensation system.

Entitled "Report of Special Committee to Study and Evaluate the Keeton-O'Connell Basic Protection Plan and Automobile Accident Reparations," T. Lawrence Jones, AIA president, stated that the plan was the culmination of a year-long study by a special committee of the AIA "which had as its purpose the analysis of present problems and dissatisfaction with the existing system of automobile insurance, and the analysis of modifications and alternative systems which might better meet the needs of the motoring public and the insurance industry."

Hypotheses of the AIA Plan

The hypotheses of the AIA's Special Automobile Committee are as follows:

1.   Fault is not a proper factor to determine reimbursement for motor vehicle accident injuries.

2.   Pain and suffering are not susceptive of objective measurement and should not be included in a reparations system.

3.   The cost of motor vehicle accidents should be borne by motorists.

4.   Any system should be operated by the present automobile insurance industry and afford it an opportunity to realize a reasonable profit.

5.   Any alternative system should cost less than the present system and should provide persons injured in auto accidents with a higher proportion of the insurance premium dollar. (See Bibliography entry No. 330).

The American Insurance Association attempted to identify in its proposal the real criticisms of the present tort liability system and found four principal points of contention:

1.   The present system doesn't pay everybody.

2.   The present system is too costly.

3.   The present system is inequitable as to distribution of costs and benefits.

4.   The present system is too slow.

It was the belief of the AIA Committee that on the basis of these criticisms its program supplied workable answers.

Unique Application to Property Damages

The AIA proposal is unique among "no-fault" plans in that it addresses itself to the problem of property damages, whereas other plans tend to restrict the no-fault concept to bodily injuries, leaving property damage claims to be handled under the tort liability system.

The proposed AIA program would include coverage for loss of or damage to property other than automobiles and their contents, arising out of automobile accidents, such loss being payable to the owner of the property as an additional insured under the motorist's policy. An exemption from tort liability for damages to other automobiles and their contents would apply to the insured motorist in all instances where the law of the state enacting the program is controlling. Motorists would assume the risk of damage of their own vehicles, with physical damage insurance being available to them at their option. Insurers would be required to offer this optional physical damage coverage.

Features of the Plan

The proposal is relatively simple. It is, essentially, a first-party pure no-fault system giving coverage for personal injury and would include coverage for loss of or damage to property other than automobiles and their contents, arising out of automobile accidents. An injured motorist would collect all of his hospital and medical costs, plus other economic loss, such as lost wages, from his own insurance company. Features of the AIA Plan are as follows:

1.   Unlimited medical expenses. Allowable expenses would consist of reasonable charges for reasonably necessary products and services. For example, hospital room and board would be limited to semi-private accommodations in the insured's area.

2.   Reasonable charges for funeral and burial expenses, not to exceed $1000, would be paid.

3.   Work income losses and expenses reasonably incurred for services in lieu of those the injured person would have performed without income (*i.e.*, expenses of hiring household help) would be covered. Loss of income from work would be adjusted to reflect income tax advantages incident to such nontaxable payments. Wage loss would be limited to $750 per month.

4.   Payment for pain and suffering would be excluded.

5.   Extra payments would be made to persons who sustain permanent impairment or disfigurement in automobile accidents to compensate them for such injuries which cannot be measured by economic loss. Level of payment in such cases would be 50 percent of the amount payable to the claimant for his hospital and medical expenses and would vary according to the degree of impairment or disfigurement.

6.   Additional insurance against serious injuries sustained in automobile accidents would be made available to motorists on a voluntary basis.

7.   "Collateral source benefits should not be subtracted in determining the amount of economic loss sustained as a result of an automobile accident; however, duplication of benefits is undesirable and should be precluded wherever possible."

8.   Loss benefits would be payable to insured persons periodically as losses accrue, subject to commutation in special circumstances. The best interests of the claimant, judicially determined when necessary, would be the controlling consideration in determining the need for, or the desirability of, commutation.

9.   Coverage would cover the owner of the vehicle and his family for their loss and in addition would cover other occupants of the car and pedestrians who are not otherwise insured.

10.   Passengers in public vehicles would be covered under the insurance on the vehicle in which they were riding.

11.   The program would be compulsory—coverage would be a prerequisite to registering or operating an automobile in a state enacting the program.

12.   Costs of rehabilitation would be covered under the plan.

Complete Immunity from Tort Liability

There would be complete immunity from tort liability. Motorists would still face the possiblity of tort actions in conflict-of-law situations, especially in connection with out-of-state driving; consequently, residual automobile liability insurance for limits of liability most commonly in use under state financial responsibility laws would be compulsory.

Uninsured drivers would be subject to liability in tort. Loss benefits would be subtracted from any tort recovery against an uninsured driver and repaid to the insurer which had made the payment under the assigned claims plan. The non-resident wishing to avoid tort liability could obtain economic loss insurance for the operation of his vehicle within the enacting state.

The right to present common law procedures, including jury trial, would be retained for settling and litigating disputes. This right would extend to disputed claims for economic loss benefits as well as to disputed claims involving residual automobile liability insurance.

Damage to Property

Coverage for loss of or damage to property other than automobiles and their contents, arising out of automobile accidents, would be paid. The owner of the property would be treated as an additional insured under the motorist's policy.

Motorists would assume the risk of damage of their own vehicles, with physical damage insurance being available to them at their option. Insurers would be required to offer this optional physical damage coverage.

Assigned Claims Plan

The plan includes an assigned claims provision, which would make payment even in automobile cases involving uninsured or hit-and-run vehicles. Insurers writing economic loss insurance in the state would be required to pay claims assigned to them on an equitable basis under a plan approved by the Insurance Commissioner.

Pedestrians would be covered for economic loss under their own policy, or, if a non-owner, under the driver's policy. In cases of injury involving nonresident or hit-and-run drivers, the pedestrian's claim would be handled through the assigned claims plan.

Application to Commercial Vehicles

The Committee recognized that the plan could be viewed as an unsound and undesirable windfall to commercial vehicles. The Committee contemplated essentially that the motorist would be responsible for people in his own car, and it is clear that commercial vehicles (except public-carrying vehicles) would have little exposure because of the absence of family and guests in commercial vehicles.

Thus, the cost borne by commercial vehicles under the ordinary tort liability system would be shifted to a considerable extent to private passenger vehicles. The AIA Plan does not endeavor to redistribute those lost costs, except as respects passengers in public vehicles where the insurance on the public vehicle would be primary.

Because of the desire to make commercial vehicles bear their proportionate share of the economic losses, the Committee suggested that the AIA proposal could perhaps be modified to provide that the mandatory insurance on commercial vehicles should afford a primary basic protection benefit to occupants of private passenger vehicles injured in the accident. (See Bibliography entry No. 18).

NATIONAL ASSOCIATION OF INDEPENDENT INSURERS
"Dual Protection Plan"

The "Dual Protection Plan" was proposed on December 14, 1970, by the Chicago-based National Association of Independent Insurers, whose affiliated companies write over half the nation's automobile insurance. The plan provides for a limited first-party no-fault system. It preserves the right of tort action for damages in excess of policy limits.

According to the NAII president, "This program will provide the public with a broad, basic loss protection and speedy benefit payments, while stabilizing or reducing premium costs. It is responsive to the major criticisms of the present reparations system, and yet it does not destroy the principle of personal accountability for negligent driving or the other vital rights and concepts underlying that system."

Features of the Plan

The program provides for the following features:

1.   Broadening of the automobile insurance policy to afford basic immediate-pay coverage up to $2000 in medical expense benefits, including medical, hospital, and funeral expenses, for each person injured while riding in or struck by the insured automobile. Excess limits coverage would be available as an option.

2.   Coverage up to $6000 for wage loss with a maximum of $4380 payable for services otherwise performed by an injured non-wage earner. Excess limits coverage would be available as an option.

3.   Catastrophe coverage would be offered to all policyholders and their families, extending the scope of the basic immediate-pay protection to at least $100,000 per person for medical expenses and

wage loss, and $25,000 in death benefits. Optional coverage available under the "Dual Protection Plan" provides the following benefits up to $100,000 per person:

  a) All medical, hospital and rehabilitation expenses.

  b) A maximum of $750 a month for lost income from work, or $12 a day for other disabled persons.

  c) A maximum of $750 a month or a total of $25,000 in survivors' benefits.

  d) A minimum $5000 death benefit to the named beneficiary.

4. Preservation of an innocent accident victim's right to recover damages from a wrongdoer, including economic losses beyond those afforded by the immediate-pay coverage, as well as reasonable compensation for non-economic losses.

5. Streamlining of the judicial process by providing special arbitration of small claims procedures for quick, economical disposition of cases under $3000.

6. Further minimizing the cost of the system by adopting standards governing the amounts recoverable for pain and inconvenience in the less serious cases, and requiring that awards for wage loss be computed net of income taxes. For nonpermanent injuries (not involving death, permanent disability, disfigurement, loss of limb, *etc.*), damage awards for pain and suffering would be governed by a formula of up to 50 percent of medical and hospital expenses of $500 or less; up to 100 percent of medical and hospital expenses of more than $500. The right to sue would be preserved in serious injury, death or exceptional cases.

7. Benefits would be payable as accrued, subject to a two-week waiting period for lost wages and reimbursement for services otherwise performed by an injured non-wage earner.

8. Court supervision of the lawyers' contingent fee system in jurisdictions where it is not now regulated.

9. More stringent penalties for fraudulent claims.

10. Increased research and action to reduce the frequency and severity of accidents, to improve automobile design, and to cut automobile repair costs.

NAII Rationale for the Plan

A.D. Sappington, Chairman of the National Association of Independent Insurers, stresses the limited value of a no-fault provision which applies only to the bodily injury portion of the premium dollar, excluding property damage coverage. "We recognize," the NAII Chairman said, "that any reduction of automobile insurance rates resulting from the adoption of such plans would affect only the bodily injury portion of the premium dollar, and that, unless traffic accidents and injuries are reduced in number as well in severity, changing the methods of reparations will have little effect in reducing the overall cost of the insurance product."

The NAII "Dual Protection Plan," according to its supporters, in addition to compensating more injured persons faster and more efficiently, sets forth actions and proposals aimed at:

1. Curbing the accident toll through research, public education, and stronger traffic laws and enforcement.

2. Reducing the severity of injuries by fostering improved automobile safety design.

3. Developing economic incentives for the production and purchase of more damage-resistant automobiles.

4. Cutting the costs of automobile damage repairs through advanced repair technology.

5. The NAII proposal is aimed at treating "the causes of our problems rather than the symptoms." (See Bibliography entries Nos. 220, 336, and 363).

AMERICAN MUTUAL INSURANCE ALLIANCE
"Guaranteed Protection Plan"

The American Mutual Insurance Alliance which in March of 1968 inaugurated the "Illinois Experiment in Guaranteed Benefits" (discussed elsewhere in this book), in December of 1970 proposed the enactment of a new "Guaranteed Protection Plan." Dealing only with the bodily injury portion of automobile insurance, which typically accounts for about one-third of the total premium cost, the plan is a combination of retention of tort liability and the expansion of first-party coverages. Full third-party liability would be retained for property damage.

Features of the Proposal

Features of the proposal are as follows:

1. State laws would be amended to require that every automobile policy contain a mandatory $2000 minimum for first-party medical coverage, irrespective of fault. Higher limits would be available as an option of the insured.

2. Persons injured by the negligence of third parties could file liability claims for expenses not covered by the basic coverages. They could also seek compensation for disability and other general damages

not reflected in direct monetary losses. Such general damages include compensation for loss of limbs, permanent scars, prolonged suffering and disruption of the insured's personal life.

    3.   Persons eligible for basic benefits would include the policy-holder, resident members of his household, occupants of his car and pedestrians injured by his car.

    4.   Mandatory $6000 minimum for wage loss up to $12 per day for non-wage earners. Both would retain their right to bring a tort liability action for full economic losses.

    5.   Pain and suffering benefits in minor cases would be limited to a formula of 50 percent of medical expenses up to $500; 100 percent of medical expenses exceeding $500.

    6.   Mandatory arbitration would be used to settle small claims (under $3000), to reduce the costs of handling them and to speed their disposition without adding to court congestion.

    7.   Courts would regulate the fees charged by attorneys for handling personal injury lawsuits, as is already being done in the state of New York and in some other states.

    8.   Stricter law enforcement and licensing controls advocated.

    9.   Benefits would be paid as accrued for first-party benefits. Lump sum would be paid for liability benefits, subject to deduction of voluntary advance payments by insurers.

    10.   There would be no statutory limit on maximum payments, except that death benefits would be limited in some states which have statutory limitations. There would also be the limits on pain and suffering payments. First-party benefits would be deducted from third-party settlements. (See Bibliography entries Nos. 334 and 336).

Minimal No-Fault Features

The "Guaranteed Protection Plan" does little to affect the traditional remedies of the tort liability system. Mandatory first-party coverages would be provided, but the tort liability system would be retained.

The primary effects of the plan on tort rights of action would be the following:

    1)   Limitations on pain and suffering in minor cases.

    2)   Mandatory arbitration would be used to settle small claims (under $3,000).

    3)   First-party benefits would be deducted from third-party recoveries.

MAIAB PLAN
(Massachusetts Association of Insurance Agents and Brokers)

The Massachusetts Association of Insurance Agents and Brokers proposed a plan that would:

1.   Require a revised form of compulsory Medical Payments coverage.

2.   Make that coverage the primary source for the first $1000 of benefits.

3.   Prevent injured persons from collecting for any benefit due under that coverage in a tort action.

4.   Preserve the company right to subrogate against another involved insurer after paying such benefits.

5.   Restrict the insured's right to make claim for pain and suffering in most cases where out-of-pocket loss was less than $500.

6.   Create a Motor Vehicle Accident Indemnification Corporation to pay revised Medical Payment benefits to persons without regular access to such coverage, and

7.   Continue to require proper liability coverage.
(See Chapin, No. 70).

CONNECTICUT ASSOCIATION
OF INDEPENDENT INSURANCE AGENTS
"Basic Benefits for Victims of Auto Accidents"

The Connecticut Association of Independent Insurance Agents in early 1971 sponsored a bill for revision of the present system of automobile insurance and accident benefits in Connecticut. The purpose of the bill was to provide for automobile insurance reform, affording quick payments of basic economic losses on a no-fault basis, but preserving the right of recovery under the tort liability system for damages in excess of the basic coverage.

Features of the Plan

The plan includes the following features:

1.   Automatic medical and hospital expense coverage within six months after the accident up to $2000 and subject to an optional deductible of $250.

2.   Automatic income replacement coverage equal to 85 percent of the gross income lost during the period commencing 30 days after the accident and continuing for 52 weeks, subject to a maximum of $500 per month.

3.   Creation by rules of court of a mandatory small claims ar-

bitration system for cases under $3000.

4. Pain and suffering provisions in the bill allow an additional 50 percent to claimants whose medical and hospital expenses amounted to $500 or less, or an additional sum up to 100 percent of the expenses if they exceeded $500.

5. In cases of death, permanent disfigurement, loss of body member, permanent loss of a bodily function and other exceptional circumstances, a court or jury may exceed the standards of the measure.

6. The establishment of a system of comparative negligence.

Similar to 1969 Plan

Many of the elements of the plan, including the interpretation of comparative negligence, were contained in "A Program for Auto Insurance and Accident Benefits Reform" proposed to the Connecticut General Assembly by the Connecticut Insurance Department in the 1969 legislative session. (Bibliography entry No. 480).

DELAWARE ASSOCIATION OF INDEPENDENT AGENTS

A no-fault plan developed by the Delaware Association of Independent Agents was introduced into the state legislature in early 1971. The plan incorporated the following features:

1. An injured party would recover from his own insurer up to $5000 for medical and similar expense under first-party coverage.

2. An aggregate limit for all persons injured in the insured's car would be $50,000.

3. Included in the first-party coverage would be payment for up to 75% of lost earnings.

4. An injured party would retain his right to sue *if his damages exceed $5000.*

5. The insurer providing the first-party coverage would have the legal right to recover its cost from a negligent party other than its own insured.

6. Uninsured motorist coverage would be expanded to permit the purchase of additional coverage for injury or death up to $100,000. Property damage protection would also be provided, with a $250 deductible.

7. The insured would be permitted to purchase loss-of-use coverage to reimburse him for the rental of a vehicle if his own is damaged by any peril covered under his automobile policy. (Under present policies, such payments are made only if the insured's vehicle is

stolen.)

8.   There would be compulsory arbitration of property damage claims up to $5000. In cases where the insured and insurer disagreed about the amount of loss, the insurance commissioner would appoint a panel to make a ruling.

9.   An uninsured motorist fund would be established through funds collected from uninsured vehicle owners. (See Bibliography entry No. 111).

NATIONWIDE INSURANCE REFORM PLAN
(Bibliography entry No. 529)

The Nationwide Mutual Insurance Company of Columbus, Ohio, in 1971 proposed a plan completely eliminating fault in automobile claims settlements, as "the best solution to current auto insurance problems—and their causes." The plan would "assure continuation of the established network of state regulation, but with additional provisions for broad federal guidelines to establish reasonable country-wide uniformity." It is a "pure" no-fault plan.

Key Provisions of Plan

The key provisions of the Nationwide Plan are as follows:

1.   Compensation of all automobile victims, regardless of fault.

2.   Payment of all medical expenses for as long as necessary. Unlimited coverage.

3.   Reimbursement of victims for wage loss at the rate of 85 percent of their regular earnings, up to 200 percent of a state's average weekly wage. Persons earning more than the average could buy additional income protection.

4.   Reimbursement for all economic losses, including expenses incurred for services which the victim cannot perform because of his injury.

5.   Payment of all necessary costs of rehabilitation and, at the same time, provision of incentives for the injured person to return to work.

6.   Survivorship benefits up to $30,000, paid in monthly installments for a specified period.

7.   Payment for property damage—up to the cash value of the policyholder's automobile, and up to $5000 for other damaged property.

8.   Automobile insurance would be the primary source of reimbursement for auto injuries and disabilities, rather than excess cover-

age over and above collateral benefits.

9. The elimination of liability actions for catastrophic losses.

10. Death benefits would be tailored more to the needs of survivors, and these benefits would be paid in equal monthly installments for a specified period.

11. A provision for the equitable distribution of high-hazard risks among all companies through a reinsurance facility.

12. State insurance departments would continue to provide direct regulation of insurance companies, within prescribed federal guidelines adopted to encourage reasonable uniformity among state insurance laws or plans.

13. Provision for the sale of automobile insurance on a group plan because it would foster economies, improvement in service, and safety programs.

Evaluation of the Plan

The claimed beneficial aspects of Nationwide's plan are as follows:

1. More prompt and timely benefits for economic loss.

2. Closer correlation between the amount of loss and the amount of recovery.

3. Policyholders could obtain the amount of insurance needed for each person's protection; ability to recover would not be restricted to the liability limits of a third party's insurance policy.

4. All persons would be eligible for recovery, thus solving the pressing social problem caused when no compensation is provided because a "wrongdoer" cannot be found.

5. It is a consumer-oriented plan because the motorist always would be dealing with the company of his choice, rather than the company of someone else's choice.

6. Insurance would be available to all motorists, and not simply to selected groups. (See Bibliography entry No. 523).

Criticisms of Proposal

The Nationwide Plan presents certain features which suggest difficult administration problems. Critics suggest that provision of unlimited coverage provides difficulties in loss reserving and carrying open claims indefinitely. Tying wage loss to a state's average weekly wage is novel, but nevertheless fraught with some problems of administration, plus the question of public acceptance of the concept. The handling of survivorship benefits up to $30,000 in monthly installments could present definite problems. If optional settlement methods are granted the insured, certain life insurance programming assistance would be advisable. Otherwise, an inflexible pay-out schedule would hardly appear to be superior to a lump sum settlement.

The Nationwide plan has received considerable criticism because it restricts compensation to measurable economic loss. General damage claims would not be covered, although optional "pain and suffering insurance" would be available. Access to the liability system and insurance company subrogation rights would be prohibited.

Nationwide Comparison in Appendix

The Nationwide Mutual Insurance Company in April of 1971 published a reference manual on no-fault automobile insurance. In the manual is presented a comparison of the Nationwide Plan with that of six other plans presented elsewhere in this book. Among the plans compared with that of Nationwide are the proposals made by the National Association of Independent Insurers, the American Mutual Insurance Alliance, the American Insurance Association, the Massachusetts Plan, Keeton-O'Connell Plan, and the Hart-Magnuson proposal.

Inclusion of this material in the appendix should help the reader to understand Nationwide's Insurance Reform Plan and provide for a useful comparison guide for understanding not only the other six plans discussed, but it will serve the reader in understanding other proposals as well.

CHAPTER VIII

FEDERAL, STATE, AND CANADIAN PLANS

A variety of proposals for reform of the automobile accident reparations system has been made on the federal and state level. In addition, Canadian provinces have experimented with systems which they label as "no-fault." The Saskatchewan Plan, of course, (discussed in earlier chapters) provides the most extensive application of the no-fault principle in the provinces. (See Appendix for comparison chart on Canadian automobile insurance plans.)

The New York Insurance Department Plan ("The Stewart Plan") perhaps has been the most controversial of the recent state proposals. Providing unlimited benefits for expenses, but at the same time excluding recovery for pain and suffering as well as collateral source benefits, the plan drew little legislative support.

More recent developments on the federal level—the Department of Transportation Report, the Nixon proposal, and the Hart No-Fault bills—will be discussed in a subsequent chapter. An earlier federal proposal made by Daniel Moynihan leads off the presentation of plans in this chapter.

MOYNIHAN PLAN

Daniel P. Moynihan, Ph.D., Director of the Joint Center for Urban Studies of M.I.T. and Harvard and chairman of a federal advisory committee on traffic safety research during the Johnson Administration, proposed a federal approach to the automobile accident reparations problem. Mr. Moynihan was special assistant to President Nixon until 1971 and served as architect of Nixon's "Family Assistance Plan."

On the subject of automobile insurance reform, Moynihan challenged the Bar and the insurance industry to reform or to get out of the "traffic accident business" and let the government take over.

A National System

If the government takes over, Moynihan suggested that the simplest way to accomplish the transformation would be for the government to automatically provide all licensed drivers with insurance against injuries and property loss—regardless of fault. A national system of accident compensation would be established, modeled perhaps on the existing accident compensation system for Federal employees or on state Workmen's Compensation plans.

Financing might be via using some of the tax money originally intended for the interstate highway system, but which may not be used for that purpose, plus an extra "penny or so" on the gasoline tax.

The new federal program would involve considerable dislocation for those now employed by or involved with the private insurance industry, "but these are, generally speaking, valuable workers for whom an orderly transition could be arranged." (See Moynihan, No. 314; Marryott, No. 294; and *Time*, No. 57).

NEW YORK STATE INSURANCE DEPARTMENT PLAN
"The Stewart Plan"

Richard E. Stewart, Superintendent of Insurance of the State of New York Insurance Department, on February 12, 1970, submitted to Governor Nelson A. Rockefeller a report entitled "Automobile Insurance... For Whose Benefit?" The report was a culmination of instructions given by the governor in 1967 to a special committee, at which time the governor remarked:

> "Our present tort liability system for compensating the victims of automobile accidents has been authoritatively criticized as slow, expensive and unfair. The system has remained essentially unchanged while the nation has passed from the horse and buggy era to an age dominated by the automobile—with the highway accident an all-too-common occurrence.
> "The time has come for a thorough study of how automobile victims are affected by the lengthy and difficult process of determining fault and resolving claims following automobile accidents, with a view to possible changes in the system."

The responsibility for preparing such a report was subsequently transferred from the committee to the State Department of Insurance. The proposal combines elements of first-party no-fault and strict liability. It is a compulsory system, retaining tort action in death cases.

Features of the New York Plan

Features of the New York Plan provide:

1. Every person who sustains net economic loss arising out of the use of a motor vehicle in the state of New York is fully compensated for such loss, excluding (a) occupants of another motor vehicle, (b) the owner of a motor vehicle by reason of property damage to his motor vehicle, or (c) the operator of a motor vehicle while committing a felony or operating with the specific intent of causing injury or damage. Owners and operators are included under the compensation without regard to fault.

2. There are no statutory limits. Medical, funeral, and other economic losses would be paid in full.

3. Collateral source benefits would be excluded, including reimbursement of medical, hospital, and rehabilitation expenses. Net economic loss under the plan would exclude the amount of any reimbursement available from other insurance or similar sources except from general public revenue.

4. The owner of a commercial vehicle (other than a motor coach for carrying passengers) or a taxicab are liable without regard to fault to reimburse an insurer of any other kind of motor vehicle for payments made under the plan "on account of net economic loss as a result of property damage to any other kind of motor vehicle, where such payments arise out of the use of such commercial vehicle or taxicab in this state."

5. There is no provision for recovery for pain and suffering. Under the provisions of the proposal "there shall be no cause of action for personal injury or property damage based on negligence in the use or operation of a motor vehicle in this state."

6. The plan calls for three basic compulsory coverages:
   1) The first-party coverage.
   2) $10,000/$20,000/$5,000 liability coverage for out-of-state bodily injury and property damage claims and for in-state wrongful death claims.
   3) Non-vehicular property damage coverage.

The plan provides deceptively simple coverage—personal injury insurance and coverage for damage to non-automotive property. This places the responsibility on the motorist to provide his own automobile property damage coverage.

Criticisms of the Stewart Plan

Criticism of the New York State Insurance Department Plan has been vocal:

1. "It will deprive at least 7.5 million people of rights that go all the way back in the history of Anglo-Saxon law."

2. Pain and suffering awards are eliminated so that a person

losing a limb or other faculty would receive no compensation. Under the plan an innocent traffic victim would be denied compensation for partial and permanent disability, loss of earning capacity, disfigurement, dismemberment, loss of bodily senses, or the pain, inconvenience and suffering associated with the injury. "All of these must be borne with Spartan endurance because damages for these items of loss are not easy to compute and are therefore eliminated."

    3.   The plan covers an accident victim only for his "net economic loss" (medical bills and loss of salary). This neglects 7.5 million "forgotten people" (welfare recipients, children, housewives and senior citizens) who would receive little reimbursement.

    4.   The plan will "decimate the legal profession—lawyers and claim investigators get about 23 percent of the $686 million in injury liability insurance premiums paid in the state each year."

    5.   The plan is unduly benevolent to owners of non-vehicular property, to the detriment of automobile owners.

    6.   The plan specifically excludes the owners of a motor coach for carrying passengers, but it would appear that trucks, taxis and passenger cars "used for commercial purposes" would be subject to the plan's absolute liability provision; this is discriminatory.

    7.   There is a strange inconsistency that pain and suffering damages are eliminated and yet the right to recover under tort liability is retained in the event of wrongful death.

    8.   The New York Plan is fuzzy about how it will pay for future wage losses of children, students and workers who have not yet realized their full economic potential.

    9.   The compulsory policy would pay for damage to clothing, buildings, and other property but not for car damage. This is irrational in theory.

    10.   The plan lacks a mechanism for effective administration of the law and enforcement of the rights of individuals.

    11.   It is improper to permit an insurer to charge a premium for net loss of income but to escape payment where there is other coverage, such as Blue Cross, workmen's compensation, disability insurance or union welfare fund coverage.

    12.   Since collateral source benefits are eliminated except those sources funded from general public revenues, it would appear that the latter might include Medicare, Medicaid, Social Security and other public welfare programs. Why persons receiving benefits from public sources will be allowed what amounts to a double recovery and those who receive similar benefits from private sources will not, is unexplained.

    13.   "Under this proposal, persons injured by a negligent driver not only couldn't collect from him—they couldn't even collect from

the auto insurance policy they had been forced to buy until they had exhausted all of their other available resources. This means they would collect nothing until they had used up all of their personal accident and health insurance, all of the sick leave they had accumulated, all of their wage-continuation benefits, union health and welfare benefits, social security payments, Medicare, Medicaid, disability benefits, V.A. benefits, welfare payments and all other sources of payment. This ought to be called 'Last Resort Insurance', since many auto accident victims would collect little or nothing from it." (Statement by Paul S. Wise, President of American Mutual Insurance Alliance, see Bibliography entry No. 286. Other references: See Ghiardi, No. 171; Connor, No. 83; Bibliography entries Nos. 346, 396, and 444).

Commentary on Other Coverage

Criticisms No. 12 and No. 13 are inconsistent. As noted in No. 12, the Stewart Plan proposes elimination of collateral source benefits, *except those sources funded from general public revenues.* Mr. Wise, however, in No. 13 includes social insurance plans which technically are not funded from general public revenues. This particular provision of the Stewart Plan creates some confusion and ambiguity, since it is not made clear what is intended in "those sources funded from general public revenues." A collateral source exclusion embodied in no-fault legislation would necessarily have to clarify this point.

CALIFORNIA PLAN
(Compensation Plan by the Financial Responsibility Study Committee—March 17, 1967)

The California Plan is similar to the Keeton and O'Connell approach with some variations.

Features of the Plan

Every auto owner, as a condition of registration, would be required to obtain *medical payment and disability insurance* (Clause A) and *negligence liability insurance* (Clause B). This insurance would be for the benefit of himself, his passengers, and any pedestrians injured by his car.

This plan offers everyone injured in an automobile accident, regardless of fault, a chance to obtain scheduled disability benefits and "out-of-pocket" medical payments from the policy of the owner of the car in which he was riding or, in the case of a pedestrian, the policy of the owner of the automobile involved.

The plan would cover medical costs, including rehabilitation, temporary disability, permanent disability, and death benefits. Medical, hospital, and rehabilitation benefits would be limited to a ceiling of $5000, with a $200 deductible applicable. Temporary disability would start after one week and would be limited to 240 weeks.

Waiver of Tort Claim

Acceptance of benefits would waive any tort claim. An injured person, however, could forego the scheduled benefits and risk a traditional negligence suit. Payment from collateral benefit sources would be deducted. This plan does not otherwise significantly alter the present tort liability system.

A liability insurance policy would be required to have fairly high limits, *e.g.*, $100,000 per accident; $20,000 per person. This insurance would be similar to the existing "uninsured motorist" insurance.

Other Changes

The guest statute might be abolished as not necessary; suits between members of the same family or household would be prohibited.

Property damage would be handled in the traditional manner.

A person who intentionally injures himself would not be able to recover accident payments. (See Bibliography entry No. 60).

"THRESHOLD PLAN—GUARANTEED LIMITED BENEFITS"

The "Threshold Plan—Guaranteed Limited Benefits" is an amalgam of several ideas which came out of the 1967 session of the Massachusetts legislature. This plan was put into bill form and was considered during the 1968 session.

Features of the Plan

Under the provisions of the "Threshold Plan," those sustaining only minor bodily injury in automobile accidents would be barred from recovering under tort law. In lieu thereof they would be guaranteed a payment measured by the reasonable value of the "medical expense" incurred, plus a portion (70%) of the reasonable economic value (limited to $750) of time lost from employment. Payments would be made regardless of fault.

A "threshold" is defined which would establish the cut-off between minor injuries and presumably major injuries. If medical expenses did not exceed $150, the injury would be considered minor. Those who "build up" their expenses to exceed the threshold are barred from recovery under the plan and must fall back on the uncertainty of trying to recover under tort law.

The "threshold" amount and the amounts of the "no-fault" benefits can be moderately changed without changing the concepts.

Payments from Insurer of Third Party

"No-fault" payments will come from the insurer of the "other car." If two or more motor vehicles are involved, the operator and passengers of a motor vehicle shall have such payments made by or on behalf of the owners or operators of the other vehicle. If only one vehicle is involved, the operator, passengers, and any pedestrians struck by the vehicle, shall have payments made by or on behalf of the owner or operator of that vehicle.

Proponents of the plan believe that it will unclog claims handling machinery, to reduce the bickering and the uncertainties on small cases, and to reduce the cost of insurance. (See Marryott, No. 294).

RHODE ISLAND PLAN

The Rhode Island Plan was a bill patterned on the Keeton-O'Connell Plan introduced in 1968 in the legislature of Rhode Island. Under this proposal, no automobile could be registered unless it was covered by at least the minimum basic protection policy. Coverage would be $10,000/$100,000 for injury to the driver and occupants of the insured car, $15,000/$30,000 liability to others, and $5000 property damage, excluding first-party collision or damage to another car insured under this plan. Car owners would have two options on collision coverage and could obtain higher limits at the option of the insurer.

Coverage for General Damages

Coverage for pain and suffering, inconvenience, and other items currently protected against by the existing system would be optional, as would be self-insurance for pain and suffering. Pain and suffering would not be recognized in the basic plan, but facilities would be provided whereby the owner could buy such coverage for himself and his passengers rather than for the driver and passengers of the other car if he were at fault in a collision.

Effect on Collateral Benefits

Collateral benefits would be deducted from basic protection benefits, but an insured with such collateral benefits available would pay a lower premium for basic protection. The premium schedule would also fix higher rates for applicants with adverse driving or accident records. (See Damman, No. 97).

THE GORDON "NO-FAULT" BILL

In April of 1971 the New York Senate Insurance Committee reported out a no-fault bill, S. 4400-4, the only bill of its kind to reach the floor in either house in early 1971. The bill, sponsored by Senator Bernard G. Gordon, the key legislator on the subject of automobile accident reparations in the state of New York, received more favorable attention by the legislature than the Stewart-Rockefeller no-fault proposal. The latter proposal is a broad, all-encompassing revision of the present tort system.

The Gordon bill did not win full support from industry spokesmen at a March 24 hearing, although it was characterized as being "a balanced and realistic approach toward solving the state's auto insurance problems."

Features of the Bill

Under the Gordon proposal, the driver's own insurance company would provide medical and disability payments to victims of automobile accidents up to a maximum of $2000. The plan proposed some limitations on pain and suffering claims. One party in an accident would be permitted to sue another for pain and suffering, but when the medical and hospital expenses of the victim total less than $400, he would not be permitted to sue for an amount in excess of these expenses, except for certain types of injuries. However, when medical and hospital expenses exceed $400, a suit could be instituted for any amount for pain and suffering.

The plan provides for reimbursement of two-thirds of a person's lost income, and there are a number of optional deductibles which can be selected by insureds.

It was anticipated that the bill would undergo considerable amendment. (See Bibliography entries Nos. 177, 348, and 367).

CANADIAN "ACCIDENT BENEFITS PLAN"

The Canadian "Accident Benefits Plan" is the result of amendments made to the Canadian Insurance Act in 1968. Under these amendments, provisions were made to establish plans similar to the Saskatchewan Plan but on a voluntary basis in the provinces. By November of 1970 some eight provinces had adopted the plan. The program provides for limited accident benefits with optional additional third-party liability coverage. It is a voluntary program.

Features of the Plan

Features of the plan provide the following:

1. Up to $5000 payment for death, dismemberment, or loss of sight, plus $1000 for each surviving dependent.

2. Medical expenses are paid as accrued with no maximum limit.

3. Funeral expenses are paid up to the amount subscribed to by the insured.

4. Up to $35 weekly disability is paid for a period of two years, with further coverage of two additional years of disability payments if the injury proves permanent.

5. Since tort liability is retained over the first-party benefits, third-party liability claims are paid up to the limits of the optional additional third-party liability policy.

6. There are no statutory limits set on amounts recoverable for pain and suffering, but collateral source benefits are excluded.

BRITISH COLUMBIA "ENRICHED ACCIDENT BENEFITS"

The British Columbia "Enriched Accident Benefits" plan which is in effect in that province largely resulted from the recommendations of a British Columbia Royal Commission report on automobile insurance. Presented in 1968, the report resulted from exhaustive hearings carried over a period of 14 months during 1966 and 1967. The most important recommendation of that report provided for the creation of a new program of compulsory automobile insurance.

Studies Show Need for Reform

A number of studies cited by the Commission indicated an urgent need for reform. In one study of 1253 traffic accident cases chosen at random from 1963 police files in British Columbia, the Commission members found that compensation of only $900,000 had been paid on actual losses of $2.7 million, and that claims were settled more quickly for collision and property damage than for personal injuries or deaths.

The Commission observed, "The conclusion that this discrimination is undesirable hinges only on the belief that individuals deserve treatment at least the equal of that accorded bent fenders—a belief few people would care to quarrel with."

During the prolonged hearings, the Saskatchewan government volunteered extensive evidence of the experience of the plan in that province. The study Commission observed that in present-day British Columbia conditions are somewhat different from those in Saskatchewan, and the resultant legislation passed in British Columbia was not as extreme as that of the Saskatchewan system.

Features of the Plan

Features of the British Columbia Plan include the following:

1.   Personal injury accident benefits under a fixed schedule, including a $5000 death benefit for loss of the household head, plus $1000 for each surviving dependent. A scale of weekly payments is available to the surviving spouse.

2.   Medical and rehabilitation payments are made as expenses are accrued, subject to a fixed schedule. Rehabilitation benefits are available up to the policy limits of $50,000.

3.   Funeral expenses of $5000.

4.   Weekly disability indemnity of $50 for up to four years. Payments then continue for life if the injury is permanent.

5.   The first-party coverage does not apply to property damage. There is full third-party liability for property damage, with a minimum mandatory property damage liability policy of $50,000 required of insureds.

6.   There are no statutory limits on recovery for pain and suffering, but collateral source benefits are not permitted. (See Findlay, No. 161).

THE ONTARIO PLAN—1964
(Not to be confused with the existing Ontario Law)

This 1964 proposal provided for basic compensation on a schedule of benefits without discarding the jury trial. The proposal included in the standard automobile policy, as an integral part of the policy, accident benefits providing medical payments, death, dismemberment and total disability weekly benefits to be paid pursuant to a schedule, without regard to fault. No coverage would be provided for partial disability or for pain and suffering. Claims would be presented against the injured party's own insurer. Death within 90 days of the accident would be compensated. The amount payable would be graded according to the age, sex, and marital status of the deceased. Total disability benefits were provided for 104 weeks after a seven-day waiting period.

The proposal was supported by the Osgoode Hall study on Compensation for Victims of Automobile Accidents, conducted in Ontario in 1964. The study found that only 42.9 percent of those hurt or killed received any reparation under the tort liability system, and only 28.8 percent recovered all of their economic loss.

Deprived of Right to Sue

The Ontario plan is a true "no-fault" proposal, since it provides for mandatory accident benefits coverage as part of a standard third-party automobile policy and stipulates that the injured person would be deprived of his right to sue except for an amount in excess of the accident benefits.

Criticisms of the Plan

The Ontario Plan has been opposed on the grounds that the motorist should not be legally obligated to pay the premiums on a policy which provides accident benefits to persons other than occupants of the insured vehicle. Other criticisms were that there would be consumer resistance to the inclusion of third-party pedestrians, and the further criticism that implementation of the proposal would require legislative changes to the common law. Inadequate benefits for the very serious personal injury cases is another point of criticism. (See Hodosh, No. 194 and Murray, No. 317).

Note: Hospital costs in Ontario are largely borne by general social insurance.

THE ONTARIO LAW—1972

The Ontario government has passed legislation requiring automobile accident benefits as a mandatory part of all auto insurance policies sold in Ontario. Motorists involved in an accident can still proceed through the courts or through negotiation with the third party to secure additional benefits. However, the amount of first-party accident benefits already received by the claimant must be taken into account in any subsequent tort liability settlement.

Features of the Law

The major provisions of the Ontario law which will become effective January 1, 1972, are as follows:

1. Disability benefits of 80 percent of the total earnings of employed persons, with a maximum $70 weekly benefit. Payments

commence on the day of disability and continue throughout the disability period. Maximum benefits represent double the previous rate of $35.

2. Disability payments of $35 weekly to the spouse or principal unpaid housekeeper residing in the household not otherwise engaged in occupation or employment for wages or profit.

3. Upon death of the head of the household, $5000 to the principal dependent and $1000 to each additional dependent. Benefits are paid when death occurs within 180 days of the accident, or within two years if the disability has been continuous. The head of the household is defined as the spouse earning the greater income.

4. Medical and rehabilitation benefits of $5000 per person, covering the expenses within four years that are not covered by other medical or other hospitalization programs.

5. Benefits of $2500 upon the death of a spouse, where such spouse is not the head of the household.

6. Benefits of $500 upon death of a dependent child 5 years of age or under, and $1000 upon the death of a dependent child 5 to 21 years of age.

7. In the case of temporary total disability, there is no waiting period between the time of disability and date of payment. Payments cover a two-year period.

8. Funeral expense benefits are paid up to $500.

Modifications Increase Previous Benefits

The new law modifies previous benefits by increasing the coverage. It also removes the waiting period of seven days or more which existed on disability benefits.

All insured motor vehicles, including motorcycles, motorscooters, snowmobiles, trucks and buses are covered. Passengers, pedestrians struck by an insured vehicle, or members of the family of the owner of the insured vehicle, while still living at home, are eligible for benefits if involved in a motor vehicle accident.

To insure prompt payment of disability benefits, full payments will be made during the first two weeks regardless of additional income available to the disabled person. After that, a pro-rata adjustment will be applied so the benefits under the plan and benefits received from other sources do not exceed the person's normal weekly earnings.

No Premium Increases

It is predicted that under the new Ontario law there will be no increase in insurance rates, despite the increased benefits. According to Financial and Commercial Affairs Minister, Arthur A. Wishart, the government has received assurances from insurance company representatives that, despite higher benefits, there will be no increase in accident benefit rates in 1972.

NATIONAL ASSOCIATION OF INSURANCE COMMISSIONERS

On June 17, 1971, the National Association of Insurance Commissioners, the organization of insurance department heads from all the states, endorsed "modified no-fault" coverages and resolved to recommend to the states the enactment of legislation based on guidelines drawn up by the group. The guidelines are contained in the following resolution.

The N.A.I.C. Resolution

WHEREAS the auto reparation systems currently in force in the various states do not uniformly and adequately compensate all injured parties in auto accidents for their economic loss, and

WHEREAS such reparation systems fail to equitably distribute the claims dollar among all victims and claimants, and

WHEREAS such reparation systems often fail to provide prompt payment of insured losses, and

WHEREAS no-fault insurance is now available for medical payments, comprehensive, and collision coverages, and

WHEREAS the National Association of Insurance Commissioners feels keenly its responsibility to use its influence and expertise to meet the changing needs of society,

NOW, THEREFORE, BE IT RESOLVED that the National Association of Insurance Commissioners recommends to the legislatures of the several states, which have not already enacted such legislation, enactment at a minimum of "modified no-fault" insurance coverages which provide coverage for economic losses suffered in auto accidents including the following:

(1) Prompt payment for economic loss;

(2) Distribution of the auto insurance claims dollar in such a manner that a close relationship is developed between the benefits delivered to each injured party and his actual economic loss;

(3) Distribution of a larger percentage of the premium dollar to parties suffering economic loss;

AND BE IT FURTHER RESOLVED that the auto reparation systems continue to remain under state regulation and that there be no federal government implementation of any auto reparation system or federal alteration of the tort system;

AND BE IT FURTHER RESOLVED that the NAIC continues to support and endorse state-by-state experimentation with various forms of no-fault coverages and the right of the states to enact systems with differing characteristics.

Evaluation of the "Guidelines"

About the only thing positive to say about the "guidelines" submitted by the National Association of Insurance Commissioners is that they truly afford remarkable latitude for "state-by-state experimentation." Otherwise, the "guidelines" should prove to be virtually valueless in helping states solve their automobile insurance reform problems.

Predictably, the resolution calls for continued state regulation of the system with no interference of any kind by the federal government.

If this is the best the N.A.I.C. can produce in the way of guidelines for the individual states to follow, the "states' rights" advocates are in serious straits. Hopefully, the N.A.I.C. will provide more enlightened leadership in the future months as individual states provide helpful experience with no-fault plans. Otherwise, lack of standardization and uniformity due to the leadership vacuum on the state level could well goad the federal legislators into solving the states' problem.

NOTE: As this book went to press, the United States Department of Transportation reportedly was working with the National Conference of State Governors and the Conference of Commissioners on Uniform State Laws on a model state no-fault law. Completion of the drafting was expected sometime before the end of the year.

PART III
EVOLUTION OR REVOLUTION?

CHAPTER IX

REFORMATION WITHIN THE LIABILITY SYSTEM

Criticisms of the present tort liability system with its adversary-jury method of determining liability based on fault in lawsuits arising from automobile accidents, have prompted the intense evaluation of the present tort liability system. Although there are strong arguments for the abandonment of the liability system in the handling of automobile accidents, there are, nevertheless, strong philosophical arguments advanced by defenders of tort liability for the retention of that system.

THE EVALUATION

Defenders of the liability system predicated upon fault, awarding the innocent but punishing the wrongdoer, believe that the tort liability system is the best way to assure that justice will be done. Further, to assure that justice will be the end result, the procedure of determining liability in the adversary-jury court system is believed to be the best method to obtain the nearest human approximation of what is truth. Such an end, in the viewpoint of defenders of the tort liability system, is most likely to be gained by contest, where apposing attorneys, committed to the causes of their clients, present the best possible evidence for consideration by jurymen who reach decisions through argument and counter-argument.

Defenders of the tort liability system argue that the foregoing fundamental process should not be replaced by some system of compensation which rewards all injured regardless of fault. The moral principle of reward for good and punishment for wrong is universally accepted, and justifiably so, in their viewpoint. Further, it is the belief of the proponents of tort liability that administrative decision which determines the rights of litigants is not an adequate substitute for the thorough means provided by the courts. Such a substitution can be only expedient rather than remedial and would be recognized as an omen of governmental rule which is not the path of a free people with full rights based upon Constitutional guarantees.

Change Is Inevitable

Defenders of the tort liability system, nevertheless, recognize the fact that change is an inevitable feature in society, and it would be fruitless to maintain the status quo. Indeed, the whole character of a legal system is its dynamic nature. Societal pressures, concurrent with changing conditions, dictate that a legal system must be pliable and amenable to change. Accordingly, if threats to the adversary system are to abate, in the opinion of the defenders of the tort liability system, these threats must be countered by positive reform programs rooted in defensible principles.

Problems Recognized under Tort Liability

The defenders of the tort liability system recognize the fact that mounting problems have focused increasing criticism upon the status quo, and that reform is necessary and desirable. The specific problems, in their viewpoint, result from:

　　1.　A growing population and expanding economy;

　　2.　Growing claims consciousness, resulting in an excessive number of nuisance cases;

　　3.　Unwarranted refusal to settle meritorious cases;

　　4.　Questionable tactics to secure large and undeserved awards as damages;

　　5.　Public and legislative apathy to existing problems, notably insufficient judicial personnel, inadequate court facilities, and failure to enact adequate traffic safety programs. (See Bibliography entry No. 108).

A number of proposals have been advanced by individuals and organizations, suggesting various means by which the tort liability system can be salvaged but at the same time preserving the advantages inherent in the system.

"RESPONSIBLE REFORM—A PROGRAM TO IMPROVE THE LIABILITY REPARATIONS SYSTEM"

The Federation of Insurance Counsel, the Defense Research Institute, the International Association of Insurance Counsel, and the Association of Insurance Attorneys, have proposed a program which they entitle "Responsible Reform—a Program to Improve the Liability Reparations System."

The basic thesis of the program is that the public believes that "fairness requires that the one who causes harm to another must pay for it. What the public is saying is that the present accident reparations system has failed in some respects to keep pace with the needs of our exploding population, and that it can and must be improved.

"But this does not mean it wants to destroy or abandon the underlying legal substructure for untested, highly theoretical alternatives in a rush to revolution."

Rather than drastically altering the present tort liability system, these organizations of attorneys advocate a reform of the present system.

Proposals of Reform

The following are some of the most important proposals of the program advocated by these associations of attorneys:

1.   A vigorous highway safety program concentrating on the driver.

2.   Minimum, optional first-party coverage for medical and hospital expenses, income disability and the like.

3.   Changes in the collateral source ruling allowing juries to consider all benefits and services received by a claimant in assessing damages.

4.   More judges to eliminate court congestion and delay, and mandatory arbitration of lawsuits involving claims under $3000 in jurisdictions where court delay is a problem.

5.   Adoption of specific practices and procedures to streamline the administration of justice.

6.   Adoption of the Wisconsin form of comparative negligence in those jurisdictions where the application of the rule of contributory negligence has given rise to legitimate concern as to the justice of the system.

7.   Formulation of a plan which can serve as a guide to the appraisal of fair compensation for pain, suffering, and inconvenience sustained through the fault of another.

Fairness of the Tort Liability System

According to William C. Harvin, President of the Federation of Insurance Counsel, "There is strong evidence that the public believes it is only just and fair that one who causes injury to another should adequately compensate him for the injury. This sense of fairness is basic to the fault-liability system. It is totally inconsistent, however, with the no-fault concept proposed by those who would scrap our liability reparations system for something akin to compulsory health and accident insurance."

Addressing himself to the specific proposals of the program advocated by the four attorneys' groups, Mr. Harvin stated, "As lawyers, we intend to lend our support to the implementation of these proposals and to any others which are in the public interest. We also will continue to examine today's problems in the light of future developments and will make additional positive suggestions and proposals from time to time." (See Bibliography entry No. 158).

ADVANCE PAYMENTS AND REHABILITATION

Another method of preserving the tort liability system, assuring the system of justice which supporters believe is inherent in the tort liability system, is the use of advance payments techniques. Advance payments and rehabilitation preserves the basic "fault principle" while speeding up payments to claimants who deserve compensation. Companies using these methods seek out claimants and offer quick payment of medical bills and property-damage costs, and they replace lost income. There is no longer a wait for court decisions or maneuvers in cases where the companies figure that they will eventually have to make payment. (See Bibliography entry No. 8).

Under advance payment, immediate advancement of funds is made for medical expenses, loss of earnings, and other expenses to third-party bodily injury claimants, without release, where such payment ultimately will be made on behalf of the insured. A number of companies are using forms of advance payments in handling tort liability claims. Several methods are in use.

Open-End Releases

The open-end release is a technique of handling third-party liability claims. It has been adopted in recent years to overcome the objections of tort liability critics who contend that under the liability system considerable delay is experienced before final payment is made in a liability claim. The critics contend, and in many cases rightly so, that a claimant will be confined to a hospital with medical bills accumulating, with his damaged automobile sitting in a garage with no funds available for its repair, with living expenses piling up at home, and with no hope of obtaining money until the bodily injury and property damage claims are settled simultaneously, sometimes months or years after an accident. The delay and the resultant financial pressures often force a claimant to settle prematurely in an appreciable number of cases.

To avoid this delay, the open-end release is used. Under it an insurance company will make advance payments to a claimant to take care of medical bills, property damage costs, and advance funds to take care of living costs for the claimant's family. The amount advanced is applied to the final settlement, and when the claimant is finally ready to make final settlement, it can be consummated. There is no need to subject the claimant to inordinate delay and prejudice his rehabilitation because of lack of funds.

Making Payments without Release

Some companies use the advance payment technique of making quick payment of medical bills and property damage costs, and, in addition, pay for other expenses or make money advances where the claimant has a legitimate need, and these payments will be made without obtaining a release.

The rationale behind making payments without release is that the release itself is seldom needed. Companies have determined that claimants seldom break their oral agreement and sue later on for their liability claim. Thus, the rationale for advance payments without release is that it works better in the long run—it removes to a great extent the adversary relationship existing between the liability insurer and a claimant; it removes the delay in making payment; and it is excellent public relations for insurance companies.

Authorization of Insurance

Technically, the authorization of insurance technique is not part of the advance payment procedure. It involves the use of accident and health, life, and annuity insurance in cases where the future course of the claimant's medical recovery is in doubt. Insurance is purchased by the defendant and becomes part of the consideration for a release.

Insurance can be utilized in the settlement of a variety of cases, including claims for wrongful death, where there are unknown elements involved in the claims, such elements being for the most part future developments which cannot be foreseen with any degree of accuracy.

Example of Advance Payments Use

A typical advance payment plan is that adopted by Hartford Insurance Group in the 1960's. Initially experimented with in the New York, San Francisco and Chicago areas, advance payments were made only to those claimants where it was believed that payment would be ultimately forthcoming.

Automobile property damage payments were made to claimants as soon as loss was determined. Advances of money were made to pay bills incurred for medical treatment as a result of the accident. In addition, the company provided reimbursement at regular intervals for wage loss resulting from the accident. Up to $100 per week was paid for physical and emotional suffering during each week of total disability caused by the accident. (See Barker, No. 39).

IMPROVEMENT OF THE ADVERSARY-JURY SYSTEM

This is a proposal made in 1967 by Edward C. German, Philadelphia attorney, then president of Federation of Insurance Counsel and vice-president of public relations of Defense Research Institute.

Features of the Proposal

1.   Effective deployment of manpower to improve the performance record of the judiciary.

2.   The naming of judges who have proven ability as "settlement judges" to reduce the backlog of personal injury cases where delay exists.

3.   Appoint judges to office for life so they do not have to engage in politics, and establish a Commission on Judicial Qualifications to pass on the conduct of judges in their posts.

4.   After retirement, judges should be named as "senior judges" to perform in special areas which they are willing to undertake.

5.   Relieve judges of purely clerical tasks, modernize the court buildings, and install data processing for more complete and accurate record keeping in the courts.

6.   Establish a system of compulsory arbitration for injury claims which, in effect, would be tried by lawyer panels, subject to court review, in order to reduce the number of minor cases which are on file. (See Bibliography entry No. 29).

FUCHSBERG PROPOSAL

Jacob D. Fuchsberg, attorney and past president of the American Trial Lawyers Association, proposes the following:

1.   Compulsory liability insurance;

2.   Unlimited coverage;

3.   Using the comparative negligence standard instead of contributory negligence;

4.   Compulsory medical payments feature in the compulsory liability policy;

5.   Consideration of permitting direct suit against insurers;

6.   Selling of liability insurance to cover individual people instead of car owners;

7.   Massive safety campaigns as "our first order of business";

8.   An expanded advance payment and rehabilitation program;

9.   An insolvency insurance fund to cover fly-by-night companies;

10.   Abolition of guest laws and governmental and charitable and

intra-family immunities;

11.   Work for "an adequate court system, instead of starved courts"; and

12.   Tough traffic law enforcement, and against the car involved, thus putting family pressure on the careless driver. (See Bibliography entry No. 467).

SPECIAL MASTERS

Under this proposal, auto-accident cases, rather than going into court, would be assigned first to groups of unpaid referees, including prominent lawyers and insurance company representatives.

These referees, or special masters, would study the papers in each case, confer with the respective lawyers for the plaintiff and the defendant and try to persuade them to reach an agreement. (See Bibliography entry No. 94).

HAYWOOD PLAN

This is a plan proposed by Egbert L. Haywood, former president of the International Association of Insurance Counsel, a prominent Durham, N.C., defense attorney.

He proposes the following steps aimed at updating the negligence liability system: modernization and codification of the rules of evidence; appointment of a "bar proctor" at every personal injury trial; improvement of the jury selection process; and more frequent separation of the issues of liability and damages.

These proposals should be coupled with other positive steps whose undertaking rests with the insurance industry: wider use of the advance payment technique; a broadening of uninsured motorist and medical payments coverages, and greater utilization of rehabilitation programs. (See Haywood, No. 193).

THE MILEY PLAN

This is a plan devised by Frank R. Miley, C.P.C.U., Vice President, Alexander & Company, Chicago, Illinois, director of the Chicago Board of Underwriters.

1.   The plan provides for payments from the insured's own insurance company for accidental death, dismemberment and disability

for all occupants of an automobile and for pedestrians. Such coverages are superimposed on the present automobile liability policy only to the extent they do not serve as payments in lieu of payments which would otherwise be made under liability insurance.

    2.   No reduction for collateral source benefits.

    3.   The basic automobile policy is retained with changes incorporating an accident insurance approach. Uninsured Motorists coverage would be altered by substituting accident coverage providing $10,000 for one person, and an aggregate of $20,000 for more than one person, indemnity for accidental death or dismemberment, and disability coverage.

    4.   Automatic right to insurance for all drivers—basic limits.

    5.   The Plan should be supplemental with compulsory automobile insurance legislation. Physical damages should be included.

    6.   The Plan may be initiated and adopted by the regulatory authority not only agreeing with it but actively persuading automobile insurance companies to conform to it, or it may be effectuated by legislation.

    7.   A reinsurance pool for all companies for basic limits and abolition of the Assigned Risk Plan.

    8.   The inclusion of property damage liability in the basic limits and the reinsurance pool is necessary if we are to abolish the Assigned Risk pools.

    9.   Automatic establishment of basic limits rates from statistical results of the pool.

    10.   Right to pursue remedy under tort law is retained. Tort law would not be revised.

    11.   Insurers would have the right of subrogation for payments made under the plan. If the insured should not exercise the option of proceeding against a third party within a reasonable period of time, the insurer could subrogate.

    12.   The Plan would be compatible with any rating system in use. It would conform to territorial differentiations, classifications and merit system of rating.

    13.   Retention of rating system's flexibility permits rating penalties on wrongdoers which is the present effective civil penalty system. (See Miley, No. 309).

MARRYOTT PLAN

    This is a proposal made by Franklin J. Marryott, vice president of Liberty Mutual Insurance Company, that medical payments coverage be made mandatory and broadened to include pedestrians injured by the insured driver. (See Bibliography entry No. 33).

Medical payments coverage would be expanded to make it applicable to pedestrians who happen to be members of non-car owning families. The coverage would be available in larger limits than are presently commonly sold, and it would be a mandatory part of every policy. (See Marryott, No. 295).

THE MORRIS AND PAUL PLAN
"Supplementary Compensation in Economic Disaster Cases"

Professors Clarence Morris and James C. N. Paul of the University of Pennsylvania Law School in 1962 suggested a state-collected and administered fund to reimburse victims of automobile accidents for 85 percent of their otherwise unreimbursed loss of income in excess of $800, without regard to fault. There would be a payment limitation of $600 per month maximum for loss of income.

The authors of the plan believed that some reform was necessary, but they were convinced that abolishment of liability for fault was doomed to failure for lack of popular support. In addition, they wanted to avoid over-compensation of those suffering little in the way of tangible losses. Thus, their plan emphasized "economic disaster cases." The plan proposed the establishment of a fund for economic disaster cases only.

The common law remedy for pain and suffering would be retained, and attorneys' fees—set at a percentage of the damages—would be recovered from the fund.

Features of the Plan

The plan proposed the following features:

1. A deductible feature would eliminate all claims for economic loss under $800.

2. Collateral source benefits would reduce tort liability awards.

3. Special provisions on attorneys' fees would establish a schedule of fees—roughly one-third of a tort liability recovery—this would recognize the value of lawyers' services.

4. Legal fees, like medical expenses, according to the authors of the plan, should be compensable only under the 85 percent rate.

5. There would be no automobile physical damage coverage.

Sketchy on Details

The details of the Morris and Paul plan are extremely sketchy.

No details are provided on how to handle disputes. (See Morris & Paul, "The Financial Impact of Automobile Accidents," *110 University of Pennsylvania Law Review*, vol. 110 (1962), pp. 913-33; see Morris & Paul, No. 313).

CALIFORNIA STATE BAR PLAN

A special Committee on Personal Injury Claims of the California State Bar Association in 1965 proposed a basic private compulsory insurance system.

The plan provided for compulsory insurance coverage as a prerequisite for vehicle registration. That coverage would provide payments for medical and economic losses, permitting the insured to retain his tort liability right of action, but with the stipulation that repayment must be made to the insurer for the medical and economic losses out of the policyholder's tort liability recovery. The insured could actually use proceeds of the medical payments coverage to finance litigation under tort liability. In this respect, the plan resembles the plan in effect in the Canadian province of Saskatchewan.

The plan provided for periodic payments as losses accrued. Loss insurance which would cover the insured and occupants of the insured's vehicle would provide for medical expenses to $500 and other economic losses to $10,000. Liability insurance and medical payments coverage would be provided under the policy.

It is a misnomer to label this plan as a "no-fault" proposal. It simply added loss insurance on top of tort liability coverage. (See Hodosh, No. 144 and MacKay, No. 289).

THE LOGAN PLAN

The Logan Plan is presented in an undated paper (about 1967), citing research of the Federation of Insurance Counsel conducted by its automobile insurance committee. Results of the research were presented during a workshop in the spring of 1967 and reported in the 1967 issue of the *Federation of Insurance Counsel Quarterly*.

Driver Insurance with Emphasis on Licensing

Logan defends the fault concept as being "sound, logical and beneficial." His proposal for automobile insurance reform embodies two approaches:

    1.   A new automobile insurance concept—a driver insurance

policy.

2.   Emphasis on driver licensing and automobile insurance law.

Under this proposal, liability insurance policies would be issued to individual drivers only, eliminating the omnibus clause which covers relatives and others driving the vehicle with permission of the named insured. Each driver would have his own policy and his own record upon which he would be rated, thus eliminating the rating penalties which are imposed upon a safe driver-owner who nevertheless permits others to drive his automobile. Drivers in high-risk classifications who are now being partially paid for by the over-charging of others would necessarily be rated up. Thus, poor drivers in a family would jeopardize their own insurability rather than that of the entire family. The owner of an automobile could be held liable for others under his own policy only in cases involving vicarious liability.

The rationale of the Logan Plan is:

> "To make certain that each accident victim is compensated for an injury, is it better to expand insurance coverage and overload a smaller number of persons, or is it better to expand the number of persons paying premiums and charge each a smaller and fairer amount?"

The Plan proposes a model policy, prepared by Logan and Mr. Norman Risjord, Vice President and General Counsel of Employers Reinsurers Company of Kansas City, Missouri. The policy, according to its framers, would reduce costs by eliminating "all kinds of frills not necessary to the basic problem and already covered by collateral insurance"—medical payments and uninsured motorist coverage and "the expanded coverages within the liability contract."

Basic to the implementation of the Logan Plan are a number of reforms in handling insurance claims but primarily in reforms in the legal system. A key feature of the reforms would be changes in driver licensing laws.

Changes in Driver Licensing Laws

To obtain a driver's license, an individual would have to prove that he has an individual liability insurance policy. The license and policy would have the same inception and termination dates. Cancellation of the policy would automatically cancel the individual's driver's license. The license would be stamped with the name of the insurer.

Other Suggested Reforms

1.   Advance payments and rehabilitation
2.   Collateral source limitations

3.   Bifurcated trials
4.   Court-assigned medical experts
5.   More use of pre-trial procedures
6.   Special courts for automobile case litigation
7.   Assignment of more judges

(See Logan, No. 286).

Criticisms of the Plan

The Logan proposal has considerable merit in recognizing the contribution of individual drivers to the automobile accident toll. It proposes a more mature approach to the handling of irresponsible drivers on the nation's highways. The inability or the unwillingness of states to eliminate the dangerous driver from the highways by taking away his driving privileges would be accomplished by the Logan proposal.

The plan could, however, create some highly undesirable consequences for the insurance industry and the motoring public. For example, it would place the onus of driver cancellations upon the insurance industry, creating a worse public relations problem than it has under the current system. It would also subject the American public to the vagaries of individual company underwriting standards as the foundation for driver license cancellations. The lack of uniformity in those standards would suggest that the nation would end up with a more confusing and inequitable system than it has under the present system.

"KNOCK-FOR-KNOCK"

The no-fault automobile insurance that has been in effect in England for almost half a century is not applied by law. It operates under voluntary "Knock-For-Knock" agreements among the insurance companies. It is subscribed to by all the insurance companies in the United Kingdom, with the exception of only a handful of more recently established companies.

Under the English "Knock-For-Knock" agreements, the insurer assumes full liability for damage sustained by his own insured, without recourse to any third party. Both physical damage and the cost of medical and hospital treatment of personal injuries are covered under the agreements.

Operation of the System

The system is relatively simple. After an accident, automobile owners notify their respective insurers. Repair costs are then paid by each company, with no attempt to determine responsibility for the accident.

Supporters of the system believe that it has eliminated the potentially crushing volume of automobile accident litigation in England that overwhelms the courts in the United States. In addition, it is believed that an automobile owner realizes a great savings in premium costs, compared with those levied in the United States.

The underlying philosophy of the "Knock-For-Knock" agreement is that British insurers as a whole insure the total market, not just their own select group of policyholders. This means that their results are averaged out to a great extent and tend to follow the total loss experience of the country rather than each company's individual experience.

Weaknesses

In order to encourage careful driving, a no-accident bonus system prevails on premiums. However, trouble can arise when, after an accident, the insured finds that he has lost his no-accident bonus even though he was in no way at fault. In theory, the no-claim bonus is determined solely on liability for the accident, but in practice this does not always work well because very few drivers ever like to think that they were the ones at fault in a collision. (See Dammann, No. 97 and Shaw, No. 428).

Canada Uses "Knock-For-Knock"

In Canada in most provinces (Saskatchewan is a notable exception) the various automobile accident reparations programs provide for first-party benefits. These benefits in no way affect an individual's right to sue, but any amount so recovered is reduced by the amount paid as accident benefits.

According to the Insurance Bureau of Canada, as of June 29, 1971, "practically all" Canadian insurance companies have signed a "Knock-For-Knock" agreement, waiving their subrogation rights for accident benefits payments against other companies that are signatories to the agreement.

CHAPTER X

DOT STUDY, NIXON PLAN, AND HART'S NO-FAULT

As the nation entered into the 1970's, perhaps the most interesting developments in the no-fault controversy were the United States Department of Transportation reports, the 1971 Nixon proposal, and the Hart automobile insurance reform bills.

The Department of Transportation "Automobile Insurance and Compensation Study" reports have stimulated the most active discussion of the nation's automobile accident reparations system and have provided a wealth of materials for the proponents of reform. The impact of the studies has been or will be felt in every state legislature as the nation grapples with its automobile insurance problem.

Particularly interesting to observers, and frustrating to the DOT research team, was the Nixon Administration's reaction to the conclusions contained in many of the reports. President Nixon's subsequent charge to the states to pass their own reform legislation dismayed proponents of a federal approach to reform, but implicit in his charge was the implication that federal legislation would set standards for the states if they failed to act in a timely fashion.

Senator Philip A. Hart (Democrat from Michigan), chairman of the Senate Subcommittee on Antitrust and Monopoly and an ardent consumer champion, disdainful of a state-by-state approach to the nation's automobile problems, introduced federal legislation in both 1970 and 1971. His "Uniform Motor Vehicle Insurance Act" provides for a scope of federal involvement which goes beyond that of most plans and is particularly unpalatable to "states' rights" advocates. If the national political climate for automobile insurance reform continues unabated or accelerates, it is likely that Hart-type legislation will be enacted by the federal government, barring unprecedented expeditious legislative action on the part of the states.

The following pages examine the DOT Study, the Nixon proposal, and Senator Hart's no-fault proposals as most fascinating developments in the no-fault dispute.

THE DEPARTMENT OF TRANSPORTATION STUDY
(See Bibliography Entries Nos. 117-140)

The widespread national attention devoted to the subject of automobile safety, insurance company insolvencies, insurance policy cancellations, and lack of availability of coverage, combined with public interest generated on no-fault automobile insurance plans, such as the Keeton-O'Connell proposal, focused Congressional concern on the subject of automobile insurance. That concern culminated in action on the part of the United States Congress to enact a law late in the Johnson Administration, directing the Department of Transportation to conduct a $2 million, two-year automobile insurance study to explore the entire area of automobile indemnification or reparations systems in the United States.

Law Authorizing DOT Study

The preamble of Senate Joint Resolution 129, which forms the authority for the Department's automobile insurance study, reads as follows:

"Whereas Congress finds that suffering and loss of life resulting from motor vehicle accidents and the consequence of social and economic dislocations are critical national problems;

"Whereas there is a growing evidence that the existing system of compensation for such loss and suffering is inequitable, inadequate, and insufficient, and is unresponsive to existing social, economic and technical conditions;

"Whereas there is needed a fundamental re-evaluation of such system, including a review of the role and effectiveness of insurance and the existing law governing liability;

"Whereas meaningful analysis requires the collection and evaluation of data not presently available, such as the actual economic impact of motor vehicle injuries, the relief available, both in public and private sources, and the role and effectiveness of rehabilitation..."

The resultant legislation, P.L. 90-313 (1968), directed the Department of Transportation to conduct a comprehensive study of the motor vehicle insurance and compensation system based on tort law (negligence liability).

Contracting Out Research Projects

The DOT study staff spent its initial time deciding on the areas to be studied in depth and on the nature of the specific research projects which should be awarded. Insurance people were added to the staff to give a balanced perspective to the study results.

After areas of study were determined, the Department of Transportation awarded contracts for 19 separate research projects, mostly to academicians and professional research corporations. A number of projects were farmed out through the Federal Trade Commission.

The Study Reports

The various contractors and the Federal Trade Commission submitted their reports beginning in March 1970 and culminating in a final report submitted by Department of Transportation Secretary, John A. Volpe, in March of 1971 (See Bibliography entry No. 131).

The entire study is made up of 24 different reports in 26 volumes. Copies of individual reports may be obtained by writing to the Superintendent of Documents, Government Printing Office, Washington, D.C. 20402. Individual reports vary in cost from 30 cents to $2.75; the entire series of reports can be obtained for $30.40.

Title of the individual studies are as follows:

An Analysis of Complaints in Selected Automobile Insurance Markets

Automobile Accident Litigation

Automobile Personal Injury Claims, Vols. I & II

Causation, Culpability and Deterrence in Highway Crashes

Comparative Studies in Automobile Accident Compensation

Constitutional Problems in Automobile Accident Compensation Reform

Compensation for Motor Vehicle Accident Losses in the Metropolitan Area of Washington, D.C.

Driver Behavior and Accident Involvement: Implication for Tort Liability

Economic Consequences of Automobile Accident Injuries, Vols. I & II

Economic Regulation of Insurance in the United States

Insolvencies among Automobile Insurers

Insurance Accessibility for the Hard-to-Place Driver

Mass Marketing of Property and Liability Insurance

Motor Vehicle Assigned Risk Plans

Motor Vehicle Crash Losses and Their Compensation in the United States

The Origin and Development of the Negligence Action

The Price and Availability of Automobile Liability Insurance in the Nonstandard Market

Price Variability in the Automobile Insurance Market

Public Attitudes Supplement to the Economic Consequences of Automobile Accident Injuries

Public Attitudes toward Auto Insurance

Quantitative Models for Automobile Accidents and Insurance

Rehabilitation of Auto Accident Victims

Structural Trends and Conditions in the Automobile Insurance Industry

A Study of Assigned Risk Plans

The entire series of studies encompasses some 4,673 pages of materials, and it is not within the scope of this book to provide an exposition and analysis of the various studies. Findings and conclusions from several of the studies are cited elsewhere in this book.

Basis for a No-Fault Plan

The series of studies provides the basis for the recommendation of a no-fault plan which would incorporate the following features:

1.   Require every car owner to carry insurance that would provide protection on a first-party basis to him, his family and to every uninsured passenger or pedestrian for all economic losses they incur from an accident involving the car, subject to reasonable limits and deductibles. The insurance also would protect him and his family while they are pedestrians or passengers in another vehicle.

2.   Provide full coverage for all medical benefits with a relatively small permissible deductible per accident but with very high mandatory limits. Coverage would be primary as among private insurance systems.

3.   Afford coverage for a relatively high percentage of earned income, with a short permitted waiting period at the option of the insured and a permitted monthy benefit ceiling by the insurer of perhaps as much as $1000.

4.   Provide coverage for the cost of necessary replacement services for non-employed persons, such as housewives, up to a benefit of perhaps $75 per week, with a permitted waiting period for benefits at the option of the insured.

5.   Contemplate ultimate coverage of damages to property, including that of the insured, if experience under first-party personal injury coverage is successful. There would be a permissible deductible referable to the vehicle only at the option of the insured of up to perhaps as much as $1000 or a third of the value of the car, and with a permissible limitation of coverage by the insurer of $10,000 per accident.

6.   Bar recovery for any loss covered by required insurance in any private damage action. The existing right to sue for damages resulting from negligence would be severely curtailed. A person could recover for intangible losses only if he established that he suffered permanent impairment or loss of function or permanent disfigurement, or that he incurred personal medical expenses—excluding hospital expenses—as a result of the accident in excess of a rather high dollar threshold.

Commentary on the Study Reports

There are wide differences in both the quality and the importance of the Department of Transportation reports. Some treat the subject matter superficially, while others have added greatly to the body of knowledge of the automobile compensation and insurance systems. Some are highly theoretical and have little practical application. Some of the reports make little or no attempt at hiding the bias of their authors. (See discussion in Maisonpierre, No. 291).

An author of one of the Department of Transportation reports, Calvin H. Brainard, makes the following observation about the entire project: "Through the assembly and organization of impressive amounts of research material, the DOT investigation has made an important contribution to the study of the automobile accident problem. But its findings are neither exhaustive nor infallible. In the public interest, it is to be hoped that predetermined arguments and ends will not act as guides to those having recourse to its vast storehouse of data and information for legislative reform or counter-reform." (See Brainard, No. 51).

NIXON AUTO INSURANCE PROPOSAL
March 18, 1971

The Nixon Administration, discarding the recommendations of a United States Department of Transportation study implemented by Congress by a law enacted late during the Johnson Administration, recommended an automobile insurance reform plan that would leave the legislation to the states.

It was widely believed that John A. Volpe, the Secretary of Transportation who presented the Administration's views to the Senate Commerce Committee, had favored a stronger approach but was overruled by the White House.

The Administration plan included a recommendation that the Senate and House pass a resolution declaring it to be "the sense of Congress" that the states should enact no-fault legislation.

Implied Threat of Federal Intervention

Volpe's proposal for a "Concurrent Resolution" for adoption by Congress that would express its support of a no-fault system was noticeable for its lack of any Federal strings attached. There was, however, an implied threat of a Federal takeover if the states failed to act within a reasonable time—such as two years. The Secretary proposed reviewing the accomplishments of the states after 25 months had elapsed and then deciding whether they had demonstrated the "feasibility of attaining a satisfactory and compatible motor vehicle accident reparations system without further Federal legislation."

Volpe stated that, although reform should be achieved through state action without imposing a uniform single reform system upon all the states, and without shaking the foundation of state regulation and state control of decisions regarding their own reparations systems, "some kind of broad national goals or standards, which are advisory, would seem to be very useful and appropriate." He did remark, however, "Our basic philosophy is opposed to any single set of uniform standards. The problems are different in the different states. But, if the states don't act, then perhaps we ought to provide standards which the states should follow and hopefully exceed. The language of the resolution pretty well tells the states what they can expect if they don't do the job."

Volpe also stated, "We believe that the states should begin promptly to shift to a first-party, no-fault compensation system for automobile accident victims. We believe that this might be done gradually and in such a way that we can reverse ourselves if the actual performance of the system doesn't meet our expectations."

The Proposed Resolution

The proposed resolution submitted by Secretary Volpe cited the inequities of the current system and concluded:
> "that it is the sense of the Congress that the regulation
> of insurance should, in general, continue with the states,
> subject to the admonition, however, that Congress can-
> not, and will not, long ignore the need for evolving new
> and updated approaches to insurance and accident com-
> pensation."

Critics of the Nixon Approach

The most vocal critic of the Nixon proposal was Richard J. Barber, who resigned by request in December of 1970 as Deputy Assistant Secretary of Transportation. Mr. Barber, a Johnson Administration appointee, who directed the Department of Transportation study, characterized "the White House-dictated approach" as "pale, anemic, and lacking in substance." He alleged that in a series of White House conferences, in which insurance company officials participated, the Department "was forced, not to retreat, but into a near rout. The unprogressive, unresponsive forces in the insurance industry have won a major victory at the White House," he alleged.

Barber called the Administration's proposals "a disgraceful sham," and was joined by most of the members of the Senate Commerce Committee.

Considerable criticism was expressed because the Administration's plan:

1.   Gave no suggestions for a model bill to guide the states.

2.   Gave no advice on what might be the best way to handle insurance of commercial vehicles under no-fault plans.

3.   The state-by-state approach permitting the states "to experiment" raises the spectre for risk managers handling large fleets of interstate vehicles that they will be required to deal with 50 different "experimental" methods of handling their culpability in accidents.

4.   Gave the states no guidance on how to integrate no-fault auto insurance with workmen's compensation.

5.   Was not particularly helpful in suggesting how to handle corporate liability to injured employee drivers.

State Option "Depressing"

Senator Philip A. Hart expressed no confidence in the state-by-state approach to handling the automobile reform problem. He argued that the states cannot be expected, on the basis of past performance, to act within a reasonable time. A fact often cited is that it took 37 years—from 1911 to 1948—for all of the states to adopt workmen's compensation laws. He stated that "the track record" of most bills in state legislatures has been "depressing," even when there had been no opposition. As for the unique problems confronted by individual states, alleged by Secretary Volpe, Senator Hart asked, "What's the difference whether an accident occurs in Wyoming or Idaho, in New York or California?"

The Nixon Administration plea that a state-by-state approach to implementation of no-fault is necessary because "the problems are different in different states" is repudiated by the Department of Transportation Automobile Accident Litigation study conducted by the Federal Judicial Center. (See Bibliography entry No. 118). That report states: "The factors influencing automobile accident litigation—

population, vehicle ownership, accident rates, ratio of suits filed to injuries and damage, the resources allocated to processing cases once they have entered the system, and the manner in which urbanization affects the legal process—these factors are simple, straightforward, relatively uniform across the U.S.... Many commonly held views about factors influencing accident litigation have been tested, and the majority have been rejected as false." The Federal Judicial Center report was one of the better studies conducted in the Department of Transportation project.

Senator Warren G. Magnuson (Dem., Wash.), Chairman of the Senate Commerce Committee, stated that he feared it would take at least two and a half to three years before many states could pass such legislation if they were of a mind to do so. He asked Secretary Volpe if the situation is as critical as the Secretary pictures it, why should not the initial stage to provide recovery of all medical and economic loss on a first-party basis be implemented at the federal level—especially since there is across-the-board agreement on the need for prompt remedial action and on the no-fault approach as the most practical method?

Federal v. State Issue Clouds Reform

The question of federal versus state regulation and establishment of standards for no-fault systems seems to be very much an issue. American Insurance Association President T. Lawrence Jones pinpointed the problem when he remarked, "The question whether reform of the automobile insurance system shall be accomplished by state or federal unfortunately has tended to overshadow" the fact that there is a need for "a complete first-party, no-fault system of compensation for auto crash victims. Through the most thorough examination, resulting in the most conclusive evidence, the existing tort liability system has again been proven to be lacking as a fair, efficient and satisfactory instrument of compensation for people injured in auto accidents."

Mr. Jones expressed opposition to a Federal approach to the subject and declared, "We believe it to be in the over-all interest of the property-casualty insurance industry as a whole to recognize that a system of extensive first-party, no-fault benefits has been established as a national policy and objective and to encourage the states to adopt such a system as swiftly as possible." (See Bibliography entries Nos. 3, 178, 213, 355, 534, 356, 382, and Morris, No. 525).

Accusations of Bias

James Ridgeway points out in an article that Mr. Volpe, a three-time Massachusetts Governor who has also been Federal Highway Administrator and Massachusetts Public Works Commissioner, opposed reform of automobile insurance while he was governor of Massachusetts. Ridgeway also alleges that President Nixon himself has maintained close ties with insurance people, most recently as a director of Mutual of New York and over the years through a friendship with the Kemper family, which runs Lumbermans Mutual, a prominent auto insurer. (See Ridgeway, No. 404).

The evidence indicates, however, that at the time of Volpe's report to Congress he was in full support of Federal standards for a no-fault insurance proposal, possibly backed up by pressure on the states to conform through a mandatory effective date or Federal penalties. The White House opposed legislative standards, and Mr. Volpe abandoned the concept on the eve of testimony before the Senate Committee. Instead, he suggested the resolution urging the states to act. (See Karr, No. 510).

HART NO-FAULT PROPOSAL

Senator Philip A. Hart (Dem., Mich.) introduced legislation on September 14, 1970, to reform the automobile liability insurance system, including a measure to establish a no-fault system and two bills to pave the way for speeded-up development of group automobile coverage plans. The bill proposing the no-fault program, S. 4339, would put into effect a Uniform Motor Vehicle Insurance Act. The bill did not pass. Senator Hart's package of reform legislation was the result of a three-year study of automobile insurance conducted by the Senate Judiciary Anti-Trust Subcommittee of which he is chairman.

Bill Re-Introduced in 1971

On February 24, 1971, Senator Hart reintroduced his bill in a slightly modified version (S. 945), but bearing the same title. Senator Warren Magnuson (Dem., Washington) joined as co-sponsor of the bill. The 1971 bill proposed the establishment of a first-party, no-fault system with tort liability retained only "in cases of catastrophic harm," *i.e.*, permanent and total disability, permanent and partial disability of 70 percent or more, and permanent, severe and irreparable disfigurement. Up to $30,000 would be payable in the case of death. Survivors of non-wage earners and those suffering economic loss in excess of $30,000 still would be able to sue under the tort system. Summary of the Uniform Motor Vehicle Insurance Act follows.

General Approach

The Hart proposal provides for a first-party, no-fault system, with tort liability retained only "in cases of catastrophic harm," *i.e.*, permanent and total disability, permanent and partial disability of 70 percent or more, and permanent, severe and irreparable disfigurement. The insured, occupants of his vehicle, and pedestrians injured by his vehicle would proceed, regardless of fault, directly against the insured's own company for personal injuries (including death) arising out of the operation or use of that vehicle.

An exemption from tort liability is provided except for "catastrophic harm," where there may be recovery for "economic loss" in excess of that received under the bill.

No-fault coverage is compulsory for motor vehicle owners, and a criminal penalty is provided for registering a vehicle without the insurance, or for knowingly operating or using an uninsured vehicle on the public highways.

As long as a person has a valid driver's license, is willing to pay the premium, and the company's solvency would not be impaired, companies cannot refuse to sell, and once the policy is sold, it cannot be cancelled nor non-renewed. An assigned claims plan would provide no-fault benefits, for example, to victims of hit-and-run accidents. At the insured's option, coverage for "catastrophic harm" liability shall be offered by the company in limits of at least $50,000 per person and $300,000 per accident.

If the insured buys the "catastrophic harm" coverage, the company must offer uninsured motorist coverage in the same limits as the "catastrophic harm" coverage purchased. Additional coverages, for example, for damage to property, may be offered, subject to the approval of the Secretary of the Department of Transportation.

Coverage under the Plan

No-fault benefits apply to personal injuries (including death), but do not apply to damage to property. A lump sum is paid for death, and other benefits are paid as accrued.

There are no limits to the medical or rehabilitation benefits. Only expenses not compensated from any other private or public sources are covered, unless such sources provide that their benefits shall be supplemental to those paid under the bill.

The plan provides wage loss benefits of 85 percent of monthly earnings at the time of the injury or $1000, whichever is less, up to thirty months; maximum amount for death cases would be $30,000. As with medical and rehabilitation, only lost earnings not compensated from any other private or public sources are covered, unless such sources provide that their benefits shall be supplemental to those paid under the bill.

Compensation is provided for other economic losses, for example, housekeeping, babysitting, transportation and telephone. There are no dollar amount limitations on this coverage.

No coverage is provided for pain and suffering.

Financing, Rating and Regulation

Insureds provide the financing by purchasing coverage from private insurance companies.

A common, uniform statistical plan is proposed for the gathering and compilation of (1) claims, and (2) loss experience data for the classes of risk in each rating territory for each coverage under the bill. The insurance companies would be allowed to continue to pool their loss experience data, but would not be allowed to continue to pool their expense data.

The Secretary of DOT shall require standard uniform and standard minimal (1) policy provisions, (2) classes of risk, and (3) rating territories, for each coverage under the bill. The Secretary shall analyze the claims and loss experience data filed by the companies, for the purpose of making available to the public the rate (or pure premium) indicated by such data. By comparing this indicated rate (or pure premium) among the various companies, the prospective buyer will be able to obtain some indication of the claims payment practices of the companies. By reviewing the actual rate being charged, as well as the indicated rate (or pure premium), the public will be in a position to shop for price and quality.

Other than the provisions for the statistical plan, the States will continue to regulate the rates. (From the *Congressional Record*, See Bibliography entry No. 449).

Criticisms of the Hart Plan

Predictably, the Hart proposal has come under considerable attack, because it establishes a federal program with uniform provisions applicable throughout the nation. This, according to critics, prevents the states from experimenting and from creating programs which would meet local, individualized problems of the several states. The threat of Federal incursions into the insurance business has drawn heated criticism from all segments of the insurance industry—including the American Insurance Association, which has proposed one of the most radical "no-fault" proposals. The National Association of Insurance Commissioners, fearful of Federal pre-emption of State prerogatives, has denounced the Hart Plan.

The special provision shifting proportionate total insurance costs onto the operators of trucks and other large vehicles has created considerable controversy. No-fault supporters, however, claim that charging such owners more is equitable, since large vehicles usually cause more damage than ordinary passenger vehicles.

The Hart Plan is backed by an impressive array of statistics compiled by the Senate Judiciary Anti-Trust Subcommittee, and, although it has drawn extensive fire from critics, Hart-type federal legislation, of some form, can be anticipated if the states fail to heed the warnings of Congress to provide a uniform, national insurance program which provides necessary reforms of the present system.

PART IV
ARGUMENTS FOR AND AGAINST
CHANGE TO NO-FAULT

CHAPTER XI

RATIONALE OF THE TORT LIABILITY SYSTEM

Basic to most of the automobile insurance reform proposals has been the substitution of "no-fault" for the tort liability system. Such a drastic reform, if "no-fault" is adopted, would materially alter the manner in which automobile accidents are handled and the way that accident victims themselves are compensated.

FUNDAMENTAL CHANGES

A change to a no-fault system would largely eliminate the adversary relation inherent in the insurance claims-man/tort-claimant relationship. It would substantially eliminate a large body of potential litigation or pre-trial business for the legal profession, because many of the automobile accident tort liability cases would be eliminated. A "pure" system would eliminate all cases.

"Pure" vs. Mixed System

The number of eliminated cases and the extent of the reduction of business experienced by attorneys would be dependent upon the nature of the "no-fault" system adopted. A "pure" system, embodying "no-fault" principles, which eliminates all automobile accident tort liability claims, would have a dramatic effect on the legal business handled by many attorneys. It would greatly de-emphasize the need for liability specialists among insurance claims adjusters, particularly in those cases where the adjuster spends most or all of his time handling automobile liability insurance claims. The multiple-line adjuster, particularly one handling liability claims under other than automobile insurance, would still require tort liability expertise.

Since most of the "no-fault" proposals are not "pure" systems—rather, residual tort liability is preserved over a basic specified coverage—there will still remain the need for liability specialists for the residual cases, both among the insurance claims adjusters and among the legal profession.

The Issue of Morality

Perhaps more subject to controversy is the issue of responsibility for fault. Basic to the American Puritan Ethic has been the unimpeachable tenet that each man is responsible to his own God for his transgressions. The concept of accountability and punishment for bad conduct with reward for good conduct has been a fundamental principle of the nation's value system for generations. Tampering with that system appears to many observers to be a serious mistake which signals a deterioration in American morality.

Proponents of change to a "no-fault" system argue equally convincingly that there is nothing moral about the present operation of the tort liability system in the case of automobile accidents. They point out with much conviction that the tort liability system was never designed for situations arising out of high-speed ground transportation.

Where accidents occur with split-second timing; where the question of fault is difficult and illusory; and where victims of automobile accidents are burdened by the delay, expense, and uncertainty of a capricious system of affixing blame and determining damage, this is certainly no crowning triumph in morality.

Arguments for and against Change

Many arguments have been advanced attacking or defending the application of the present tort liability system to the automobile accident problem. The rationale of that system and its application to the motor vehicle should be examined. Accordingly, to aid the reader, some of the most popular arguments advanced for and against a change to a "no-fault" system are presented.

LOGIC OF THE FAULT SYSTEM

For Change

Damage awards under the fault insurance system operate through thousands of legal and extra-legal forums that apply its rules unevenly and unpredictably. Some 99% of the claims are settled in a proliferation of forums outside the judiciary—typically in unrecorded private sessions between the claimant or his attorney and an

Against Change

Liability for fault is an intrinsic part of the reparations system for automobile accidents, where each driver should be held responsible only for accidents which are his fault. The process of determining fault in tort liability, as in the case of criminal law, requires careful weighing of the issues and a proper adjudication. It is a credit

insurance adjuster. "Part lottery and part bazaar, the fault insurance system is unreliable and unpredictable." (See Bibliography entry No. 351).

* * *

The final cause of law is the welfare of society. The rule that misses its aim cannot permanently justify its existence. (Cardozo, Benjamin, The Nature of the Judicial Process 66).

* * *

A typical driver has a better than even chance of having an accident every three years; just about every driver will have an accident sometime. "Safety experts have concluded that automobile accidents have become so widespread that virtually every family can expect to experience personally the tragedy of automobile-inflicted death or injury." (See Bibliography entry No. 351).

* * *

Human error is inherent in the operation of a motor vehicle. One study has shown that the automobile driver must make 200 observations and 20 decisions each mile he drives. The potential is so great that it would be natural for even the most care-

to the system that it provides a prompt disposition of liability claims through the insurance claims process. It is only in the claims of disputed liability where the court adjudications are required to resolve the issues.

* * *

No-fault would inevitably put an end to the moral and legal responsibility of individuals who inflict injuries upon their fellows. The regimentation of all injured persons in no-fault plans without regard to guilt or innocence would certainly lead to the simultaneous destruction of the dignity of the individual and the evenhanded justice of the common law. (See Bibliography entry No. 90).

* * *

Those people who argue that everyone will have an accident, and therefore, everyone should pay equally for the cost of automobile accidents distort the fact that there are careful drivers who go for many years without experiencing accidents. They also distort the fact that a minority of reckless, inexperienced, and intoxicated drivers cause a disproportionate number of accidents.

* * *

ful of drivers to make errors in judgment. The average driver does make errors—one per each two miles driven. (See Bibliography entry No. 449).

* * *

A substantial but largely unmeasurable number of violations and crashes occur which involve generally competent drivers who are suffering temporary lapses from their normal adequate levels." (See Bibliography entry No. 120).

* * *

Even professional drivers at the General Motors proving grounds—despite their superior training and supervision and the carefully engineered highways—persistently have accidents. (See Bibliography entry No. 449).

* * *

In 1959 almost half of what was paid to traffic victims came from non-fault sources such as accident and health insurance, life insurance, social security, *etc.* This raises the question that, if it is morally repugnant to pay automobile insurance to a traffic victim without reference to fault, why is it morally acceptable to pay the same victim from accident and health insurance, from wage replacement insurance, from Social Security disability insurance, and indeed from the widespread medical payment and collision coverages of the automobile insurance policy itself, all of which are payable without reference to fault?

"Literally, the principle of liability for fault is derived from the religious belief that each of us is responsible to his God for his own conduct." The concept that damages should be paid to a traffic victim only upon proof of a driver's negligence is "a crowning triumph of reason and morality." (See Keeton and O'Connell, No. 253).

* * *

"Our law and our whole political thesis is based on a sense of fair play." (See Logan, No. 286). The position taken by proponents of the present system and the tort liability law on which it is based is that in the majority of cases an auto accident is a result of controllable human actions: hence, the

(See O'Connell, No. 377).

* * *

Using the tort liability system in automobile accidents is no more rational than having to prove that you didn't cause the fire before collecting insurance when your house burns down. It makes no more sense than seeking out the fellow who sneezed on you in order to sue his insurance company for hospital costs for your pneumonia. (See Bibliography entry No. 64).

* * *

We do not refuse to pay the hospital bill for the patient who did not wear his rubbers in the rainstorm or a fire insurance claim for the homeowner who dropped a cigarette, yet in both cases these individuals were negligent. (See Bibliography entry No. 449).

* * *

When you die, your life insurance company does not refuse to pay your widow on the ground that you contributed to the unfortunate result by smoking too many cigarettes. (See Bibliography entry No. 351).

* * *

The tort liability system is illogically perverse. Palliatives which attempt to "reform" the system by ameliorating one or another of the defects are bound to fail. *Arbitration*, for example, would help precisely those claimants who already do best under the fault insurance system, and, since arbitrators' decisions are

party responsible should be made to pay for the damages caused and should have to care for his own losses. (See Hold, No. 196).

* * *

"To bring out a plan for less law and order or less personal responsibility . . . seems to us somewhat less than good planning." (George W. Nordhaus, Bibliography entry No. 18).

* * *

Before discarding the aged, yet vital, "reasonable man" and adopting such a drastic innovation, we should ask whether a civilized society can maintain itself without its members being accountable for their conduct, *i.e.*, a reasonable society without a reasonable man?

* * *

Dean Roscoe Pound wrote, "The import of abdicating personal responsibility centers on the issue of freedom versus equality, on democracy versus a socialist state." (Pound, Law in the Service State: Freedom Versus Equality, 36 A.B.A. J. 977, 981, 1050 (1950).

* * *

"Change within the framework of tort jurisprudence has worked remarkably well up to the present. Within our lifetime, we have observed the defense of contributory negligence softened by the doctrines of last clear chance and comparative negligence either by law or by fact in the hands of a jury. We have been fascinated by

not binding on the parties, nothing would be accomplished to reduce court congestion. Adopting the *comparative negligence* doctrine, likewise, is without merit. It merely makes the process of deciding claims more complicated than it is today. It has been used in several of the states for a number of years, and it has not solved the problem of the automobile accident victim. In addition, increasing medical payments and providing for income loss reimbursement on a first-party basis as an overlay on top of the fault insurance system would merely increase the inefficiency of the overall reparations system, resulting in substantial premium increase. It is inherent in the palliative proposals, with their offsets of first-party benefits against liability awards, that the consumer would be required to pay to operate two reparations systems instead of one. They make little sense. (See Bibliography entry No. 351).

* * *

Common-law doctrines of immunity are antiquated. While some of these doctrines are being discarded, they are still part of the law in many states. For example: (a) sovereign immunity, (b) charitable immunity, and (c) intra-family immunity (claims between husband and wife and between parent and child). (See Marryott, No. 295).

* * *

The doctrine of contributory negligence is antiquated, cruel and

new rules of discovery and pretrial practice. Surely we are not going to destroy this inspiring institution for the sake of a sociological experiment." (LeRoy E. Kennedy, Vice President, Northwestern National Group).

* * *

unrealistic. Therefore, it is largely ignored. The result is an intellectually dishonest basis for verdicts and damages. (See Marryott, No. 295).

* * *

Why did we abandon our previous reliance upon the "fault" system in the case of work injuries? Essentially, it was because the system did not provide fair, prompt and economical reimbursement. Also, it was because it had become clear that on-the-job injuries often were not really anybody's fault. People felt it was unrealistic to continue a system which, for each injury, sought to identify and punish a negligent party. It has become unrealistic to carry on a system based upon identifying the guilty and the innocent. In most states about 90 percent of all drivers carry automobile liability insurance. Judgments against presumably negligent parties are secured, but nine times out of ten the source of the money is an insurance company, rather than the negligent individual personally. (See Cass, No. 65).

* * *

"Courts have better things to do today than try to decide whether a light was red or green five years ago." (See Paulson, No. 383).

* * *

We should reserve our courts for matters which merit adjudication by freeing them from problems that could be handled bet-

Those who attack the fault system as a basis for determining responsibility for an automobile accident would apparently scrap the entire concept of individual responsibility which cuts across not only automobile liability but all types of tort situations, as well as the underlying premise upon which criminal liability is predicated.

* * *

"Is the concept of personal responsibility outmoded? If so, is it outmoded for drivers only, or should it be abolished in other areas of human conduct as well?" How about the responsibility for fault in the far more numerous injuries suffered in other types of accidents? (Paul S. Wise, President of AIMA, See Bibliography entry No. 18).

* * *

ter under another system. Furthermore, we could free our doctors for more profitable uses—such as improving emergency accident treatment—rather than sitting in courthouses or otherwise being tied up in the fault-finding process. (See Bibliography entry No. 362).

* * *

The present system is vulnerable. It is a system which pits the parties against each other as adversaries, with the outcome hinging upon such things as the skill and persuasiveness of the opposing attorneys, the personality and economic position of the plaintiff and defendant, and upon the amount of insurance carried by the defendant. The system always puts the insurance company in the unenviable position of opposing the injured party. It is drastic and unwise for the insurance business to rigidly defend the status quo, while refusing to consider reasonable, evolutionary changes consistent with the changing world in which we live. (See Crane, No. 93).

* * *

A "no-fault" system would eliminate almost all controversy between insured and insurer, except those controversies arising from differences in the valuation of damages. (See Hold, No. 196).

* * *

The fault insurance system is damaging to the insurance industry. "Much of the bitterness toward automobile insurance com-

A program that does not discriminate between the accident victims and the accident causers with respect to claim payments is a threat to the theory of insurance, removing the deterrents for accident prevention and safety practices and a basic concept of the free enterprise system of insurance of "rating commensurate with the risk," rewarding the careful and penalizing the negligent and unsafe in insurance and in all the fields of human endeavor that it affects. (See Bibliography entry No. 370).

* * *

A large number of insurance companies have labeled the "no-fault" system as contrary to public policy and the public interest.

Legally-trained personnel fear the danger that the "no-fault" concept will present for traditional American values—the concept of right and wrong, the maintenance of a sense of duty and responsibility to others, the sense of justice—ingrained in the U.S. system of jurisprudence.

* * *

panies, and the rates they charge, can be traced to the underlying imperatives of our common law tradition of liability based on fault. The system is not reliable which does not compensate you adequately and promptly when you find yourself compelled to make use of it." (Testimony of Pennsylvania Insurance Commissioner, David Maxwell, in Hearings on S.Res. 233 before the Subcomm. on Antitrust and Monopoly of the Senate Comm. on the Judiciary, 90th Cong., 2d Sess. 714-18 (1968).

* * *

A revolutionary approach to reform is irrational; it is not in the public interest. "While the present system has its obvious faults, we should not hastily move to a system merely because it is new. Caution, common sense, and consideration of sound public policy demand that we carefully assess the full range of alternatives and move gradually in the direction of reform, checking actual experience as we proceed." (U.S. Secretary of Transportation, John A. Volpe, See Ghiardi, No. 172).

* * *

Instead of following the non-fault principle throughout, many plans, such as the Saskatchewan Plan and the Keeton & O'Connell proposal, incorporate the fault principle for the allocation of damages above and below the stated insurance limits and for types of losses, such as property losses, which are not covered. (These are covered in the Saskatchewan Plan). This creates a "liability illusion"; yet it is effectively removed. It is but a single step from it to a pure non-fault system. If the public is willing to accept a halfway non-fault system, the public would also accept a pure non-fault plan. Retention of the tort system for serious cases, as advocated in plans such as the Keeton & O'Connell proposal, is inconsistent with arguments against discarding the "liability for fault" concept.

* * *

A no-fault plan is a compulsory form of excess accident and health insurance with a form of disability income insurance attached. One may wonder why it is needed. As the burden of a motorist's responsibility for damages other than to himself is removed, there is little need for anything other than an extension of the present forms of accident or health insurance. There is no need for the element of compulsion unless it is assumed that persons do not recognize their exposures or that for some reason government is obliged to force people to protect themselves. (See Hold, No. 196).

* * *

No-fault would not motivate people to drive more carefully, would not prod Detroit to build safer cars, would not reduce the cost of auto insurance, and would not help law enforcement. (Vestal Lemmon, President of the National Association of Independent Insurers, See Lemmon, No. 514).

DETERMINATION OF FAULT

For Change

Criteria for determining fault under the present system are highly unrealistic.

Because of inability of people to remember what happened in traffic accidents, many lawyers will agree that traffic cases are unique in the extent to which parties and witnesses, as well as lawyers in conferring with them, are subject to inducements to exaggerate, to resort to half-truth, and to skirt the boundaries of outright perjury. (See Keeton & O'Connell, No. 256).

* * *

Witnesses indulge in imaginative reconstruction of events imperfectly perceived and even more imperfectly remembered. (See Rokes, *Human Relations in Handling Insurance Claims*, Richard D. Irwin, Inc., 1967. Chapter 3, "The Imperfect Human"). The result of all this is that automobile litigation is more fraught with both innocent misrepresentation and outright perjury than any other area of contested litigation.

* * *

Professor William L. Prosser, the foremost authority on tort law, states:

"The process by which the question of legal fault, and hence of liability, is determined in our courts is a cumbersome, time-consuming, expensive, and almost ridiculously inaccurate one. The

Against Change

Ascertainment of fault is an integral feature of a legal system. It is the foundation of the judicial process of distinguishing between the aggrieved victim of wrong-doing and the wrongdoer. Determination of fault is basic to a society's concept of right and wrong, identifying the party who has violated society's rules, specifying punishment and providing retribution for his deleterious act or omission.

The ascertainment of fault is basic to the criminal law, to contract law, and to many facets of man's relationship with his contemporaries. What possible social triumph is achieved by eliminating the fault concept in the operation of motor vehicles? We have determined the legal question of fault in the United States ever since the automobile entered the picture. The system has worked well for three or four generations.

The current assault against the fault-finding process is symptomatic of a social deterioration in personal responsibility for one's conduct. Abandonment of the fault concept based upon the premise that determination of fault is impossible ignores the simple fact that we have succeeded in doing the "impossible" for the past seventy years, and we can continue to adjudicate issues of fault for the next seventy years.

evidence given in personal injury
cases usually consists of highly
contradictory statements from the
two sides, estimating such factors
as time, speed, distance and visi-
bility, offered months after the
event by witnesses who were never very sure just what happened
when they saw it, and whose faulty
memories are undermined by
lapse of time, by bias, by conver-
sations with others, and by the
subtle influence of counsel. Upon
such evidence, a jury of twelve inexperienced citizens, called away
from their other business if they
have any, are invited to retire and
make the best guess they can as
to whether the defendant, the
plaintiff, or both were 'negligent,'
which is itself a wobbly and un-
certain standard based upon the
supposed mental process of a hypothetical and non-existent reasonable man. European lawyers
view the whole thing with utter
amazement; and the extent to
which it has damaged the courts
and the legal profession by bringing the law and its administration
into public disrepute can only be
guessed." (See Bibliography entry
No. 95).

* * *

"The inherent weakness of the
jury system lies precisely in these
psychological factors within the
jury itself. Sympathy, bias, credu-
lity, gullibility, susceptibility to
impression, to a good speech, a
good display and a good show, lead
all too often to the wrong verdict."
(Prosser; See Bibliog. entry No. 433).

Applying fault law to automobile accidents is completely unrealistic. Determination of fault turns on comparing of what the participants did at the time of the accident with what a hypothetical, reasonable man might have done, and then on connecting their acts with "foreseeable" damages. Both in determining fault and in determining the causal relationship between a particular negligent act and a particular injury, therefore, fault law is led into a focus on extraordinary incidents and into some highly abstruse reasoning.

* * *

Accidents often occur because of a split second error of judgment or a lapse of attention. Involvement in such an accident is largely a matter of chance; there will always be automobile accidents, for there will always be human error. Thus, the consequences of such accidents should properly be borne by society as a whole. (See Rokes, No. 413).

* * *

The nightmare of trying to find the culprit in a chain-reaction pile-up on a freeway involving six, ten, twenty or fifty cars is one of the greatest absurdities of all time. (See Bibliography entry No. 10).

* * *

ANTIQUITY OF THE TORT LIABILITY SYSTEM

For Change

The notion that negligence has deep roots in antiquity is in error. Legal scholars are well agreed that negligence law constitutes a relatively recent development in Anglo-American law. Superseding a strict liability regime, the ascendancy of the negligence principle can be traced only to the Industrial Revolution. Its rationale was that the needs of society demanded that the growth of industry and the expansion of commerce should not be impeded by the onerous financial liabilities inherent in a strict liability regime. (See James, No. 132).

* * *

Out of the early days of the automobile came the negligence concept that liability for fault would be a morally flavored compromise between earlier strict liability concepts and the total abnegation of responsibility for harm flowing from socially desirable activities. It was felt that liability should be predicated upon fault, and it was better for the victim of an accident not provably the "fault" of some other individual to bear the financial consequences of his injury rather than to deter others from engaging in socially useful activities because of the risk of having to bear the costs of accidents that might occur. (See James, No. 132).

* * *

Against Change

The tort liability system "has existed hundreds of years—a system older than this country." (Dan Loring, former president of the National Association of Insurance Agents, see Wilson, No. 558).

* * *

A "no-fault" plan will deprive at least 7.5 million people of "rights that go all the way back in the history of Anglo-Saxon law." (See Connor, No. 83).

* * *

The shift back toward strict liability, as evidenced in many areas of tort law, is more consistent with early common law. As stated in a 1681 English case, "In all civil acts the law doth not so much regard the intent of the actor, as the loss and damage of the party suffering . . ." (Lambert v. Bessey, 83 Eng. Rep. 220).

* * *

The tort liability system was not intended to serve a nation in which millions of vehicles are on highways at speeds exceeding 60 miles per hour. (See Bibliography entry No. 409).

* * *

SHIFT TO COMPENSATION EMPHASIS

For Change

"Clearly, the social objective of the present auto insurance system is to reimburse the injured person. Every important legal or statutory development in the past 30 years has been in that direction. But try to think of a system which by its basic principle (*i.e.*, fault) could impede its objective more effectively.

"In this comic opera, the hero is the plaintiff's lawyer, who is seeking to obtain an adequate award for his injured client. The villain is the insurance company. Under the rules of the game, the insurer defends and one might say seeks to thwart the socially desirable goal of reimbursing the auto accident victim. This would be

Against Change

Says American Insurance Association head, T. Lawrence Jones:

"If it were to be judged on that basis, admittedly the present tort liability system is not an efficient system of making reparations to all traffic accident victims . . . It was not designed or intended for that purpose." (*Business Week*, April 20, 1968).

* * *

amusing if it did not place such a
serious drain on the financial resources of the motoring public.
For the insurance industry, it has
been a public relations nightmare.
No-fault auto insurance puts the
industry where it should be—providing direct insurance benefits."
(See Bibliography entry No. 174).

* * *

The social emphasis has shifted
from punishing the wrongdoer to
protecting the automobile accident
victim. "The old morality that had
as its premise that only wrongdoers should be punished, and that
any degree of fault on the part
of the claimant would bar his recovery of damages, has been crum-
bling. It is fighting a losing battle
with the quest for security." (See
Marryott, No. 296).

* * *

The fault system is unrealistic.
The auto accident is a social problem somewhat like that of old age
or unemployment, and persons
damaged in auto accidents should
be compensated irrespective of
fault. In the great majority of
cases the automobile accident is
the fault of no one; an auto accident is the inevitable result of the
speed of automobiles, human
frailties, and the rapid pace at
which people live. If the auto accident is viewed as a more or less
inevitable event and a product of
our environment, the accident may
be compared to a disease. (See
Hold, No. 196).

* * *

Auto insurers are selling the wrong product. Policies were initially designed primarily to protect the holder against the risk of liability, but most of the public clamor today is not concerned with this. Instead, the bulk of complaints concern compensation for accident victims, and the business can't afford to ignore this "growing level of criticism"— even though it may not have been responsible for the problem. (See Diamond, No. 141).

* * *

Public expectations have shifted more and more toward protecting the person who is injured. (See Bibliography entry No. 320).

* * *

Says H. Clay Johnson, president of the Royal-Globe Insurance Companies:

"We live in a time when the idea is widely accepted that the injured party deserves redress or compensation, regardless of fault. As a consequence, we find that courts and juries, by interpretation, are constantly broadening the terms of insurance contracts beyond the original intent of the insurer and insured. More and more often, we find that 'extra-contractual' obligations are being placed upon insurance companies." (See Bibliography entry No. 433).

* * *

An insurance system should not be a "tool of the penal code." Difficulties over establishing fault have twisted the present system into something it was never intended to be—a reparations system—"because judges and juries believe that people should be paid for their injuries suffered in crashes. In this way, the tort liability system has been amended virtually out of existence; and with good reason, because it just doesn't serve modern life." (T. Lawrence Jones, President of AIA, See Slattery, No. 549).

* * *

Punishment for wrongdoing should not be a role of the compensation system—it should become the sole function of the law enforcement agencies and the courts. (See Hold, No. 196).

* * *

CHAPTER XII

ECONOMY, EFFICIENCY AND EQUITY

Much has been written and said about the inefficiency of the tort liability system in the handling of automobile accident reparations. Charges of gross wastes and inadequacies stem out of a system which specifies as a condition precedent to recovery the establishment of fault.

LEGAL AND INSURANCE MACHINERY

Since the ground rules are specified, the legal machinery for fault determination comes to play and the trappings of that machinery necessarily extract their pound of flesh. Issues of fact and of law which must be resolved in order to determine questions of fault must use the judicial forum or a comparable forum in order to produce what the American society expects in the way of justice.

An Expensive Middleman

The judicial forum is a centuries-old human institution which has served man well. But it is expensive, and it is time-consuming, for it requires highly trained specialists to help assure the administration of justice. Judges trained in law and dedicated to impartial fact-finding must be paid. Extensively schooled counselors or attorneys at law are needed to gather evidence and present it in a manner most conducive to the best interests of their clients.

The legal system is an expensive middleman in the tort liability system. That it perhaps drains an inordinate fee for its services has been extensively discussed as critics clamor for reform of the contingent fee system. That it is fraught with delay and other excesses is perhaps true.

The basic issue, however, is the legitimacy of the middleman in the automobile accident reparations system. The middleman's legitimacy is apparent within the mandates of the present tort liability system.

The Insurance Distribution System

"The American Way" dictates that private enterprise can do things better and more economically than government enterprise. Yet there are those critics who look at the insurance distribution system as a model of inefficiency and exorbitant profit—single-mindedly devoted to profit-making in an activity where other objectives deserve at least equal consideration.

Raw statistics of excessive administration and distribution costs, capricious policy cancellations, inadequate insurance coverage and pitiful recoveries have focused the glare of antagonism against the private insurance industry as the institution charged with the responsibility to handle the automobile accident reparations problem.

Compounding the problem is the unenviable record of some states in failing to assure that the private industry does its job. State regulation as the media for protecting the public and the industry itself against untoward business conduct has in some cases aggravated the system under which the present automobile accident reparations system operates.

Arguments for and against Change

Proposals for reform vary tremendously on the extent of modification of the tort liability system. They also differ substantially on what role the private insurance industry should play.

Arguments for and against change to a "no-fault" system are particularly interesting when related to the subjects of economy, efficiency and equity. Those arguments follow.

ADMINISTRATION OF SYSTEM

For Change

The costs of administering the present system are too high. The following tables illustrate the great waste inherent in the tort liability system in what essentially amounts to the delivery of medical care to injured victims of automobile accidents.

Against Change

The assertion is made that the whole process will be far simpler than at present—"Just like dealing with your own fire insurance company." There is little true basis for this comparison. A fire insurance claim is for a definite ascertained amount and it is settled in a lump sum. Claims under a no-fault system, such as the Keeton & O'Connell plan, would involve significant variables, such as the existence of collateral source payments, claimant income levels, extent of rehabilitation and recovery, and the like. Even explaining how the figures are computed to the average claimant would be a difficult task. In addition, the retention of tort liability in the more serious cases makes every case involving more than superficial injuries a potential lawsuit to be investigated by the liability carrier. (See Kemper, No. 265).

* * *

For Change

TABLE 1. — *Where $5,700,000,000 of automobile bodily injury liability insurance premiums went, 1969*

	Amount	Percent
Premiums[1]	$ 5,768,000,000	100
Company expenses:		
Selling	1,043,286,000	
Overhead	295,374,000	
State taxes	167,817,000	
Total company expenses	1,506,477,000	26
Claim adjusting expenses	789,586,000	14
Claimants lawyers fees	947,839,000	16
Court costs	111,102,000	2
Total expenses, fees, and costs	3,355,004,000	58
Net benefits to claimants	2,412,996,000	42

[1] Earned by over 1,000 stock, mutual, and reciprocal insurers.

Note: "Premiums," "Company expenses," and "Claim adjusting expenses" derived from Bests Aggregates and Averages (1970, 31st ed.), and The Spectator (Chilton Co., Philadelphia, Pa.); "Claimants lawyers fees" and "Court costs" derived from U.S. Department of Transportation, "Automobile Personal Injury Claims," pp. 73, 80 (1970), and "Automobile Accident Litigation," p. 7 (1970).

Source: U.S. Senate Antitrust and Monopoly Subcommittee

TABLE 2. — *Where each $1 of automobile bodily injury liability insurance premium goes*

Premium	$1.00

Company expenses:	
Selling	.18
Overhead	.05
State taxes	.03
Total company expenses	.26
Claim adjusting expenses	.14
Claimants lawyers' fees	.16
Court costs	.02
Total expenses, fees, and costs	.58
Net benefits to claimants	.42

Note: "Premiums", "Company Expenses", and "Claim Adjusting expenses" derived from *Bests Aggregates and Averages* (1970, 31st Ed.), and *The Spectator* (Chilton Co., Phila., Pa.); "Claimants Lawyers' Fees" and "Court Costs" derived from U.S. Dept. of Transportation, *Automobile Personal Injury Claims,* pp. 73, 80 (1970), and *Automobile Accident Litigation,* p. 7 (1970).

Source: U.S. Senate Antitrust and Monopoly Subcommittee.

TABLE 3. — *Breakdown of the 42 cents of net benefits to claimants out of each $1 of automobile bodily injury liability insurance premium*

	Cents
In excess of out-of-pocket loss (*viz.* general damages, such as pain and suffering)	21
Duplicate recovery[1]	7
Out-of-pocket loss not otherwise compensated	14
Net benefits to claimants	42

[1]*i.e.,* benefits received from other sources, such as Blue Cross, Blue Shield, Social Security and sick leave, *etc.*

Note: Derived from Statement of Professor Robert E. Keeton, Harvard Law School, before the U.S. Senate Antitrust and Monopoly Subcommittee Hearings on Automobile Insurance, December 9, 1969; U.S. Dept. of Transportation, *Economic Consequences of Automobile Accident Injuries* (1970).

Source: U.S. Senate Antitrust and Monopoly Subcommittee.

TABLE 4. — *Comparison of private insurance systems—*
Cost of delivering $1 of benefits

	Auto bodily injury liability insurance	Work-men's compen-sation insurance	Group accident and health insurance
Total dollar input....................	$2.40	$4.50	$1.22
Administrative expenses.....................	1.40*	.50*	.22**
Benefits..	1.00	1.00	1.00

*Includes insurance company expenses, and all costs of litigation.
**Includes property and liability insurance company expenses;
    excludes costs of any litigation.

Sources: U.S. Senate Antitrust and Monopoly Subcommittee as to bodily injury liability insurance: "Crisis in Car Insurance," pp. 89-90. (Keeton, O'Connell, and McCord, University of Illinois 1968) as to workmen's compensation insurance, "The Spectator," p. 33, September 1970 (Chilton Co., Philadelphia, Pa.) as to group accident and health insurance.

TABLE 5. — *Comparison of selected insurance company costs* of deliv-*
ering $1 of auto bodily injury liability, workmen's compensation, and
group accident and health benefits in 1969

[In cents]

	Auto bodily injury liabil-ity— Fault and nongroup	Work-men's compen-sation— nonfault and nongroup	Group accident and health— nonfault and group
Stock companies:			
Aetna Life & Casualty.................	38	28	12
Allstate...	39	27	7
U.S.F. & G.	38	30	22
Mutual companies:			
American Mutual Liability............	35	27	16
Employers Insurance of Wausau....	35	21	13
Liberty Mutual.............................	33	19	11

*"Costs" mean all underwriting and claim adjustment expenses, including any defense lawyer fees, but excluding claimants lawyers fees and court costs.

Source: Best's Aggregates and Averages—Property and Liability, pp. 120, 122-123, 126-129, 199, 200, 202-204 (1970, 31st ed.)

TABLE 6. — *Automobile Insurance Premiums Written and Losses Paid 1960-64, 1965-69*

[Dollar amounts in billions]

Auto bodily injury

	Premiums	Losses	Losses to premiums (percent)
1960-64	$16.4	$ 8.5	51.9
1965-69	25.0	12.9	52.7
Combined 1960-69	41.4	21.5	51.8

Auto property damage

	Premiums	Losses	Losses to premiums (percent)
1960-64	$ 6.6	$ 3.8	56.9
1965-69	10.5	6.4	61.2
Combined 1960-69	17.1	10.2	59.5

Auto physical damage

	Premiums	Losses	Losses to premiums (percent)
1960-64	$11.7	$ 6.4	54.5
1965-69	18.8	10.9	57.8
Combined 1960-69	30.5	17.3	56.6

Source: U.S. Senate Antitrust and Monopoly Subcommittee: derived from "The Spectator" (Chilton & Co., Philadelphia).

For Change

The costs of administering the present system are too high. In the aggregate, the total burden is more than twice the net benefits delivered. At the other end of the scale is Social Security (OASDI), where the operating expense ratio appears to be about 3 percent of the benefits delivered. (See Keeton & O'Con-

Against Change

nell, No. 256. Also see Robert J. Myers & Francisco Bays, "Old Age, Survivors and Disability Expenses," *Social Security Bulletin*, vol. 29, no. 7, July, 1966).

* * *

The fault insurance system is inherently expensive to operate. There is a striking contrast between the administrative cost of 3 cents in Social Security, 7 cents for Blue Cross, 17 cents for health and accident plans, and 58 cents of the premium dollar for automobile insurance, leaving only 42 cents to pay victims' costs. (Included in the 58 cents is 40 cents for insurance company expenses, including claim adjusting costs, and 18 cents for attorneys' fees and court costs.) (See U.S. Senate Antitrust and Monopoly Subcommittee chart, Bibliography entry No. 449).

* * *

Automobile liability insurance today is so inefficiently administered that the public pays $2.20 in premiums for every $1 provided in net benefits to injured persons. (See Keeton & O'Connell, No. 253).

* * *

A no-fault plan will speed up claim payments, because all claims will be two party (between insured and his insurer), eliminating the time-consuming third-party claims. Payments will be made as losses occur.

* * *

Critics of the "no-fault" concept complain of the complexity of such no-fault plans as the Keeton & O'Connell proposal. Rather than criticizing specific aspects of that proposal, which were incorporated largely to placate critics of radical reform, a change to a purely no-fault system, utilizing medical payments coverage, would be less expensive and would be simpler to administer than the Keeton and O'Connell Plan. (See Keeton & O'Connell, No. 256).

* * *

Rates are rising everywhere, and in some states they are skyrocketing. In 11 years, average rates for a minimum level of automobile liability insurance covering bodily injuries rose by 112 percent in Michigan, 95 percent in South Carolina, 83 percent in Virginia, 77 percent in Arkansas, 56 percent in North Carolina, and 54 percent in Massachusetts and Mississippi, to give a few examples. (See Keeton & O'Connell, No. 253).

* * *

ELIMINATING ATTORNEYS AND COURTS

For Change

"Motor vehicle accident litigation in the court system was estimated to occupy 17 percent of the system's available resources." (See Bibliography entry No. 118).

* * *

Total paid losses of all auto liability insurers on all liability claims were about $7 billion in 1968, the year in which the Department of Transportation places attorneys' fees at about

Against Change

Critics contend that juries are too costly. They claim that the longer trial time involved in jury cases increases the expense for litigants and the public. Facts do not support this charge. For example, for a year ending May 31, 1967, jury expense amounted to only 13 percent of the total cost of the New York State judicial system. (See DRI, No. 108).

* * *

$1 billion. Thus, eliminating attorneys from the reparations system could result in a price cut for the public of about 14 percent. (See Bibliography entry No. 125).

* * *

The total cost of attorney participation in the tort reparations system was put at over $1 billion in 1968. (See Bibliography entry No. 119).

* * *

In the 220,000 lawsuits arising from 1968 auto accidents, the victims collected a total net after legal fees and other expenses of $700 million while lawyers collected $600 million plus expenses.

* * *

New York Times (July 18, 1971) describes one Boston attorney who grossed $250,000 in automobile tort work in 1970, but anticipates a gross of less than $20,000 in 1971 under the Massachusetts no-fault system.

* * *

Lack of a solution to the present crisis will necessarily result in disrespect for law, lawyers, and insurance companies. (See Keeton & O'Connell, No. 253). The system now pays more for the overhead of insurance companies, lawyers, and courts than for the compensation of victims, and inequitably distributing the compensation it does pay. In sum, it provides too little, too late, and does it unfairly, wastefully and corruptly. All traffic claims today are dominated by attitudes of dis-

No-fault plans do not usually provide for arbitration; disputes would have to be taken to court. You would have to hire a lawyer to sue your insurer. (See Kemper, No. 265).

* * *

Since no-fault plans typically provide for retention of the tort liability concept over the no-fault floor of benefits, a no-fault plan would actually increase litigation and attorneys' fees, because many more people would file suits for damages in excess of the amounts provided under the plan. (*i.e.*, everyone would claim damages in excess of the specified amount for pain and suffering, and it would not be proper to exclude recovery in cases of severe injuries where there was extensive pain and suffering).

* * *

cord, distrust and even outright hostility accompanying any negligence lawsuit. (See Keeton and O'Connell, No. 256).

* * *

The average claim takes sixteen months to settle. Under a no-fault plan, claims would be paid quickly and the nation's badly over-crowded court dockets would get relief.

* * *

The contingent fee charged by attorneys results in inordinate and excessive legal fees and robs the claimants of substantial amounts—it is an anachronistic system of payment, particularly used in automobile accident cases. It is also instrumental in swelling the volume of automobile accident litigation in this nation.

* * *

Most costs of litigation and attorneys' fees are unnecessary and could be eliminated under a no-fault plan.

Wasteful bickering over fault—with all the cost of investigators, lawyers and the courts—would be eliminated in the great majority of cases. (See Keeton & O'Connel, No. 253).

* * *

A study of traffic injuries in Michigan found that 68 percent of those who recovered from the other party incurred "collection expenses" ranging up to 60 percent of their settlement, with a mean of 32 percent in all cases in which expenses were incurred. (See Keeton & O'Connell, No. 256).

There has been no public complaint against the contingent fee. Claimants—when given a choice between paying hourly rates usually charged or taking the contingent fee—have selected the contingent fee. (See Bibliography entry No. 89).

* * *

Says Whitney North Seymour, an eminent Wall Street lawyer and former president of the American Bar Association, "I'm very disturbed about the negligence situation. But, whenever I bring it up, they tell me about the lawyers all over the country who would be forced out of the profession." (See O'Connell, No. 377). An example of opposition of the legal profession was afforded in 1967 when the Keeton & O'Connell Plan unexpectedly was passed by the lower house of the Massachusetts legislature. A strong lobby of attorneys, spear-headed by the American Trial Lawyers Association, helped to kill it in the state Senate. (See *Time*, No. 57).

COMPENSATION ADEQUACY

For Change

In 1967 the half million cases of seriously injured or killed victims incurred economic losses of $5.1 billion. But the fault auto liability insurance system paid them only $813 million—with an additional $248 million coming from coverage such as medical payments and collision. For each $5 lost, auto insurance—of any kind—paid back only $1. (See Bibliography entry No. 362).

* * *

Against Change

Accident victims are not left standing so naked as one might be led to believe. They have recourse to one or more of the following sources of compensation:

Medicaid, available to all whose medical expenses make them medically indigent;

Medicare, for the elderly;

Automobile medical payments coverage, for car-owning families and guests;

Employer-provided medical and hospital plans;

Government medical benefits to servicemen and government employees;

Workmens' compensation coverage;

Wage continuation and unemployment compensation programs;
Blue Cross and Blue Shield;
Individual accident and health insurance.
(See Bibliography entry No. 280).

* * *

Many automobile victims don't collect for pain and suffering under the present system. Judgment-proof uninsured drivers have left many victims with uncompensated pain and suffering claims. In addition, a Department of Transportation study has indicated that serious losses are under-compensated—claimants with $25,000 or more in losses get back only 30 percent of their losses under the tort liability system.

* * *

The present tort liability system is not compensating individuals with permanent disability. A Department of Transportation study showed that claimants with a permanent total disability had an average total economic loss of $78,000. Yet, they received an average insurance payment of $12,556—only 16 percent of their loss.

* * *

Of those seriously injured in auto accidents (or survivors of those killed), only 45 percent receive benefits from the present liability system. One out of ten receives nothing from any form of reparation.

* * *

The tort liability system leaves about 50 percent of all victims and perhaps more than 50 percent

The fact that one-in-four auto accident victims collects nothing from auto liability insurance "is hardly surprising, since about 25 percent of auto accidents are single-vehicle crashes." (Paul S. Wise, A.M.I.A.) This is no indictment of the tort liability system. It was never intended to compensate the careless, drunken, or suicidal driver.

* * *

of the aggregate victim loss without recovery. (See Bibliography entry No. 125).

* * *

The fault insurance system hinders rehabilitation. It pays proportionately least to the seriously injured. Many techniques of rehabilitation have to be started promptly. They cost money. The fault insurance system pays slowly. (See Bibliography entry No. 351). The system is unreliable and unpredictable as to whether and, if so, how much it will pay. Moreover, it makes its payments all at once in a lump sum.

The present system prescribes lump sum payments not only for those damages that have already accrued but also for all the damages that will ever occur in the future, under an estimate at the time of the award that is *final*. Ordinarily the amount cannot be re-determined even if it is found to be woefully inadequate or grossly excessive. (See Keeton & O'Connel, No. 256).

* * *

System of payment in one lump sum under the present system is bad. Several studies have shown that most automobile accident victims are unaccustomed to the management of relatively

Rehabilitation can be accomplished promptly and adequately under the tort liability system. A number of insurance companies are utilizing the techniques of advance payments, whereby claimants are given quick payments of medical bills, property damage costs, and lost income. There is no longer a wait for court decisions in cases where the companies believe they will eventually be making payment.

Under advance payments, payments are made as costs accrue, and rehabilitation is strongly encouraged as a means to cut down the ultimate expenses sustained by an injured victim.

* * *

large sums of money and will allow their awards to be dissipated.
(See Keeton & O'Connell, No. 256).

* * *

The tort liability system for
handling automobile accident
cases promotes "crude 'kangaroo'
adjustments" in which the "amount
of damages depends on who secured
the best or the most witnesses, who
has the best lawyer, the personal
prejudices of the jurors, and the
so-called 'breaks' of the trial."
(Former New York State Supreme
Court Justice Samuel H. Hofstadter.)

* * *

The tort liability system provides tremendous inequity in recovery, reflecting the lack of soph-
istication of lower income and lower educated people. In serious injury cases families with incomes
under $5000—which account for
almost one-third of the families
in this country—recovered only
38 percent of their economic
losses. However, families with incomes over $10,000 recovered 61
percent. Those with no schooling
recovered 16 percent of losses.
But, those with college training
recovered 64 percent. Yet the low
income families are likely to be
paying the highest premiums for
this lack of protection. (See
Bibliography entry No. 125).

* * *

According to Martin Mayer,
The Lawyers (Harper & Row,
1967), "the realities of the legal
consequences of accidents are an
unconscionable mess." He cites a
Pennsylvania study showing that

in 1959, 46.8% of traffic victims involved in serious accidents received nothing; among those seriously injured, with out-of-pocket loss greater than $3000, approximately 66% received nothing or less than half their loss, all this calculated *before* the subtraction of lawyers' fees!

* * *

A recent Michigan study showed that in the late 1950's, 63% of all traffic victims got nothing from automobile liability insurance, with 45% of even the seriously injured getting nothing. Those with smaller claims are often paid off relatively generously and quickly as "nuisance claims." (See O'Connell, No. 377).

* * *

Reform will eliminate inequity, inadequate payments or non-payment. The severely injured seldom recover more than a fraction of their losses. A substantial number (25%) go uncompensated, even for their out-of-pocket losses. Under a no-fault plan, all but a very small percentage of injury claims in automobile accidents would be paid. Reform will eliminate the gross injustice and inequity in payments. Under the present system, persons suffering minor injuries are commonly overpaid, receiving compensation many times greater than their losses. (See Keeton & O'Connell, No. 253).

* * *

Those slightly hurt are often promptly and overly paid, while those with serious injuries are

Those hardship cases so movingly described by proponents of no-fault to induce resentment against the present system can be countered by equally moving recitals of hardship cases produced by a no-fault plan. Is it equitable to pay benefits to the drunken driver, the convicted felon fleeing from his crime, the drag racer and the multiple accident repeater, and deny full recovery to innocent victims such as housewives and children whose economic loss will be limited mainly or entirely to medical bills, and who in many cases will recover nothing for pain and suffering?

* * *

paid, if at all, a fraction of their damages and only after long delay. Most victims come from lower income groups and are wage earners for families. The plight of the more seriously injured victim is so desperate, with continuing fixed costs in the form of food, rent, *etc.*, plus mounting medical expenses, that he is in no position to bargain; the insurance company's position conversely grows stronger with delay. On the other hand, the nuisance value of claims and the desire of insurance companies to maintain good public relations means prompt and generous payment for the trivially injured. (See Keeton & O'Connell, No. 256).

* * *

The fault system results in wildly erratic settlements. Insurers are notorious for over-paying small "nuisance" claims because it would cost more to fight them than to settle. At the same time, the seriously injured victim with high economic losses is often unable to wait for his case to come to trial and is forced to settle for whatever the company offers. If he does gamble on going to court, he may lose the case because of a capricious jury and get nothing. (See *Time*, No. 57).

* * *

Guest statutes prohibiting recovery by passengers unless the driver was grossly negligent often have the effect of leaving uncompensated victims. (See Marryott, No. 295).

Injured guests receive compensation under the tort liability system through automobile medical payments coverage. That coverage can be increased to any desirable amount without tampering with the liability system, and it will continue to pay, regardless of fault, as it now does under the present system.

* * *

Often the amount of recovery for wrongful death is so limited by statute as to leave survivors inadequately provided for. (See Marryott, No. 295).

* * *

State statutes stipulating wrongful death recovery limits can be repealed. Their existence is not an indictment of the tort liability system.

* * *

The measurement of damages in personal injury cases today is often wildly intuitive. The reimbursement plan under a "no-fault" system would eliminate this problem.

* * *

A strict reimbursement plan rules out recoveries for pain and suffering and would create worse problems than it solved.

* * *

While any dollar limit set under any no-fault plan, either in existence or under consideration, may be considered arbitrary, they are based on intelligent estimates by people who have examined insurance claims records as to what cut-off point would alleviate the existing insurance problems. By preserving the tort liability system over and above the basic limits of coverage, moreover, it is possible for the damages in excess of the basic limits on those minimal number of cases which would exceed basic limits to be recovered.

* * *

Dollar limits established in no-fault proposals are entirely arbitrary. Why apply the no-fault concept to one dollar amount but eliminate recovery for damages in excess of that amount?

* * *

COVERAGE AVAILABILITY AND COST ALLOCATION

For Change

Implementation of a "no-fault" system would reduce insurance costs motorists must pay. For ex-

Against Change

The chief actuary of the Massachusetts Department of Banking and Insurance, M.G. McDonald,

ample, it is estimated that automobile insurance costs paid by New York motorists would be reduced 15 percent to 25 percent, which amounts to $87.8 million annually at the insurance levels of 1964 (conclusion reached in a study conducted by an independent professional actuary, Frank Harwayne, a consulting actuary, a director of the American Academy of Actuaries, a Fellow of the Casualty Actuarial Society, and chief casualty actuary of the New York Department of Insurance.) Under another estimate, based on somewhat different assumptions, the savings would be as much as 25 percent. (See Keeton, No. 251).

* * *

In the Canadian province of Saskatchewan, where a "no-fault" automobile compensation plan has been in effect since 1946, automobile insurance costs two-thirds as much as comparable coverage in adjoining North Dakota. (*Time*, No. 57).

* * *

In the first quarter of operation of the Massachusetts Plan, there was a 36 percent reduction in the average claim paid. In addition, the state experienced a 60 percent drop in total claims.

* * *

estimated in September of 1967 that if a "no-fault" plan, such as the Keeton & O'Connell proposal, were introduced in Massachusetts, the cost of coverage required by statute for private passenger car owners would increase from 19 percent to 35 percent. Other actuarial studies have predicted a wide variety of results, nationally and in individual states. No estimate thus far presented is sufficiently reliable to form an adequate basis for decision. (See Kemper, No. 265).

* * *

Richard J. Wolfrum, F.C.A.S., Actuary, Liberty Mutual Insurance Company, states that proper data to evaluate a general compensation system for automobile injuries is not available today. In particular, there is a need for the insurance industry to put together official automobile bodily injury tables which will show:

1. The economic status of people injured.

2. Injuries by type of injury.

3. Disability periods for people injured.

4. The medical and hospital costs of injuries.

5. Dependency status of survivors for death causes.

Also he points to the need for: (1) distribution of overall costs among various classes of people

In 17 months of operation under the Puerto Rico Plan, 90 percent of every premium dollar was returned in benefits, and, because of reduced accident and death rates, plus operating economies, sharply increased benefits are proposed without increasing premiums

* * *

Under a no-fault plan, the rating system would make more sense. Under a related-insurer arrangement, an insurer can base rates it charges a policyholder on *both* elements of the risk of loss—how often claims will be presented (accident and claim frequency) and how much will be paid (average claim cost). At present insurers set rates while looking at only half the picture as it applies to

injured or among various segments of the public; (2) information on just how many claimants are not now compensated; (3) the amount of coverage under "collateral benefits" that have been purchased privately by the public or are available to them through group or other employer financed systems; and (4) what proportion of settlements which are paid today to the claimant does not reach his pocket. (See Bibliography entry No. 60).

* * *

Estimates of savings are often based on the cost of a bare bones protection package and do not include the cost of optional coverages which would be needed to supplement inadequacies. (See Bibliography entry No. 102). For example, savings are gained through elimination of recoveries for pain and suffering, abolition of the collateral source rule and a series of exclusions and deductibles. Some plans would reduce costs, but only through reduction of coverage and benefits. (See Bibliography entry No. 106).

* * *

Elimination of the tort liability system will provide benefits for high-risk drivers (those most likely to be responsible for automobile accidents and thus ineligible for benefits). Under a no-fault system, a limit will be imposed on recovery. Consequently, safe drivers will make a considerable sacrifice in average recovery in exchange for a modest dollar savings in price, whereas

their insureds—how often claims will be made against them (claim frequency).

The present system of negligence liability insurance and rating takes account of the first of these ways that a given motorist contributes to the overall risk but disregards the second. This follows naturally from an unrelated-insurer arrangement, because the second type of risk contribution has its impact on the other party's insurer. Under this arrangement, there is no way for an insurer to know whom its insured will injure. Because, then, the risk falls at random, it is simply ignored as a factor in rating.

A "no-fault" plan with a related-insurer relationship would immediately take care of some of our current assigned (or high) risk problems. (See Keeton & O'Connell, No. 254).

* * *

Under a first-party system, losses could be predicted with a greater degree of accuracy, since there would be fewer open-end cases such as experienced in liability claims. This would make it possible to develop more adequate rates based on moderate but realistic profit margins. (Frederick D. Watkins, President of Aetna Insurance Company, See Bibliography entry No. 358).

* * *

Some no-fault plans eliminate benefits for drunken driving, intentional infliction of injury, and injuries sustained while in the

the unsafe drivers will greatly increase their recovery expectations and also gain a considerable dollar savings in price. (See Brainard, No. 51).

* * *

For example, if the New York Stewart Plan were instituted, the high-risk drivers would be subsidized by careful motorists in an amount averaging $83.62 per vehicle. (See Bibliog. entry No. 342).

* * *

Drivers should remain financially responsible for the damage they cause because it helps to allocate the cost burden more fairly. Under such a system the auto insurance rates are based on the damage a motorist is likely to inflict on other people. Under most no-fault systems, auto insurance rates would be based largely on the amount of damage the motorist and his family would be likely to suffer in a crash, regardless of who caused it.

* * *

Persons with a bad back or other pre-existing conditions might well pay higher rates because they would be more prone to costly disability in case of a crash. (See Bibliography entry No. 64).

* * *

No-fault plans pay exactly the same benefits to every driver and passenger, right or wrong, and in some cases, drunk or sober, law-abiding or law-defying.

* * *

Some no-fault proposals make no provision to penalize negligent commission of a felony. Besides, it is the purpose of the no-fault insurance to compensate the injured, not to police the nation's highways, a function which should be undertaken by more vigorous legislation and enforcement of driving standards.

For example, the Hart bill provides that no payment shall be made to "the operator or user of a motor vehicle while committing a felony, or operating or using with the specific intent of causing injury or damage, or operating or using a motor vehicle as a converter without a good faith belief that he is legally entitled to operate or use such vehicle." (See Bibliography entry No. 449).

* * *

No-fault plans typically exclude coverage for persons under the influence of alcohol or intoxicants, or those whose injuries are self-inflicted, and drivers involved in illegal activities. In addition, most proposals retain the tort liability system to enable injured victims of the excluded class of motorists so that tort liability claims can be brought against culpable motor vehicle drivers.

* * *

Drivers with large families will not necessarily be penalized under the rating system of a "no-fault" plan. They could well receive low rates because they drive more cautiously with children in the car, or tend to remain at home more and use their vehicles less than the young, single driver. And the large

persons who cause accidents. The reckless or drunken driver would be treated as your equal in determining recovery for damages. Drunken drivers could collect more benefits than their innocent victims. (See No. 265).

* * *

The no-fault approach would benefit the driver under the influence of narcotics or intoxicating liquor, and those who intentionally injure themselves or are driving while in the commission of a felony or attempting to avoid arrest by a law enforcement officer.

* * *

The rating system under the present tort liability system is much more equitable. Liability premium rates are geared to a driver's accident potential. Young, single men, for instance, pay relatively high rates because they are involved in proportionately more accidents. In a "no-fault" system, family will get more protection for its money, because every member will always have coverage.

* * *

the burden of higher rates would be shifted to drivers with large families because their claims are likely to be larger than those of other drivers.

* * *

The no-fault system, rather than eliminating inequity, would produce widespread inequity. "It would compel the careful motorist to totally insure himself against all injuries and property losses inflicted by the careless, and to bear all the costs and hazards involved." This would create an "unjust and inequitable scheme of compensation to pay the guilty instead of the innocent. It would create an unfair and discriminatory rating system and a broad climate for careless driving. (See Bibliography entry No. 437).

* * *

The crucial question concerns the rationale for taking from some accident victims and giving to others. The rationale seems to be equality or the more even distribution of compensation. However, are equality and equity synonymous? (See Hold, No. 196).

* * *

Inequities are apparent in a no-fault plan. Under the present system, persons with the best driving records causing the fewest accidents are good risks and pay lower premiums. Under a no-fault plan, the process would be turned around. The best risks under the plan would be those persons to whom an insurer could expect to pay the smallest amount of damages in case of an accident. For example, a student with a sports car would be a good risk. A family man with a sedan or station wagon would be a poorer risk since he may have a number of persons in his auto at the time of the accident, and would have lost wages, medical expenses, *etc.*, as claims. (See Kemper, No. 265).

* * *

The tort liability system provides for cost allocation based on accident involvement instead of benefits collected. The no-fault system would penalize the family man with many children, while the long-haul truck man will pay less. (Rudolph Landolt, Kemper Group, See Slattery, No. 549).

* * *

Under a "no-fault" plan, a large portion of the insurance cost is shifted from those people most likely to collect the most money as a result of accidents. There will be a major redistribution of premium, with some socially dubious results.

* * *

Rating will create a nightmare for actuaries. The plan will require such a tremendous range in rates as to be incomprehensible to the public; that the total number of "undesirable" risks going into assigned risk plans will probably be increased; and that the reliance on honest disclosure of collateral source benefits will be so great as to introduce a permanent element of inequity into any rating system devised. (See Kemper, No. 265).

* * *

Unless collateral source benefits are eliminated, credit would have to be given to those persons having personal accident and health coverages. Such a system of debits and credits would entail a rather complex system of rating which would require constant investigation of whether insureds still owned the various health and accident contracts that they were given credit for at the time they were rated for no-fault coverage. (See Hold, No. 196).

* * *

Shall the premium be based on the number of persons in the household? As a member of a car pool, should a stiff extra premium be paid? Is a school bus operator responsible for any injury to the children, regardless of circumstances? (See Jeffrey, No. 230).

* * *

Commercial trucking companies, operating fleets of trucks over long distances, with heavy use of roadways, will pay lower rates than now because their injured employees would receive the collateral benefit of workmen's compensation. (See DRI, No. 106).

* * *

The proposal would make it more difficult, if not impossible, for insurers to devise a merit rating plan, which produces lower rates for fault-free drivers and higher rates for accident-prone. (See Bibliography entry No. 1).

* * *

Victims in single-car accidents admittedly would receive

Under the present tort liability system, those people injured in

benefits under the no-fault system. However, savings would be realized in reduction of loss adjustment expenses, attorneys' fees, and court costs which should offset any trend toward increased rates resulting from this increase in benefits.

* * *

Allowances can be made for the rating of commercial vehicles. For example, under the Hart bill, "The Secretary of Transportation shall classify all motor vehicles larger than ordinary passenger automobiles into reasonable categories, and shall assign to each category a percentage of responsibility for net economic loss sustained by occupants of other vehicles; such classification and percentages of responsibility shall be based upon the increased severity of injury caused by large vehicles in comparison to ordinary automobiles." (See Bibliography entry No. 449).

* * *

Pennsylvania's insurance commissioner, Herbert S. Denenberg, advocates absolute liability for third-party damages on the part of commercial vehicles: "There is something to be said for making fleet owners absolutely liable under no-fault. There are, in fact, some very compelling arguments to do this." In his opinion fleet single-car accidents are excluded from liability recoveries. If these persons are compensated, the cost of insurance will increase measurably. Paul S. Wise, President of the American Mutual Insurance Alliance, states that roughly 25 percent of automobile accidents are single-vehicle crashes. How can you cover these people without unduly increasing the cost of automobile insurance under a no-fault system?

* * *

The rating problem involved in assigning an equitable rate to passenger vehicles or to commercial vehicles presents an insoluble problem.

* * *

The subject of rating equity in the case of commercial vehicles provides inherent problems of inequity. In the Massachusetts program they are treated just as private passenger vehicles. However, the New York insurance proposal specifies that commercial vehicles would be exempt from no-fault and held absolutely liable for third-party damages. The New Jersey Commissioner of Insurance, Robert L. Clifford, states that absolute liability for commercial vehicles "makes no sense." He refutes the argument that fleet insureds are better able to pass on costs of insurance to consumers. "You know who pays in the long run." (See Bibliography entry No. 397).

* * *

owners are better able to control
the use and abuse of their vehicles. (See Bibliog. entry No. 397).
* * *

Property damage claims are
easily controllable from the standpoint of dollar amount determination. First-party physical damage coverage can be provided by
an insured's own insurance company with full coverage payable
regardless of who was at fault.
The no-fault concept can work as
equitably on property damage
claims as on bodily injury claims.
* * *

An estimated 8 percent to 10
percent of all drivers fit into the
"hard-to-place" insurance market.
Many drivers, especially the elderly, the young and the resident of
city centers, have trouble even
getting insurance coverage even
though they have good driving
records. (See Montgomery, No.
524).
* * *

Under the present system, insurance companies are locked in
ruinous competition to insure preferred risk drivers—people between
30 and 50 who don't drive their
cars around much and haven't had
any accidents. At best, the preferred risk group may include 30
percent of the 100 million drivers
in the country. Those not included in the prime risk category are
paying more for insurance, and in
some cases find it hard to get policies from reputable companies.
(See Ridgeway, No. 405).
* * *

No-fault plans do not pay the
innocent automobile accident victim for the damage to his own automobile caused by the negligence
of the other driver. Why eliminate
property damage claims?
* * *

Those to whom insurance is unavailable through usual channels are open to being preyed upon by shaky, sometimes shady, "high-risk" companies, an inordinate number of which have gone into insolvency amidst scandal, leaving their insureds and many traffic victims high and dry. (See Keeton & O'Connell, No. 254).

* * *

An investigation of high-risk insurance in 1965 by the Anti-Trust and Monopoly Subcommittee of the Senate Judiciary Committee disclosed that in the preceding five years, sixty-five companies had become insolvent, leaving 300,000 people with $100 million in unpaid claims. And the committee reported in January, 1967, that eight more "high-risk" companies had failed, bringing the total to seventy-three in six years. (113 Cong. Rec. S 978, daily ed. Jan. 26, 1967). This prompted the introduction of legislation to establish a Federal Motor Vehicle Insurance Guarantee Corporation, a bill introduced by former Senator Dodd.

* * *

CHAPTER XIII

OTHER AREAS OF CONTENTION

There are many issues in question in the "no-fault" controversy, besides the points of contention explored in the preceding two chapters. Additional issues are explored in this chapter.

PROBLEMS FOR LEGISLATORS

The legal mechanics of administering a "no-fault" program, the question of public acceptance of such a revolutionary change, and the effect that removal of driver responsibility would have on the "deterrent" character of the tort liability system, all pose weighty problems for the legislators considering the adoption of "no-fault" laws.

The Legal Question

Equally of concern are problems regarding the legality of "no-fault" legislation. Can "no-fault" legislation be passed to abrogate common law rights? Does such legislation contravene basic Constitutional guarantees?

The experience of the Massachusetts Plan, at least in that state, would suggest that the legal obstacles to implementation of "no-fault" legislation are more imagined than real. The Massachusetts Supreme Court on June 29, 1971, approved the "no-fault" plan in that state.

The ultimate legal test of such plans, however, will inevitably rest with the United States Supreme Court as the nation proceeds with this imaginative social experimentation in automobile accident reparations systems.

Public Opinion

A particularly thorny problem confronts the state and federal law-makers. Does the public *really* want a "no-fault" system? Even more germane, does the public know what a "no-fault" system is, and is the public willing to give up the conventional remedies of the tort liability system?

Opinion polls are cited pro and con on the issue of "no-fault," each sponsor of respective polls claiming legitimacy for its poll while stridently denouncing opposing findings of other polls. The evidence is unclear on whose poll is best.

What *is* clear, however, is that the present controversy would not have erupted into national prominence if the present system were operating in a commendable manner. Something *is* wrong, and the public believes that something *is* wrong.

Arguments for and against Change

Articulate spokesmen for and against change to the "no-fault" concept have addressed themselves to many of the implications inherent in a change. Some of the facets have been discussed in previous chapters; some have been alluded to in the introduction to this chapter. Some of the more common issues not already explored are presented in the following pages.

LEGAL-CONSTITUTIONAL QUESTIONS

For Change	*Against Change*
The Massachusetts Supreme Court on June 29, 1971, ruled as constitutional the automobile "no-fault" plan in effect in that state. * * *	*Constitutionality*—It is unconstitutional in all of the states whose constitutions prohibit any limitation of the amount recoverable for injury. It is probably unconstitutional in states like Illinois and Massachusetts whose constitutions guarantee a remedy certain for injuries or wrongs without an obligation to purchase it. The plan will be struck down as a violation of the due process and equal protection clauses of the federal and state constitutions. (See Kemper, No. 265). * * *
There will be no interstate complications under a federal "no-fault" system, nor will there be a problem under state-administered plans if they voluntarily agree to uniform legislation. Likewise, there will be no discrepan-	*Interstate Complications*—Conflict of law situations together with possible variations of interstate accident situations will produce hundreds of thousands of interstate complications. For example, if the other driver came

cies under state plans if they are required to follow federal standards.

* * *

Alleged Constitutional disabilities, particularly on the federal level, are more imagined than real. The commerce clause is a most obvious possible source of Constitutional power for legislation by Congress to deal with the problem of assuring adequate compensation for persons injured in automobile accidents. The commerce power is naturally suggested by the monumental economic dimensions of business activities centering around motor vehicle transportation in the United States, including not only the automobile manufacturing industry but also the vast array of supporting industrial and commercial operations.

Constitutional questions might arise in funding the federal automobile accident loss compensa-

from a state which did not have the plan and was injured in your state which did, he would be paid in the same manner as you, but from a fund created from a portion of the insurance premiums you pay. Further, if you injure a motorist from a state not having the plan while he is in your state, your policy would not pay him. If that injured person sued you in his own state, obtaining judgment, your policy would not protect you. If you caused an accident in a state not having a plan, any person you injured could sue you for damages. You would have to purchase liability insurance. (See DRI, No. 109).

* * *

The Seventh Amendment is a serious obstacle to federal legislation dispensing with jury trials for determining eligibility for compensation.

There is considerable question whether reforms to replace the system of administering compensation for automobile accident victims is really so very essential for the continued prosperity of the national economy as to come under the commerce clause and justify federal action. (See Bibliography entry No. 122).

* * *

tion program. A program of benefits for automobile accident victims, however, could logically be
incorporated into the Social Security system, just as disability
and medical benefits have been
added to the old age and survivors insurance. There doubtless is
an infinite variety of ways in
which a social evil in the United
States could be found to affect
the general welfare so as to justify expenditures by Congress.
(Admittedly, the economic aspects of the consequences of
shortcomings in the tort liability
method of compensating for
losses is something which would
require further documentation).

As for abrogation of common
law rights based on fault, if federal expenditures for such compensation were deemed to be for
the general welfare, then such incidental "regulation" to abrogate
the traditional remedy would surely be legitimate under the "neces-
sary-and-proper clause."

Another remedial approach to
implementing a "no-fault" system would be by restricting the
license privilege, requiring waiver
of common law rights and remedies in acceptance of the terms of
a compensation system as a condition for access to the use of
federal highways.

In addition, arguments that a
radical reform would result in denial of equal protection are without merit. Indeed, the present
tort liability system arguably results in a greater denial of equal

protection, by overcompensating small claimants and undercompensating large claimants, than would the proposals for reform. One of the purposes of such proposals is precisely to achieve greater proximity to equality of treatment among all victims of automobile accidents. (See Bibliography entry No. 122.)

* * *

Chief Justice of the United States, Warren Burger, has stated, "If our society comes to the conclusion, as it watches our system of justice work, that we have built up a process that is inadequate or archaic, too cumbersome or complex, or if society feels that we have extended certain of our basic principles too far, there is a remedy. The people have the right and the ultimate power to change a system. Neither the laws nor the Constitution are too sacred to change, and the decisions of judges are not holy writ. The Constitution and the law are tools to serve us, not masters to enslave us. We should not hesitate to make basic changes or discard mechanisms which do not work to the benefit of society." ("The Views of the Chief Justice," *Life*, August 7, 1970).

* * *

If a proposal is sound and in the public interest, Constitutional obstacles will be overcome as they were for similar reasons when workmen's compensation laws were enacted.

* * *

Most lawyers and legal scholars believe that in today's Constitutional climate the courts would be loath to strike down legislative enactments providing a comprehensive no-fault automobile accident reparations system.

* * *

PUBLIC OPINION – GENERAL

For Change

Americans over the age of 18 would prefer a no-fault automobile insurance system over the present system of tort liability by a ratio of 2½ to 1. In addittion, by a ratio of 3½ to 1 they would be willing to give up their right to sue for pain and suffering in return for prompter payment of all financial losses, immunity against lawsuits and lower automobile insurance premiums. (According to a country-wide survey conducted by OCR Caravan Surveys of Princeton, New Jersey, a subsidiary of the Opinion Research Corporation. See Bibliography entry No. 23).

* * *

Other public opinion surveys have found the public favoring non-fault over fault insurance for automobile accidents. The *Minneapolis Tribune* found 67 percent of those expressing an opinion favoring non-fault insurance; University of Illinois found 71 percent of those expressing an opinion favoring non-fault insurance; National Educational Television

Against Change

In a national consumer attitude survey conducted by Market Facts, Inc., of Chicago in some 3000 interviews conducted between March 14 and April 13, 1970 (survey sponsored by four large automobile insurers in consultation with the National Association of Independent Insurers and the American Mutual Insurance Alliance), the following findings appeared:

1. When a description of no-fault insurance was read to car owners interviewed, the majority disapproved, expressing the opinion that a driver at fault in an accident should pay for damages.

2. Six out of ten were opposed to a no-fault plan which would eliminate pain and suffering payments.

3. Over 70 percent of those who had personal experience in filing automobile insurance claims were opposed to no-fault.

4. The majority were opposed to having automobile insurance as excess coverage over other collateral benefits. (Sponsors of the Market Facts survey were Allstate,

found 70 percent of those expressing an opinion favoring non-fault insurance. (See O'Connell and Wilson, No. 380).

* * *

A public opinion poll conducted by the State Farm Mutual Automobile Insurance Company, which showed dissimilar results of public opinion, "grossly biases the results regarding the public's view of the fault criterion." (See O'Connell and Wilson, No. 380).

* * *

Kemper Group, Liberty Mutual, and State Farm Mutual Insurance). (See Bibliography entries Nos. 406 and 273).

* * *

A public opinion poll conducted by the State Farm Mutual Automobile Insurance Company of 3,090,315 State Farm policy-holders indicated that 94 percent of that number favored the tort liability system in the handling of automobile accidents. (O'Connell and Wilson, No. 380).

* * *

Public opinion polls which purport to show that the public wants this or that system are misleading; systems are too complex for the public to know what is best. (See Maisonpierre, No. 291).

* * *

A public opinion poll conducted by the Institute of Public Opinion (George Gallup) on April 3 and 4, 1971, of 1,519 adults in more than 300 scientifically selected localities across the nation, indicated that 42 percent of all those interviewed say they have heard or read about the no-fault plan dealing with auto insurance. Only about half this number, however, can give a correct description of its main features and have reached an opinion. Among this relatively small group (about one-fifth of the total adult population), opinion is four-to-one on the favorable side. When asked, "Do you approve or disapprove of the no-fault plan?" the following results were obtained, based on the total sample:

	Percent
Approve	15
Disapprove	4
Uninformed or Undecided	81

(See Gallup, Nos. 168 and 169).

* * *

A survey conducted by the University of Michigan for the Department of Transportation indicated a shift in public attitudes toward no-fault. "After various features of auto insurance were discussed" with them, "more people expressed themselves in favor of a no-fault system of insurance than in favor of the prevailing fault system." (See Bibliography entry No. 136).

* * *

There is widespread acceptance of the "no-fault" concept developing within the insurance industry itself. Individual insurance companies—such as the Insurance Company of North America and the Glens Falls Group—have come out openly with newspaper and magazine advertisements in favor of "no-fault." (See INA advertisement, *U.S. News and World Report*, Oct. 23, 1967, p. 93).

* * *

The support that some segments of the insurance industry are giving to no-fault, notably the American Insurance Association, is prompted by devious motives. "The declining position of the AIA executive committee companies in the automobile insurance market" and the fact that the AIA writes so much group insurance business, and no-fault lends itself to the group approach, suggests the self-interest of these companies. (James M. Kemper, Jr., President of the Kemper Companies, See Bibliography entry No. 18).

* * *

The trend toward Mass-merchandising of automobile insurance and group programs is already well on its way, and a number of studies, including the Stanford Report, foresee the move toward bigness in insurers and pro-

More than 800 companies compete actively for an estimated 92 percent of the total market. If the plan is widely enacted, none but the giants will be able to afford the rating uncertainties, administrative costs and retraining of per-

ducing units, irrespective of the adoption of "no-fault" automobile insurance plans.

* * *

sonnel necessary to make the plan an operative reality. Huge blocks of automobile insurance will move out of the hands of the smaller companies and their agents into mass merchandising and group programs, destroying most of the producing units in this business. (See Kemper, No. 265).

* * *

Changes are inevitable. Former Presidential Assistant Daniel Patrick Moynihan gave the example of the automobile industry, which continued to brush off proposals for making their cars safer, while warning clouds were gathering. Within a few months the automobile industry suddenly became subject to federal regulation.

* * *

Massachusetts Insurance Commissioner C. Eugene Farnam stated, "If undustry and state regulatory authorities do not provide an almost immediate solution to the automobile insurance problem, we will have Title XX—Motoraid," an allusion to the Social Security Title XIX, Medicaid. (See Bibliography entry No. 160). *New York Times* - "Unless the automobile insurance industry changes its ways, Congress will move into the picture."

* * *

As James J. Meyers, vice president for claims of the Crum & Forster insurance group, stated, the whole works may well become "a dying industry unless we reappraise our practices." (See Bibliography entry No. 87).

* * *

President Johnson called for a broad-scale investigation of the auto-insurance system, described as "overburdened and unsatisfactory."

* * *

The Department of Transportation was directed by Congress to "streamline the auto-insurance system—to make it fair, to make it simple, and to make it efficient." Auto insurance service offered to the public is "slow, incomplete and expensive." - (Staff of the antitrust subcommittee of the U.S. House of Representatives). Many states are showing interest in no-fault compensation. "Changes in the insurance system are coming. The question is not whether, but how." (See Bibliog. entry No. 37).

* * *

Congress and the Federal Government have conducted or are planning no fewer than seven separate investigations dealing wholly or in part with automobile liability insurance, involving the Department of Transportation, the Federal Trade Commission, the House Judiciary Committee, the Senate Sub-committee on Antitrust and Monopoly, the Senate Commerce Committee, the House Committee on Interstate and Foreign Commerce, and the Senate Subcommittee on Judicial Machinery. (See Hodosh, No. 194).

* * *

No-fault advocates try to stifle opposition by attributing it to lawyers who try automobile cases. There is a host of non-lawyer op-

ponents, including union representatives and members of the
clergy. Lawyers will not suffer
from no-fault because it creates
more legal problems than presently exist. (See Julien, President of
the Metropolitan Trial Lawyers
Bas Association, No. 509).

* * *

The concept of "no-fault" has
been vigorously opposed by the
American Trial Lawyers Association (plaintiffs' attorneys) and all
four major organizations of defense lawyers—the Defense Research Institute, the International
Association of Insurance Counsel,
the Federation of Insurance Counsel, and the Association of Insurance Attorneys. (See Hodosh, No.
194; DRI, No. 109).

* * *

A "no-fault" plan is the surest
road to federal regulation and federal automobile insurance. The
burdens certain to be laid upon
state regulation by the plan will
increase the pressure for federal
regulation. The plan is primarily
a system for dispensing benefits,
and therefore a natural precursor
to a complete takeover of this seg-
ment of the private sector by the
Federal Government. (See Kemper, No. 265).

* * *

"Federal incursion and possible
takeover of the liability insurance
industry, as well as the total abolition of the civil jury system in personal injury and death actions is
the predictable result of the continued distortion of the present

system and the failure to improve and modernize it." (See Ghiardi, No. 172).

* * *

PUBLIC OPINION ON PAIN AND SUFFERING

For Change

Making payment for pain and suffering is unrealistic. It is difficult to measure pain and suffering. Much that is paid for pain and suffering is really a sub rosa payment for attorney fees that should be abandoned. Payments for pain and suffering are really a waste of resources; more emphasis should be on reimbursement than revenge. (See Chapin, No. 70).

* * *

Elimination of pain and suffering in no-fault plans substitutes precise measures of damages not subject to fabrication, exaggeration, or hallucination. (See Bibliography entry No. 10).

* * *

Against Change

The proponents of no-fault insurance plans would eliminate recovery for pain and suffering. They "create the impression that any payment to auto accident victims other than net economic loss is a boondoggle—a wasteful and unnecessary cost element bordering on fraud. But the fact is that our society considers a scarred face, a shattered leg, or the loss of ability to bear children to be a very serious form of damage, and the public is likely to go on insisting that anyone causing such damage provide compensation to the victim." (Statement by Paul S. Wise, President of American Mutual Insurance Alliance, See Bibliography entry No. 268).

* * *

It is no more difficult to measure damages in personal injury cases than it is in cases involving a myriad of other loss determination situations. The issue of damages in contract matters, the value of leaseholds, intentional torts, real estate matters such as condemnation values under eminent domain, property settlements in domestic relations matters, and all other legal cases where damages are an issue have been admirably resolved in our traditional legal system. Those who attack the tort liability system and its manner of determining damages adopt an unrealistic, simplistic solution—throwing out the right to recover for pain and suffering—this throws out the baby with the bathwater.

* * *

Rules for assessment of damages are not satisfactory because, among other things: (a) a lump sum cannot properly take into account all future contingencies; (b) there is no objective standard as to the damage value of pain and suffering. (See Marryott, No. 295).

* * *

The idea of rewarding people for pain and suffering is founded on the idea that a person inflicting pain on another should be responsible for it. This idea has little merit when the punishment will in fact be transferred to an insurance company. (See Chapin, No. 70).

* * *

It is irrational to suggest the elimination of claims for pain and suffering. How else can you adequately compensate, say, a child who loses a hand in an accident?

* * *

The extreme no-fault proposals which eliminate compensation for pain and suffering, death, dismemberment, loss of sight or hearing, serious disfigurement or fracture, could result in the following socially undesirable examples:

1. A pitifully disfigured young woman would receive absolutely nothing for a lifetime of humiliation and social deprivation.

2. A young man aspiring to a career as a surgeon, a professional athlete, or a musician would

receive nothing for the destruction of his future through the loss of a hand or arm.

3. A laborer who sustains a crippling spinal fracture would receive nothing for the pain, suffering and other hardships encountered as he attempts to continue a living. (See Bibliography entry No. 363).

* * *

People simply don't understand what it is they're being asked to decide when they are asked if they would be willing to give up claims for pain and suffering. They should be asked: "In return for lower premium costs, would you be willing to give up your right to recover payment for a permanently scarred face . . . or for the loss of a leg or an eye . . . or the inability to pursue a chosen career . . . or the destruction of your ability to bear or procreate children?" (Vestal Lemmon, See Bibliography entry No. 149).

* * *

Those no-fault proposals that eliminate pain and suffering claims under a specified dollar amount are inequitable and completely lacking in rationale. For example, in the Keeton & O'Connell proposal, a dollar amount of $5000 is specified. That proposal makes the unwarranted assumption that no one should be paid for $5000 worth of pain and suffering, but that above that amount payment is socially desirable. What equitable principles dictate this assumption?

* * *

There are many cases where economic loss is negligible and pain and suffering is real and measurable. Why eliminate recovery for pain and suffering or place an arbitrary dollar figure on it? (See Chapin, No. 70).

* * *

People expect some payment in return for the indignity of being involved in an accident, in return for the nuisance and trouble that seems to be associated with recovering anything. (See Marryott, No. 295).

* * *

The public would not accept a system which arbitrarily restricted victims to recovery of their actual wage and medical losses. People expect payment for inconvenience and discomfort, especially when caused by someone breaking the law or driving carelessly. The idea that people ought to be held responsible for their carelessness is deeply ingrained in the public sense of justice. (See Wise, No. 470).

* * *

DELAY OF FAULT SYSTEM

For Change

Injured victims of automobile accidents face average delays in collecting under automobile liability insurance that are ten times as long as the delays in collecting under collision, homeowners, or burglary insurance and 40 times as long as delays under accident and health insurance. (See Bibliography

Against Change

Those who argue for no-fault systems typically discount the amount of time necessary to process a two-party claim, such as that under health insurance.

* * *

Even under a no-fault plan, claims are not paid quickly, as evidenced by the first quarter of

entry No. 351).

* * *

The fault insurance system causes inordinate delay between an accident and the transfer, if any, of the accident cost, as compared with other lines of insurance. A study by the New York Insurance Department of 7,000 paid insurance claims closed during September, 1969, (of which 1,000 were automobile bodily injury liability claims) revealed the following:

experience under the Massachusetts no-fault plan. Companies discovered that there was no reduction in the average time lag of 21 days before claims forms were returned. In many cases, the form was not accompanied by hospital and medical bills because the claimant had not received them. Thus an additional delay ensued before payment could be made. (See Bibliography entry No. 67).

* * *

INTERVAL BETWEEN CLAIM AND PAYMENT FOR SELECTED LINES OF INSURANCE

Interval Between Claim and Payment	Auto Bodily Injury Liability	Auto Physical Damage	Home-owners	Burglary	Individual Accident and Health
2 months or less	23%	79%	92%	64%	98%
6 months or less	49	98	99	97	99
1 year or less	71	99	99	99	100
2 years or less	83	100	100	99	——
3 years or less	88	——	——	100	——
Average period (months)	15.8	1.5	1.6	1.9	0.4

(See Bibliography entry No. 351).

In addition, New York data from a Department of Transportation claim survey reveals that larger claims face longer delays before payment. See the following chart:

INTERVAL BETWEEN CLAIM AND PAYMENT BY SIZE OF PAYMENT

Interval Between Claim and Payment	Under $200	$201-$1000	$1001-$5000	Over $5000	All Claims
2 months or less	63%	16%	4%	2%	24%
1 year or less	89	61	41	19	61
2 years or less	92	74	61	41	74
2 2/3 years or less	94	80	70	52	80

Source: Derived from D.O.T. Closed Claim Survey — N.Y. portion, Table 131.

* * *

Delay is inherent in the tort liability system, particularly in automobile accident litigation: (1) people delay in filing lawsuits and (2) "Court congestion reflects the priority given to criminal or other civil cases." (See Bibliography entry No. 118).

* * *

Reform will eliminate the long delay in payments caused by court congestion. In metropolitan areas the time lapse between filing of suit and trial averages more than 31 months, with a nationwide high of 69½ months in a Chicago court. If the case is appealed, an even longer wait is in store for the plaintiff.

* * *

According to Mayer, in a recent year in California, 3,346 out of 4,074 civil juries sworn were empanelled for personal injury actions. Though fewer than 5% of the actions brought ever reach the trial state, what does come into court is more than enough to clog the system. Two and a half years is the normal wait in most cities from the day a suit is brought to the day a trial begins; many calanders are so far behind (Chicago's for example) that the average delay is 5 years.

* * *

The present system imposes a heavy burden on taxpayers to support the courts in which automobile insurance claims are tried. The system is cripplingly cumbersome and costly to the public as a whole on account of the intolerable delays caused by the overwhelming number of traffic accident cases clogging court calendars. Claimants simply cannot

The claim that it will reduce court congestion is perhaps the weakest claim made for the plan. It is stoutly contradicted by a long list of judges and law professors. Court delay is confined to a small number of courts in a limited number of major metropolitan areas. Auto accident cases account for only a small percentage of the business in the congested courts. Cause of congestion, where it does exist, is a growing amount of all court business and the failure to provide the personnel and facilities to handle the increase. (See DRI, No. 109).

* * *

No-fault is likely to increase the burden on civil judges. By preserving tort suits for the more serious claims, the plan would finance the bringing of an avalanche of such actions, since the claimant will have everything to gain and little to lose if he tries for the jackpot. The problem of court congestion can be solved simply enough by just appointing more judges. (See Kemper, No. 265).

* * *

The congested courts exist only in some of the major metropolitan centers. For example, in Illinois 99 of 102 counties have no backlog and in New York there is no delay in 43 of 63 counties. (See Bibliography entry No. 102).

fight through the thicket to a court verdict. (See Keeton and O'Connell, No. 256).

* * *

An increase in judicial manpower would not help. It would only result in the elimination of the present backlog, and more of the vast numbers of claims now settled or held back from litigation because of intolerable delays will be brought forward to overwhelm the courts still. (See DRI, No. 106). Suggestions for increasing judicial manpower constitute futilely cautious patchwork on the present ailing system.

* * *

Former U.S. Supreme Court Chief Justice Earl Warren wrote, "Interminable and unjustified delays . . . are compromising the basic legal rights of countless thousands of Americans and, imperceptibly, corroding the very foundations of constitutional government in the United States." (See Bibliography entry, No. 507).

* * *

"Philadelphia tried, among others, a combination of referee arbitration things and their court docket is in just as bad shape as anybody else." (Statement by Senator Philip A. Hart—See Ghiardi, No. 172).

* * *

* * *

The injured person may accept "no-fault" benefits until the last moment, and then start suit under tort law, in those "no-fault" plans where the tort liability system is preserved over and above the compensation benefits (as in the case of the Saskatchewan Plan). Eight to nine lawsuits out of ten are filed for $10,000 or more at present courts of record. Under a new plan, the costlier tort cases may not disappear—they will more likely be in addition to the earlier payments. (See Jeffrey, No. 230).

* * *

A mandatory small claims arbitration system has been operating in Philadelphia since 1958. Prior to its adoption, the Municipal Court of Philadelphia had a backlog of more than 7,700 civil cases and delays of 24 to 30 months for many cases. Today the backlog is gone and it is possible to bring a civil case to trial in 30 days. The tort liability system can be made to work without radical reform. (See Bibliography entry No. 407).

* * *

In Philadelphia, it takes three or four years at best for an automobile accident case to come to trial, and in other large cities the delay is even longer. Nationwide, the average delay in settling claims over $2500 is 19 months. (See Denenberg, No. 115).

* * *

The problem of court congestion could be well resolved by establishment of a system of arbitration, such as that used in the Philadelphia system. This would relieve the burden on the courts and provide for a rational reform without the necessity of scrapping a legal system which has served the public well for many generations.

* * *

DETERRENCE OF FAULT SYSTEM

For Change

The "deterrence" idea is no longer valid. When personal detriment to the defendant is no longer present, deterrence does not occur (if, indeed, it ever did). See Marryott, No. 295).

* * *

There is little deterrence present when 90 percent or more of American drivers are aware that any damages they cause through their negligence will be paid for by their liability insurer. Causing monetary loss to others with a liability insurer acting as intermediary produces an impersonality to the situation so that the negligent driver does not identify with the injured party's economic and physical trauma.

* * *

Defenders of the tort liability system who allege that the cost of the accident is borne by the wrongdoer ignore the fact that under the present system the cost for the ac-

Against Change

The tort liability system making negligent drivers accountable for their fault is a deterrent to automobile accidents. Adoption of a no-fault system "would make it the announced public policy that motorists are no longer to be held accountable for injuries and damages caused by their negligence on the highway, thereby condoning if not encouraging reckless disregard of other people's safety. It would undermine driver motivation and law enforcement efforts and increase accidents, thereby offsetting or outweighing any conjectural promises of reduced insurance premiums." (See Bibliography entry No. 437).

* * *

Human life is too precious and crippling injury is too tragic to rashly trade safety for the purported loss-funding economies of a no-fault insurance system. Safety must be paramount with us, else we

cident is hardly ever reflected specifically in the wrongdoer's premium. "It becomes part of the overall loss statistics of the class of drivers into which the wrongdoer happens to fall. His premium will not reflect the fact that he was or was not legally liable for damages. It may reflect the fact that he had been in an accident. It will continue to reflect his age, sex, residence and the kind of driving he does—business or pleasure . . . Even in the most flagrant cases of driver fault, it is a myth to claim that the guilty driver pays the innocent driver for damages." (T. Lawrence Jones, President of the American Insurance Association).

* * *

"The present insurance system insulates the wrongdoer from punishment. Funds paid out to victims come not from the driver judged in the wrong but from a financial pool—created by all the policyholders of that company. The Conard study, done at the University of Michigan, showed that nearly 85 percent of all drivers had isolated themselves from financial responsibility by buying insurance. Further, only 3 percent of the defendants paid any part of the settlements from their own pockets. And in one-third of the cases where a suit was filed and settled, the defendant did not even know whether anything had been paid to the victim or claimant."

In addition, "threats of loss of

stand accessory to death and injury. The burden of proof that the behavior conditioning implicit in (tort liability insurance's) incentive structure does not now and cannot more effectively in the future contribute significantly to highway safety lies very heavily on those who advocate a non-fault insurance system. It is incumbent on them to go forward with the burden of proof.

* * *

insurance or increased rates are far down the list of what induces us to drive carefully. Much ahead on that list would be such things as fear of imprisonment, physical injury to ourselves and our passengers, damage to our cars, and sometimes a thing so simple as inconvenience—a time loss putting a schedule out of whack." (Statement by Senator Philip Hart, See Bibliography entry No. 449).

* * *

When the Puerto Rican plan was instituted, critics thought drivers would get careless and push the accident rate sharply upward. In the first year of operation the rate did go up 5 percent—but this was only half the 10 percent rise of the year before, and traffic deaths declined to 451 in the first year of operation of the plan from 541 the previous year when the no-fault plan was not in use. (See Montgomery, No. 524).

* * *

The survival instinct is a vastly stronger deterrent to recklessness than the threat of a lawsuit.

* * *

If the fault insurance system is a deterrent to anything, it is more of a "deterrent" to becoming a victim than to driving carelessly, since the system does such a poor job of compensating automobile accident victims for their damages.

* * *

T. Lawrence Jones, American Insurance Association president, states, "22 million auto accidents

"Regardless of law and underwriting systems, high-risk drivers exist. The present system identifies them; it does not eliminate them; it would merely make them anonymous . . . The present law and underwriting system places strong economic pressures on high-risk drivers, a pressure which would be relaxed by a no-fault system." (See Bibliography entry No. 134).

* * *

in a year is tragic enough evidence that the lawsuit is not effective in deterring crashes."
(See Bibliography entry No. 1).

* * *

With "no-fault," insurance companies would be encouraged to recognize the importance of safety devices in cars of their insureds. A change in the structure of insurance to a related-insurer arrangement could provide a valuable addition by leading to a greater general concern about the safety of cars on the part of the insurance industry with concomitant support of research and development in the area of automobile safety. (See Keeton & O'Connell, No. 254).

* * *

INDUCEMENT FOR FRAUD

For Change

The tort liability system encourages dishonesty. Its adversary relationship creates situations that afford no clear line between rigorous bargaining and downright dishonesty.

* * *

Daniel P. Moynihan, Presidential Assistant to both Lyndon Johnson and Richard Nixon, has said: "The victim has every reason to exaggerate his losses. It is some other person's insurance company that must pay. The company has every reason to resist. It is somebody else's customer who is making the claim. De-

Against Change

A no-fault system would cause fraud and deceit to reach new and unprecedented dimensions.

Under the present system, a claimant must be ready to swear that his claim is genuine before a court and jury. This eliminates the claims of those persons who fear the penalty which results from lying under oath. A no-fault plan is a broad invitation to fraudulent claims based upon the unwitnessed accident. It will be almost impossible to defeat a claim for any household injury, for example, if the claimant asserts he suffered it while getting in or out of his car,

lay, fraud, contentiousness are maximized, and in the process the system becomes grossly inefficient and expensive."

* * *

Under no-fault proposals, losses must be verified the same as under the tort liability system. Consequently, there would be adequate restraints placed upon the possibilities of fraud.

* * *

A no-fault plan would greatly reduce opportunities for fraud that exist in the present system. (See Keeton, No. 251).

It would eliminate built-in inducements to exaggeration and actual fraud. (See Keeton and O'Connell, No. 253).

* * *

There are adjusters who take bribes to settle cases, plaintiffs who file inflated claims, witnesses who remember the unrememberable, and physicians who commit perjury. (See *Time*, No. 57).

* * *

washing the car, or otherwise using or maintaining it. There is also a huge potential for fraud in the concealment of collateral source benefits which, if disclosed, would reduce the amount of recovery. (See DRI, No. 109).

* * *

The adversary system has served admirably in the judicial forums, in the political arena, and in the competitive marketplace, as a means to provide countervailing power and the avoidance of extremes. The checks and balances afforded by the tort liability system provide the moderation and balance which is essential to the proper determination of the issues. It inherently guards against fraud.

* * *

COLLATERAL SOURCE BENEFITS

For Change

The "collateral source" rule produces distortion to the present system of damages. In spite of the fact that personal injury damages are primarily meant to compensate for loss suffered—the damages a defendant must pay are not diminished when the claimant's loss has already been paid from some other source (such as health insurance or sick leave pay). It means that some of the insurance money available to reimburse traffic victims goes to enrich victims already paid, rather than being available for victims not reimbursed from other sources. (See Keeton & O'Connell, No. 256).

* * *

Against Change

If elimination of the collateral source rule would effect economies under a no-fault plan, the same result could be obtained under the tort liability system. A simple change of statute could eliminate collateral source benefits under a tort liability recovery without the need to revolutionize the system with the drastic changes which a "no-fault" system would bring. (See Bibliography entry No. 90).

* * *

Elimination of collateral sources of recovery would involve a reduction of benefits. Since abolition of collateral source benefits would apply in the usual basic protection, and not in the residual tort right of action (in those systems retaining tort liability), some might feel that they would have nothing to lose by proceeding with tort actions, particularly in cases of serious injury involving probable liability of a defendant. (See Bibliography entry No. 90).

* * *

Elimination of collateral source benefits or making automobile compensation excess coverage over collateral source benefits would require insureds to use up their sick leave, union-negotiated wage continuation benefits, health insurance, Social Security, retirement pay, welfare payments, disability income, Blue Cross, and other available funds. The administrative cost of determining whether other benefits had been used prior to the automobile insurance claim would place an undue burden on the system.

* * *

CHAPTER XIV

CONSUMERS UNION GOALS OF AUTO–INSURANCE REFORM

(From testimony of Robert J. Klein, economics editor of Consumers Union of United States, Inc. Adapted from the report, "Insurance: The Road to Reform," published in the April 1971 issue of CONSUMER REPORTS (pages 223-226)–Copyright © 1971 by Consumers Union of United States, Inc. Reprinted by permission).

There is no single, perfect plan. Some students of the problem even doubt that the system of privately sold insurance can be salvaged. They look toward government insurance. Certainly, the problem is made less critical by state-administered health-insurance and medical-care plans in those countries that have them. Then, at least, there is never a question of availability of medical care for all victims regardless of ability to pay and regardless of whether they are victims of automobile accidents, other accidents or illness.

THE OBJECTIVES

Consumers Union believes that this country's automobile insurance should be revamped with a view to the universal health insurance that appears to be somewhere on the horizon. With that in mind, we present a 14-point set of objectives that we think are required in a reform designed in the best interests of consumers as policyholders and as claimants.

In Consumers Union's view, the following 14 objectives should be met by any reform plan.

1.   Medical Care

All people injured in car accidents should receive, at first from private insurance, but soon, we hope, from a Federal health plan, the expenses of complete medical care, including rehabilitation. Automobile medical-insurance benefits, like other medical insurance, should be paid to all who are hurt, regardless of who caused the accident, including drunk drivers and drugged drivers. Such people must be kept from driving. But depriving them of medical care won't keep them off the road; it will only visit hardships upon their families.

Do the major reform plans meet this objective?

Keeton-O'Connell Plan—No. It limits no-fault
benefits to $10,000 per person.

American Insurance Association Plan—Yes.

New York State Plan—Yes.

Hart Plan—Yes.

DOT Plan—Not quite. It limits no-fault medical
benefits to some high but not yet specified
maximum amount.

2.   *Wage Replacement*

All disabled victims who cannot work should receive the equivalent
of their take-home pay, their earning capacity if they are students or un-
employed, or their services to their families—all such payments to be limited to an amount adequate to sustain a decent standard of living in their
community. No one should receive more money than he was taking home
before being injured, however. Social Security already pays some wage
loss to disabled persons. It should be expanded to do the full job.

Do the major reform plans meet this objective?

Keeton-O'Connell Plan—No. It limits wage replacement to $750 per month and counts that as
part of the $10,000 maximum no-fault benefits.

American Insurance Association Plan—No. It limits
wage replacement to $750 per month but does
pay it indefinitely.

New York State Plan—Yes. It goes beyond the objective by paying unlimited wage losses.

Hart Plan—No. It limits wage replacement to a total
of $30,000 but does provide up to $1000 per
month, enough for an adequate living standard
at present price levels.

DOT Plan—No. It limits wage replacement to a total
of $36,000 except for victims in "approved re-
habilitation programs," but does provide up to
$1000 per month, enough for an adequate liv-
ing standard at present price levels.

3.   *Periodic Payment*

Auto-accident-insurance benefits should be paid to victims month-
by-month as expenses and wage losses occur.

Do the major reform plans meet this objective?

Yes, although in the DOT plan it is not explicitly stated.

4. Other Insurance

Auto insurance should take care of paying only what less-costly insurance plans do not cover. Most plans, including Social Security, group hospital and medical policies, Blue Cross, and individual health policies now return a far larger percentage of the premium to the policyholders than auto insurance does.

Do the major reform plans meet this objective?

> *Keeton-O'Connel Plan*—Partly. Though it does away with duplicate payments for the same loss, it might leave automobile insurance as the primary source of benefits, at least until there is a government health-insurance system.
>
> *American Insurance Association Plan*—No. Same as Keeton-O'Connell.
>
> *New York State Plan*—Yes.
>
> *Hart Plan*—Yes.
>
> *DOT Plan*—No. It does away with duplicate payments for the same loss unless the policyholder wants to pay extra for duplicate coverage. It makes automobile insurance the primary private source of benefits, although leaving open the door for health insurance companies to compete for the business of motorists by designing their coverage to comply with automobile insurance requirements.

5. Group Auto Policies

State laws and administrative rules obstructing the sale of group automobile insurance should be overruled by Federal law. Many states have been persuaded by auto-insurance agents to hamper group sales and such mass-marketing devices as insurance for a company's employees on the payroll-deduction plan.

Do the major reform plans meet this objective?

> *Keeton-O'Connell Plan*—No. But the plan itself would encourage group selling.
>
> *American Insurance Association Plan*—No. Same as Keeton-O'Connell.
>
> *New York State Plan*—Yes, in that New York has no law against group insurance.
>
> *Hart Plan*—Yes.
>
> *DOT Plan*—No. Same as Keeton-O'Connell.

6.   Cancellation

Auto-insurance policies must be noncancelable, guaranteed renewable, and available in the open market to all eligible consumers. Everyone licensed to drive or able to register a car should be eligible as long as he pays the premiums. The situation now is that 14 percent of motorists have had their insurance canceled, and when one company cancels, other tend not to accept you. From 8 to 10 percent of car owners must now buy through assigned-risk plans because no company will deal with them voluntarily; yet an eight-state analysis of assigned-risk policyholders found that 53 percent of them had had no accidents or convictions for traffic violations. The price of being an assigned risk is very high—sometimes double the standard rate. In most states the most insurance you can buy as an assigned risk is the minimum liability coverage required by the state.

Do the major reform plans meet this objective?

    Keeton-O'Connell Plan—No.
    American Insurance Association Plan—No.
    New York State Plan—No.
    Hart Plan—Yes.
    DOT Plan—No.

7.   Pain and Suffering

The number of claims for pain and suffering should be greatly curtailed, leaving only the most serious ones. Most such claims today are paid to victims of minor injuries rather than to the seriously hurt. The average person with medical expenses of less than $100 and with a lawyer to press his claim receives six times his loss. With the elimination of petty claims for pain and suffering, the insurance system might be able to pay, in addition to out-of-pocket losses, at least some compensation to seriously disfigured and permanently disabled victims. Preferably, every such victim should be paid. If that makes insurance too costly, it may be necessary to preserve his right to sue a negligent driver.

So the major reform plans meet this objective?

    Keeton-O'Connell Plan—Yes, by means of a $5000
        deductible liability claim against a faulty driver.
    American Insurance Association Plan—No.
    New York State Plan—No.
    Hart Plan—Yes, by means of a liability claim against
        a faulty driver for permanent disability or
        disfigurement.
    DOT Plan—Yes, by means of a liability claim against

a faulty driver for permanent disability or disfigurement as well as any medical expenses beyond the no-fault limit.

8.   *Property Damage*

Damage done by automobiles to property other than automobiles should be repaired with money from the car-owner's automobile insurance even if the accident was not his fault.

Do the major reform plans meet this objective?

Keeton-O'Connell Plan—Yes.

American Insurance Association Plan—Yes.

New York State Plan—Yes.

Hart Plan—No, not unless the motorist chooses optional property damage coverage.

DOT Plan—Yes, "ultimately."

9.   *Compulsory Coverage*

Every car owner should have to carry the basic no-fault automobile insurance. Companies could offer all kinds of optional extra coverages; higher benefits for pain and suffering, higher wage benefits, *etc.*

Do the major reform plans meet this objective?

Yes.

10.   *Automobile Damage*

The consumer should have three choices of automobile damage insurance: 1) no collision insurance, 2) today's type of collision insurance, which pays for damage regardless of fault, 3) insurance that pays damage done to his car if the driver of another car caused the accident. The third choice should be offered in fairness to owners of cars with too little value to merit full collision insurance. Collision premium rates should be scaled, as some companies scale them now, to encourage construction of damage-resistant cars. Fire, theft and comprehensive insurance should be optional, as now.

Do the major reform plans meet this objective?

Keeton-O'Connell Plan—Yes. It orginated the three-choice idea.

American Insurance Association Plan—No. It offers full collision insurance or nothing.

New York State Plan—No. Same as AIA.

Hart Plan—No. Same as AIA. But this is the only plan that would require premiums based on damageability of the car.

DOT Plan—No. "Ultimately" the same as AIA

> except that the motorist could choose de-
> ductibiles under which he would pay out of
> his own pocket for repairs up to as much as
> $1000 or one-third the value of the car.

11. *Premium Rates*

They must be held down and, if possible, reduced. A system that pays benefits without attempting to establish blame can redirect to premium savings or improved benefits at least 25 percent of the cost of today's liability insurance. Elimination of automobile-insurance payments for losses already covered by cheaper insurance will cut the premium further. Elimination of pain-and-suffering claims for minor injuries will cut costs even more.

> Do the major reform plans meet this objective?
>> Yes. All claim to. But there is disagreement on
>> the savings. The Keeton-O'Connell Plan puts
>> a $10,000 limit on no-fault medical and wage
>> benefits because its actuary could not other-
>> wise foresee reduced premiums.

12. *Price Comparisons*

The driver-rating system should be standardized. A person's age, sex, where he lives, the car he drives, and how much he uses his car do appear to have a real bearing on his chances of having an accident. With no-fault insurance, companies should also design their rates around the size of the family, its other insurance and its income—in other words, those factors that would determine compensation in the event of an injury-causing accident. The important thing is for each company to use the same rating standards, including identical geographic rate zones. Companies should compete on the basic price from which all rates would be figured by percentage increases or decreases. Shoppers would then find it relatively easy to compare prices,

> Do the major reform plans meet this objective?
>> *Keeton-O'Connell Plan*—No.
>> *American Insurance Association Plan*—No.
>> *New York State Plan*—No.
>> *Hart Plan*—Yes. It originated the idea.
>> *DOT Plan*—No.

13. *Claims Service*

Insurance companies should report regularly to a Government agency their claims-paying practices, and the agency should publish data indicating how well each company satisfies its claims. Consumers Union's recent survey of claims experiences showed significant differences in the way companies handled their claims (CONSUMER REPORTS, June 1970). Full knowledge of the quality of a company's service is essential to the consumer's rational choice of a company.

Do the major reform plans meet this objective?

> *Keeton-O'Connell Plan*—No.
> *American Insurance Association Plan*—No.
> *New York State Plan*—No.
> *Hart Plan*—Yes. It originated the idea.
> *DOT Plan*—No.

14. Industry Regluation

Automobile insurance should be regulated by a Federal agency instead of by each individual state. It would be appropriate for the motoring public to finance the agency with a tax on insurance policies. Present law exempting insurance companies from the antitrust laws should be repealed. Prices should be regulated by the market under surveillance of the new Federal agency. Few states can hire the professional staffs needed to cope with their regulatory obligations. A single Federal agency could afford highly competent attorneys, accountants and actuaries and could use their services efficiently in the public interest. The American population is mobile. It travels on interstate highways, and it changes residence frequently from state to state. Americans need uniform motor-vehicle laws and uniform automobile insurance.

Do the major reform plans meet this objective?

> *Keeton-O'Connell Plan*—No.
> *American Insurance Association Plan*—
>> Does not specify.
> *New York State Plan*—No.
> *Hart Plan*—No. Insurance regulation would re-
>> main with the states in consultation with
>> a Federal administrator.
> *DOT Plan*—No. Congress would pass a resolution
>> urging the states to adopt model legislation
>> to be drafted by the Council of State Govern-
>> ments along lines suggested by Washington.

PART V
IN CONCLUSION

CHAPTER XV

IMMINENCE OF CHANGE AND ITS CHARACTER

The evidence seems compelling of a need for reform in the United States automobile accident reparations system. Under the tort liability system, the upward spiral of automobile accident costs continues unabated; attorneys continue to charge for their time and advice; insurance companies make their profit; what is left goes to the automobile accident victim; and it is little enough. Little is new in these phenomena, however. The system has worked in the past, and it has been the accepted way in American life and morals as the best way to distribute insurance proceeds to the motoring public.

Perhaps it is not so much that things have worsened—the impetus for reform could well be from other factors. Perhaps things *are* worse than they have ever been, but this may not be the major factor in the current furore raging around the no-fault vs. tort liability controversy.

PUBLIC ATTITUDES

The most significant element in the contemporary struggle is one of attitudes—the evaluation of the basic credibility of determining the pattern of health care reimbursement, disability rehabilitation awards, survivorship benefits, and other damages, upon the criteria of liability for fault. Given this shift of public attitudes towards strict liability and concern for the injured victim, combined with an emerging conviction of the inevitability of automobile accidents and the continuation of carnage on our highways, and with a sense of mistrust in the legal technique of ascertaining fault in all but the most flagrant and patently clear liability cases, a strong indication of public attitude has emerged. This is not to say that a mandate or overwhelming consensus is urging the abandonment of the tort liability system in favor of no-fault. The public opinion polls are not that clear. It is apparent that a substantial percentage of the public has never heard of the no-fault idea. Of those people who are aware of the no-fault controversy, many are unfamiliar with the features or the consequences of adoption and implementation of a true no-fault automobile insurance system.

It is accurate to say, however, that value systems of Americans are constantly metamorphosing. Many articulate and persuasive people are urging change, and a change to no-fault accomplished by a persuasive minority would be no less characteristic of the nation's method of governance than that produced in other legislative fiats.

The Attraction of Change

Nor can one discount the potential attraction of a centralized, federal-government administered plan. Social Security with its 3 percent administration expense provides a model of efficiency and economy, returning 97 percent of "insureds' " contributions to them. Verifying death, retirement age, and total disability is comparatively simple, however, compared to the administrative difficulties of verifying medical bills, avoiding "double payment" (where collateral source benefits are excluded), establishing evidence where benefits are denied drivers under the influence of intoxicants or narcotics or drivers with intentionally self-inflicted injuries, and the costs of investigating suspected fraud. Ultimately covering automobile physical damage under the no-fault system would only aggravate administrative problems of claims handling.

The Political Realities

Assuming that federal administration of a no-fault program under a Social Security-type administrative system could yield substantial economies over the present system (a not-too-unrealistic assumption), there are social, economic, and political considerations which rule out such drastic change. A federally-administered, "pure" no-fault plan, supplanting the private insurance industry and ruling out all tort liability claims and legal actions, would do irreparable economic injury to hundreds of insurance companies and tens of thousands of agents, adjusters, and attorneys.

Suggesting such a radical departure from the present system is tantamount to solving the nation's "agriculture problem" and saving Americans billions of dollars annually in government support payments by similarly eliminating, in one fashion or another, some 2.4 million excess farmers. It also proposes a scope of reform reminiscent of suggestions to purge from society the smoking habit by incidentally eliminating from the American scene the hundreds of thousands of people who depend upon the "noxious weed" for their livelihood.

The social, economic, and political realities may be too overpowering to consider seriously the proposals for radical reforms—at least in the immediate future. Time or continued deterioration of the present ailing system could materially change the outlook. Meanwhile, the radical reforms do, nevertheless, provide the impetus for reform by making the adoption of moderate proposals more likely within the system of compromise inherent in American politics.

THE PAIN AND SUFFERING ISSUE

A major issue confronting the legislative reformers of the automobile accident reparations system is the complex problem of what to do about compensation for so-called "pain and suffering" claims—the "general damages" which provide the bulk of tort liability recoveries in litigation. In order to understand the problem, we must distinguish claims for "pain and suffering"—that is, general damages—from "special damages."

We designate as "special damages" those pecuniary losses which can be substantiated by reference to specific expenditures. Examples of "special damages" are specific medical and hospital expenses, property damages, and dollar amount income losses which can be verified by reference to specific expenditures, evidenced by invoices, receipts, and other records.

Recovery for "general damages" presents a more complicated situation. General damages are those which do not require a specific showing of monetary loss, but are such losses which can be inferred from the evidence of injury. These include, among other things, damages for pain and suffering, loss of use of body members or loss by amputation of a member (hand, arm, leg, eye, *etc.*), total or partial loss of vision, and the effect of facial or bodily scarring on the injured person's future enjoyment of life, as well as the value of the loss of ability to bear children. They include losses presumably incurred when there is a loss of opportunity which conceivably might have yielded financial reward were it not for the occurrence of the accident.

General damages are such as the law itself implies or presumes to have accrued from the wrong complained of, for the reason that they are its immediate, direct, and proximate result. The distinguishing characteristic of general damages is the lack of corroboration—the lack of specific evidence—of a specific monetary loss. There is no set dollar figure which can be easily ascertained, as in the case of the "out-of-pocket" losses which form the basis for special damage claims.

Barring Recovery for General Damages

A number of interesting arguments have been advanced for eliminating recoveries for "pain and suffering." It is said that recovery for such losses should be barred because so-called "pain and suffering" is a conjectural thing, subject to fabrication, exaggeration, and hallucination, and defying the application of any rational approach to evaluation. The argument is made that payments made for such intangible "loss" are "really a waste of resources," placing emphasis upon revenge rather than upon reimbursement. Further, elimination of such recoveries would make insurance more economical for the insuring public.

Extreme critics of the principle of awarding general damages question the legitimacy of pain and suffering as an item of legal damage. Those who would eliminate recoveries adopt a neat and simplistic solution to an area of controversy which has confounded courts and juries for generations. They ignore "pain and suffering" as a proper subject for compensation.

Legal Justification for Recovery

The fundamental justification of any system of automobile accident reparations is to provide compensation for losses. Compensation requires that amounts awarded be calculated to reasonably repay an injured person for the loss which he has suffered and to place him in the same or an equivalent position to that which he occupied prior to the event which caused his injuries.

Basic to the determination of legitimacy of "pain and suffering" losses is whether ignoring such losses would in fact place an injured person in the same or an equivalent position to that occupied before the accident. A long series of legal decisions have defined "damages" or "losses" as detriment, deterioration, or injury to persons or property. To argue that loss of a body member, destruction of eyesight, or disfigurement is not a legitimate item for inclusion in any compensation system for automobile accident victims defies reason. Exclusion of these items from the realm of compensation cannot be justified on any moral, legal or rational basis.

To attack a system of making payments for temporary pain and discomfort, where full recovery is attained, may be another matter. It is one thing to use the reparations system as a symbolistic artifact of an allegedly once-operative, punitive fault system, granting nominal damages where actual damage has not occurred. It is another matter to eliminate from the compensation system a legitimate class of losses because they frustrate precise measurement and defy an expeditious system of reimbursement.

More sensible and germane to the "pain and suffering" issue is whether the tort liability system is the means by which we can best evaluate these intangible losses and determine the pecuniary figures which should be assigned to them. Aside from the issue of fault in a negligence case, is there merit in preserving the machinery of the tort liability system to evaluate the compensation payable for disability, dismemberment, disfigurement, and death?

Machinery for Reimbursing "Intangible Losses"

Basic to the adoption of a "pure" no-fault system is the complete elimination of the tort liability system—liability for fault or negligence. A concomitant of elimination of the fault system would be the substitution of some other reparations system which would provide the automobile accident victim with reimbursement sufficient to place him in the same or in an equivalent position as that occupied before the accident. Any substitute system must still grapple with the abstract of placing a pecuniary figure on intangible losses. What *is* a disfigurement worth in money? To the professional actress, it may mean hundreds of thousands of dollars in lost income. To the professional wrestler, the disfigurement may actually enhance his economic worth.

The substitute system of compensation proposed by the no-fault advocates is first-party insurance coverage. Elimination of "pain and suffering" claims—general damages—would simplify the compensation system so that losses could be easily ascertained and reimbursed. The inclusion of "pain and suffering" losses in a first-party compensation system proposes the same problem of damage ascertainment as that confronted by the tort liability system. There must still be a system of evaluation for establishing the monetary figure of these intangible losses.

Establishing the Monetary Figure

Whatever system is used in the evaluation of general damages, there are two approaches which can be taken in setting monetary awards for automobile accident victims:

1) Establishing a fact-finding and decision-making procedure which will evaluate losses on a case-by-case basis, concluding with a decision or judgment which fixes the appropriate award in each individual case.

2) The assignment of arbitrary awards to types of losses, without differentiating between individual cases. A classification system would be adopted, establishing the classes of losses and the monetary figure which would be paid in cases falling within each class. For example, a certain dollar figure would be paid for loss of specific body members (so much for an arm, a leg, loss of vision, *etc.*). A specific dollar amount would be paid for death. Some procedure could be established for ascertaining percentage of disability or extent of disfigurement, with an appropriate money award made proportionate to the percentile of disability or extent of disfigurement in each case.

Presumably, an ideal arrangement for administering these class awards would be afforded through a compensation system similar to the state Workmen's Compensation plans. Students of the history of the several states' experience with Workmen's Compensation systems, however, might point out that there are wide variations in compensation amounts and in duration of payments made in the individual states. They might argue for a uniform Federal Compensation System as a means to eliminate these weaknesses. No one, however, has determined how best to eliminate the arbitrary valuation system of assigning fixed amounts to intangible losses, regardless of whether the system is state or federal.

Criticisms of Arbitrary Awards

Defenders of the tort liability system for determining awards for pain and suffering argue convincingly that the arbitrary system of evaluating intangible losses is capricious, inequitable, and barbaric. Each case is different. Each case deserves individual consideration. Age, sex, circumstance, and a host of factors must be considered in order to provide for a rational system of compensation. This requires a fact-finding, decision-making, case-by-case approach to evaluation of intangible losses, and for a number of reasons, a compensation system based upon first-party coverage is ill-equipped to handle the task.

We have ample evidence from our experience in handling workmen's compensation and uninsured motorist's insurance claims to know that the process of establishing benefit awards is not governed primarily by consideration of the fairness and adequacy of such awards. Although individual insurance claim adjusters are well-meaning and honest, they are still economy-oriented and under obligation to their employers (the insurance companies) to construe contracts in the narrowest sense consistent with expedient legal and economical considerations. After all, business is business. Given the expertise of the law-trained insurance adjuster or claims attorney and the naïveté of the typical insured, the observer can well argue that a first-party method of evaluating intangible losses does not dispense with the adversary system. All it does is to leave one of the adversaries in a weaker and unequal bargaining position.

It is better to assign the fact-finding, decision-making valuation process to a more impartial, equitable forum. The nation's judiciary system, with its adversary approach, its provision of skilled champions (attorneys) for each of the adversaries, its safeguards built into procedural and evidential rules, may provide for the most appropriate and efficient means to administer the evaluation system of intangible losses.

COMPROMISE PRESERVING THE BEST OF BOTH SYSTEMS

Unquestionably, compromise is indicated in the controversy which rages on the no-fault issue. It is difficult to defend the preservation of the status quo, and it is unrealistic to assume that the American public will continue to countenance the expenditure of 58 percent of every automobile insurance premium dollar to return the remaining 42 percent in benefits to the insuring public, particularly in the case of losses which are easily measurable in pecuniary figures. Nor is it convincing to argue that the moral outrage of the public in the United States cries out to save the fault system. The notion that the American policyholder still embraces the fiction that the wrongdoing motorist is in fact being punished for his negligence, and that the policyholder will thus clamor to preserve the fault system, is a notion bred on the panic of those who have a great financial stake in resisting change.

More realistic is the notion that the fault system is an anachronism in a majority of the cases involving automobile accidents. It provides a grossly inefficient method of compensating the accident victims, despite the unconvincing justification of the expense as necessary to a system which is a tribute to the eternal efficacy of traditional American values—"a triumph of reason and morality." The argument resounds with the ring of nostalgia, but it is lacking in logic, reason, or relevance.

The Compensation Emphasis

The whole thrust of the evolution of automobile insurance, the emergence of financial responsibility laws, and the clamor for no-fault systems, has been to focus on the plight of the injured party in the automobile accident. Punishment of the guilty driver is a secondary consideration and a minor one at that. An attempt at prevention of culpable conduct is a prelude and a corollary of punishment for such conduct, and Americans have been noticeably lax in removing bad drivers from the highways by a system of tough law enforcement and driver licensing. There is little evidence that punishment is a national cause in *criminal cases* involving motor vehicle operation. Why continue to argue that punishment is a national cause in *civil cases* involving motor vehicle operation?

With the emphasis being placed on compensating the automobile accident victim, intense scrutiny should be focused on the assertion that first-party coverage could completely and adequately meet the demands of a sensible reimbursement system.

Preserving the Fact-Finding Machinery

Suggestions have been made for establishment of compensation boards, eliminating litigation from the trial courts. Any attempt, however, to set limits of recovery would still bear the onus of absolutism—it would still be arbitrary. Further, there would still be a need for fact-finding on the issue of damages. How much *should* be paid the automobile accident victim?

Those who argue to supplant the court system pre-suppose that the issue of damage evaluation can be resolved amicably without an adversary proceeding. Nevertheless, controversy persists; bargaining inequality prevails; some cases can't be handled amicably. An impartial, fact-finding tribunal becomes imperative.

There would appear to be merit in preserving the fact-finding machinery of the American judicial system in evaluating those intangible losses which defy assignment of pre-arranged values. Much can be said for retaining tort liability rights in the judicial system making it possible to recover in court proceedings for "catastrophic losses"—those involving disfigurement, dismemberment, disability, death, and cases where the arbitrary figure provided in a compensation system would shock the conscience of the public.

NEED FOR OBJECTIVITY

Whatever system is selected by the American public, reform cannot long be delayed. The stresses are too obvious to be ignored, despite the futile hopes of the reform obstructionists who believe that the problem will simply go away if a holding-action can be sustained long enough. Economic exigencies compel the automobile insurers to tighten their underwriting selectivity and to speed up the tempo of cancellations. These actions reinforce the public disenchantment with an automobile accident reparations system which appears to be designed to serve everyone except the public which must bear the burden of its cost and the consequences of its misallocation of resources.

The indemnification system has long been under the strain of inflationary pressures of rising medical costs, increasing court and jury awards, and other bodily injury variables aggravated by time and circumstances. These factors, however, have combined with the rapidly accelerating damageability factor and gross increase in repair costs deliberately incorporated into the motor vehicle by manufacturers since World War II, and have exhausted the patience of the motoring public. No single institution has created the current phenomenon of unrest, but each shall feel the impact of remedies which are forthcoming.

A large number of the "reform" proposals thus far made are patently unworkable palliatives which merely serve as "patchwork on the presently ailing system." The depth of their purported "reform" is not lost on the knowledgeable observer, regardless of deceptive labels assigned to them.

It is incumbent upon those who have a legitimate interest in the reparations problem to abandon their strictly self-serving stance in the public deliberations which the "no-fault" controversy has generated. There is need for a sensible recognition of reality. Radical legislative reaction to the resistance of stubborn allegiance to the status quo could well result in sacrifice of values contributed by legitimate institutions—institutions which presently participate in the automobile accident reparations system. Their sacrifice would be the nation's loss.

APPENDIX

APPENDIX A

THE MASSACHUSETTS LAW

APPENDIX A
THE MASSACHUSETTS LAW

Chapter 670

AN ACT PROVIDING FOR COMPULSORY PERSONAL INJURY PRO-
TECTION FOR ALL REGISTERED MOTOR VEHICLES, DEFINING SUCH
PROTECTION, RESTRICTING THE RIGHT TO CLAIM DAMAGES FOR
PAIN AND SUFFERING IN CERTAIN ACTIONS OF TORT, REGULATING
FURTHER THE PREMIUM CHARGES FOR COMPULSORY AUTOMOBILE
INSURANCE, AND AMENDING CERTAIN LAWS RELATING THERETO.

Be it enacted by the Senate and House of Representatives in General
Court assembled, and by the authority of the same, as follows:

SECTION 1. The first paragraph of section 34A of chapter 90 of the
General Laws is hereby amended by striking out, in line 2, as appearing in the
Tercentenary Edition, the words "thirty-four J" and inserting in place there-
of the following words: — thirty-four N.

SECTION 2. Said section 34A of said chapter 90 is hereby further
amended by adding the following paragraph: —
"Personal injury protection," provisions of a motor vehicle liability
policy or motor vehicle liability bond which provide for payment to the
named insured in any such motor vehicle liability policy, the obligor of any
motor vehicle liability bond, members of the insured's or obligor's household, any authorized operator or passenger of the insured's or obligor's
motor vehicle including a guest occupant, and any pedestrian struck by the
insured's or obligor's motor vehicle, unless any of the aforesaid is a person
entitled to payments or benefits under the provisions of chapter one hundred
and fifty-two, of all reasonable expenses incurred within two years from the
date of accident for necessary medical, surgical, x-ray, and dental services,
including prosthetic devices and necessary ambulance, hospital, professional
nursing and funeral services, and in the case of persons employed or self-
employed at the time of an accident of any amounts actually lost by reason
of inability to work and earn wages or salary or their equivalent, but not
other income, that would otherwise have been earned in the normal course of
an injured person's employment, and for payments in fact made to others,
not members of the injured person's household and reasonably incurred in
obtaining from those others ordinary and necessary services in lieu of those
that, had he not been injured, the injured person would have performed not
for income but for the benefit of himself and/or members of his household,
and in the case of persons not employed or self-employed at the time of an

accident of any loss by reason of diminution of earning power and for payments in fact made to others, not members of the injured person's household and reasonably incurred in obtaining from those others ordinary and necessary services in lieu of those that, had he not been injured, the injured person would have performed not for income but for the benefit of himself and/or members of his household, as a result of bodily injury, sickness or disease, including death at any time resulting therefrom, caused by accident and not suffered intentionally while in or upon, or while entering into or alighting from, or being struck as a pedestrian by, the insured's or obligor's motor vehicle, without regard to negligence or gross negligence or fault of any kind, to the amount or limit of at least two thousand dollars on account of injury to or death of any one person, except that payments for loss of wages or salary or their equivalent or, in the case of persons not employed, loss by reason of diminution of earning power, shall be limited to amounts actually lost by reason of the accident and further limited (1) in the case of persons entitled to wages or salary of their equivalent under any program for continuation of said wages or salary or their equivalent to an amount that, together with any payments due under such a program, will provide seventy-five percent of any such person's average weekly wage or salary or its equivalent for the year immediately preceding the accident, or (2) in the case of persons not entitled to wages or salary or their equivalent under any program for continuation of said wages or salary or their equivalent to an amount that will provide seventy-five percent of any such person's average weekly wage or salary or its equivalent for the year immediately preceding the accident. In any case where amounts paid for loss of wage, salary or their equivalent are reduced as a result of any program for continuation of the same and such reduction produces a subsequent loss, as when the limit of any such program for continuation of wage or salary or their equivalent is exhausted with the result that an injured person cannot recover for a later injury or illness as he would have been entitled to but for such a reduction, such subsequent loss to an amount equalling the reduction in personal injury protection made in accordance with this section shall, if incurred within one year after the receipt of the last benefit provided under this section, be treated as a loss of wages, salary or their equivalent incurred as a result of the injury to which personal injury protection applied.

Personal injury protection shall also provide for payment, to the named insured or obligor and members of their households, all amounts defined in this section in any case where such persons incur such expense or loss as a result of such injury while in, upon, entering into or alighting from, or by being struck as a pedestrian by, a motor vehicle not insured by a policy or bond providing personal injury protection unless such person recovers such expenses or loss in an action of tort. Insurers may exclude a person from personal injury protection benefits if such person's conduct contributed to his injury in any of the following ways while operating a motor vehicle in the commonwealth:

(1)   While under the influence of alcohol or a narcotic drug as defined in section one hundred and ninety-seven of chapter ninety-four;

(2)   While committing a felony or seeking to avoid lawful apprehension or arrest by a police officers; or

(3)   With the specific intent of causing injury or damage to himself or others.

SECTION 3. The first sentence of section 34D of said chapter 90, as most recently amended by section 3 of chapter 517 of the acts of 1964, is hereby further amended by adding at the end of the first sentence thereof the following words: — and the depositor shall in writing authorize the state treasurer to pay over to the insurer assigned a claim under section thirty-four N any and all amounts, including without limitation the reasonable costs of investigating and settling any such claim and such other reasonable expenses expended by it to satisfy a claim for personal injury protection made against it by any person, other than the depositor or members of his household, who is entitled to such payments as a result of the unavailability of personal injury protection benefits on said depositor's motor vehicle.

SECTION 4. Said chapter ninety is hereby further amended by inserting after section 34K the following two sections: —

Section 34M. Every motor vehicle liability policy and every motor vehicle liability bond, as defined in section thirty-four A, issued or executed in this commonwealth shall provide personal injury protection benefits as defined therein except to the extent such defined benefits to an insured or obligor or members of an insured's or obligor's household may be modified, reduced or eliminated by the purchase of the deductible authorized in this section. The benefits due and payable under any motor vehicle liability policy or bond as a result of the provisions therein providing personal injury protection benefits, and any benefits due any person entitled to make claim under the assigned claims plan established in accordance with section thirty-four N, are granted in lieu of damages otherwise recoverable by the injured person or persons in tort as a result of an accident occurring within this commonwealth.

Every owner, registrant, operator or occupant of a motor vehicle to which personal injury protection benefits apply who would otherwise be liable in tort, and any person or organization legally responsible for his acts or omissions, is hereby made exempt from tort liability for damages because of bodily injury, sickness, disease or death arising out of the ownership, operation, maintenance or use of such motor vehicle to the extent that the injured party is, or would be had he or someone for him not purchased a deductible authorized by this section, entitled to recover under those provisions of a motor vehicle liability policy or bond that provide personal injury protection benefits or from the insurer assigned. No such exemption from tort liability shall apply in the case of an accident occurring outside the commonwealth. However, if any person claiming or entitled to benefits under the personal injury protection provisions of a policy or bond insuring a vehicle registered in this commonwealth brings, in such a case, an action in tort against the owner or person responsible for the operation of such a vehicle, amounts otherwise due such a person under the provisions of section thirty-four A shall not become due and payable until a settlement is reached or a final judgment is rendered in such a case and the amounts then due shall be reduced to that extent that damages for expenses and loss otherwise recoverable as a personal injury protection benefit are included in any such settlement or judgment.

Claim for benefits due under the provisions of personal injury protection or from the insurer assigned shall be presented to the company providing such benefits as soon as practicable after the accident occurs from which such claim arises, and in every case, within at least two years from the date of accident, and shall include a written description of the nature and extent of injuries sustained, treatment received and contemplated and such other information as may assist in determining the amount due and payable. If benefits for loss of wage or salary, or in the case of the self-employed their equivalent, are claimed the party presenting such a claim shall authorize the insurer to obtain details of all wage or salary payments, or their equivalent, paid to him by any employer in the year immediately preceding the date of accident, or earned by him, and authorize the insurer to make any reasonable necessary investigation as to whether or not such loss may be reduced in whole or in part as a result of any program calling for the continuance of such wage, salary or earnings during absence from work. The injured person shall submit to physical examinations by physicians selected by the insurer as often as may be reasonably required and shall do all things necessary to enable the insurer to obtain medical reports and other needed information to assist in determining the amounts due. Noncooperation of an injured party shall be a defense to the insurer in any suit for benefits authorized by this section and failure of an insurer to pay benefits in the event of such noncooperation shall not in any way affect the exemption from tort liability granted herein.

Personal injury protection benefits and benefits due from an insurer assigned shall be due and payable as loss accrues, upon receipt of reasonable proof of the fact and amount of expenses and loss incurred, but an insurer may agree to a lump sum discharging all future liability for such benefits on its own behalf and on behalf of the insured. In any case where benefits due and payable remain unpaid for more than thirty days, any unpaid party shall be deemed a party to a contract with the insurer responsible for payment and shall therefore have a right to commence an action in contract for payment of amounts therein determined to be due in accordance with the provisions of this chapter.

Any insurer paying benefits in accordance with the provisions of this section shall be subrogated to that exact extent to the rights of any party it pays and may bring an action in tort against any person liable for such damages in tort who is not exempt from said liability as a result of the provisions of this section. Said insurer is also hereby given the right to make claim for all expenses it incurs on account of such payments, including the net amount of benefits paid, costs of processing claims for any such benefits, and the expenses of enforcing this right, against any other insurer providing a motor vehicle liability policy or bond on a motor vehicle registered in this commonwealth, whose owner or operator would, except for the exemption from tort liability provided in this section, be liable for such damages in tort. Determination as to whether any insurer is legally entitled to recover any such expense from another insurer shall be made by agreement between the involved insurers, or, if they fail to agree, by arbitration in accordance with the provisions of the General Laws.

Each insurer providing personal injury protection shall issue to any person purchasing a motor vehicle liability policy or bond, at his option, a policy endorsement, approved as to content by the commissioner of insurance and subject to such other regulations regarding said endorsement as the commissioner may from time to time make after appropriate hearing, which shall provide that there shall be deducted from amounts that would otherwise be or become due to the policyholder alone or to the policyholder and members of his household, as the policyholder elects, an amount of either two hundred and fifty dollars, five hundred dollars, one thousand dollars or two thousand dollars, again as the policyholder elects, said amount to be deducted from the amounts otherwise due each person subject to the deduction. Any person electing such an endorsement or subject to such an endorsement as a result of the policyholder's election shall have no right to claim or to recover any amount so deducted from any owner, registrant, operator or occupant of a motor vehicle or any person or organization legally responsible for any such owner's, registrant's, operator's or occupant's acts or omissions who is made exempt from tort liability by this section.

Amounts deducted from payment in accordance with the provisions of the preceding paragraph shall not have any effect upon the determination of whether or not the reasonable and necessary expenses incurred as a result of any injury exceed or do not exceed five hundred dollars, which determination may affect an injured's person's rights under section six D of chapter two hundred and thirty-one.

Section 34N. Insurers authorized to provide personal injury protection in this commonwealth are hereby directed to organize and maintain an assigned claims plan to provide that any person resident in the commonwealth, other than the owner or registrant of a motor vehicle not insured by a policy or bond providing personal injury protection or a member of

such owner or registrant's household, who suffers loss or expense as a result
of an injury arising out of the ownership, operation, maintenance or use of a
motor vehicle while the motor vehicle is upon the ways of the commonwealth
or in any place therein to which the public has a right of access, may obtain
personal injury protection benefits through said plan in any case where no
personal injury protection benefits are otherwise available to such a person
provided that the following shall not be entitled to such benefits:

(1) A person entitled to payments or benefits under the provisions of
chapter one hundred and fifty-two, or

(2) A person who is subject to exclusion from personal injury protection benefits by insurers under section thirty-four A of this chapter.
Said plan shall contain such rules and regulations for operation and for the
assessment of costs as shall be approved by the commissioner of insurance.
Any claim brought through said plan shall be assigned to an insurer in accordance with the approved regulations of operation and that insurer, after such
assignment, shall have the same rights and obligations it would have if prior
to such assignment it had issued a policy providing personal injury protection applicable to the loss or expenses incurred. Any party accepting such
benefits hereunder shall have such rights and obligations as he would have
were a policy providing personal injury protection benefits issued to him.

SECTION 5. Chapter 231 of the General Laws is hereby amended by
inserting after section 6C the following section: —

Section 6D. In any action of tort brought as a result of bodily injury,
sickness or disease, arising out of the ownership, operation, maintenance or
use of a motor vehicle within this commonwealth by the defendant, a plaintiff may recover damages for pain and suffering, including mental suffering
associated with such injury, sickness or disease, only if the reasonable and
necessary expenses incurred in treating such injury, sickness or disease for
necessary medical, surgical, x-ray and dental services, including prosthetic
devices, and necessary ambulance, hospital, professional nursing and funeral
expenses are determined to be in excess of five hundred dollars unless such
injury, sickness or disease (1) causes death, or (2) consists in whole or in part
of loss of a body member, or (3) consists in whole or in part of permanent
and serious disfigurement, or (4) results in such loss of sight or hearing as is
described in paragraphs (a), (b), (c), (d), (e), (f) and (g) of section thirty-six
of chapter one hundred and fifty-two or (5) consists of a fracture.

SECTION 6. Notwithstanding any provisions of section one hundred
and thirteen B of chapter one hundred and seventy-five of the General Laws
to the contrary, for the purposes of putting into effect the provisions of the
General Laws providing for personal injury protection, the commissioner of
insurance shall, on or before September the fifteenth in the current year,
fix and establish the same classifications of risks and premium charges at

least fifteen percent lower for each classification of risk within each territory from the following rates: —

Territories	Class 10	Class 12	Class 20	Class 22	Class 24
1	$117.00	$140.50	$351.00	$374.50	$193.00
2	108.00	129.50	324.00	345.50	178.00
3	100.50	120.50	301.50	321.50	166.00
4	96.50	116.00	289.50	309.00	159.00
5	88.00	105.50	264.00	281.50	145.00
6	79.00	95.00	237.00	253.00	130.50
7	68.00	81.50	204.00	217.50	112.00
8	63.50	76.00	190.50	203.00	105.00
9	59.00	71.00	177.00	189.00	97.50
10	54.50	65.50	163.50	174.50	90.00
11	49.00	59.00	147.00	157.00	81.00
12	43.50	52.00	130.50	139.00	72.00
13	37.00	44.50	111.00	118.50	61.00
14	30.50	36.50	91.50	97.50	50.50
15	24.00	29.00	72.00	77.00	39.50

Territories	Class 26	Class 30	Class 40	Class 42	Class 50
1	$164.00	$169.50	$222.50	$304.00	$234.00
2	151.00	156.50	205.00	281.00	216.00
3	140.50	145.50	191.00	261.50	201.00
4	135.00	140.00	183.50	251.00	193.00
5	123.00	127.50	167.00	229.00	176.00
6	110.50	114.50	150.00	205.50	158.00
7	95.00	98.50	129.00	177.00	136.00
8	89.00	92.00	120.50	165.00	127.00
9	82.50	85.50	112.00	153.50	118.00
10	76.50	79.00	103.50	141.50	109.00
11	68.50	71.00	93.00	127.50	98.00
12	61.00	63.00	82.50	113.00	87.00
13	52.00	53.50	70.50	96.00	74.00
14	42.50	44.00	58.00	79.50	61.00
15	33.50	35.00	45.50	62.50	48.00

Said premium charges shall be the maximum charges to be used and charged by companies in connection with the issue or execution of motor vehicle liability policies or bonds, both as defined in section thirty-four A of chapter ninety of the General Laws for the ensuing calendar year or any part thereof but any company may make written application to the commissioner of insurance for permission to use, in place of the premium charges fixed and established by him as aforesaid, such lesser charges as are now permitted by the provisions of section one hundred and thirteen B of chapter one hundred and seventy-five.

The rates of all other motor vehicle insurance coverage including those motor vehicle insurance rates filed according to the provisions of chapter one hundred and seventy-five A of the General Laws and established under the provisions of section one hundred and thirteen C of chapter one hundred and seventy-five of the General Laws shall be at least fifteen percent lower than all rates for such coverages now in effect for the year nineteen hundred and seventy.

All the reduced rates in this section shall be deemed and accepted as adequate, just, reasonable and nondiscriminatory rates for the calendar year nineteen hundred and seventy-one, based on the current relevant costs. Any future increases in these rates shall be allowed only in relation to increases in such relevant costs; and any reduction in such relevant costs shall result in corresponding reductions of the insurance rates.

SECTION 7. Section 113B of chapter 175 of the General Laws, as most recently amended, is hereby further amended by inserting after the first paragraph the following paragraph: —

In fixing and establishing classifications for premium charges to be used in connection with motor vehicle liability policies or bonds for the calendar year nineteen hundred and seventy-two and each calendar year thereafter, the commissioner shall establish reasonable surcharges, above the premium charges otherwise due, for each conviction for a moving violation committed, within the period herein specified, by the policyholder of such a policy, or the obligor of such a bond, or any other driver who resides in the same household as the policyholder or obligor and is included among those authorized to drive any vehicle covered by such policy or bond. The commissioner shall also establish reasonable discounts to be applied when neither the policyholder nor obligor, nor any other driver who resides in his household and is authorized to drive any vehicle covered by such policy or bond, has been the driver of a vehicle involved, within the period herein specified, in an accident required to be reported under the provisions of section twenty-six of chapter ninety. The period to be considered in fixing the surcharges and discounts for a calendar year shall be the period closing on August the thirty-first next preceding the calendar year to which such surcharges and discounts apply; it shall be a period commencing no sooner than September the first, nineteen hundred and seventy and in no event exceeding five years in length; and, with respect to calculating a discount, it shall be the period commencing on September the first next after the last reportable accident involvement. In the absence of a finding otherwise by the commissioner, based on data accumulated under this merit system and such other evidence as the commissioner considers relevant and material, reasonable surcharges and discounts shall be presumed to be the following: for each conviction of driving under the influence of intoxicating liquor or narcotic or hallucinogenic drugs, a surcharge of one hundred percent; for each conviction of speeding, a surcharge of twenty percent; for each conviction of any other moving violation, a surcharge of ten percent; for each full year free of reportable accident involvement, a discount of two percent.

SECTION 8. Said chapter 175 is hereby amended by inserting after section 22D the following section: —

Section 22E. No company shall issue any policy of insurance which provides coverage against loss or damage to, or loss of use of, motor vehicle resulting from collision, fire, lightning, any larceny, pilferage, theft, malicious mischief, vandalism or any other perils usually insured against, or which insures any person against, legal liability for loss or damage on account of the bodily injury or death of any other person or on account of any damages to property of another, arising out of the ownership, maintenance, control or use of motor vehicles, including motor vehicle liability policies as defined in section thirty-four A of chapter ninety, unless said policy contains a provision that it shall be automatically renewed by the company except for fraud, conviction for use of unlawful drugs or driving under the influence of liquor, or nonpayment of premiums. Further, no insurance company, and no officer or agent thereof on its behalf, shall refuse to issue or execute as surety a motor vehicle liability policy or bond, or any other insurance based on the ownership or operation of a motor vehicle because of place or garaging of the vehicle.

SECTION 9. Section 113C of said chapter 175 is hereby amended by striking out the second paragraph, added by section 3 of chapter 643 of the acts of 1968, and inserting in place thereof the following paragraph: —

No company shall be authorized to issue such motor vehicle liability policies or to act as surety upon such motor vehicle liability bonds unless it makes a mandatory offer to issue to any person purchasing such policy or bond at his option, additional coverage, beyond that required by section thirty-four A of chapter ninety, of at least fifteen thousand dollars on account of injury to or death of one person and at least forty thousand dollars on account of any one accident resulting in injury to or death of more than one person, and of the combination of bodily injury liability off the ways of the commonwealth and liability for guest occupants on and off the ways of the commonwealth, of medical coverage, so-called, and of property damage, so-called, to a limit of at least five thousand dollars, of fire and theft coverage, comprehensive coverage and collision coverage, so-called. The rates for other than fire, theft, comprehensive and collision insurance shall be subject to the approval of the commissioner, under the provisions of section one hundred and thirteen B.

SECTION 10. Section six of this act shall take effect upon passage; all other sections of this act shall take effect on January the first, nineteen hundred and seventy-one and for the purpose of the issuance of motor vehicle liability policies or bonds for the calendar year nineteen hundred and seventy-one all things necessary to be done prior to said effective date may be done.

SECTION 11. The provisions of this act are severable, and if any of its provisions shall be held unconstitutional by any court of competent jurisdiction, the decision of such court shall not impair any of the remaining provisions.

Chapter 744

AN ACT RELATIVE TO THE RENEWAL OF CERTAIN MOTOR VE-
HICLE INSURANCE POLICIES AND PROVIDING FOR THE SUSPEN-
SION OF THE LICENSE OF INSURANCE COMPANIES REFUSING TO
ISSUE OR RENEW COMPULSORY MOTOR VEHICLE LIABILITY IN-
SURANCE POLICIES.

Whereas, The deferred operation of this act would tend to defeat its purpose, which in part is to guarantee the continued availability of automobile
insurance supplied by private enterprise, therefore it is hereby declared to be
an emergency law, necessary for the immediate preservation of the public
convenience.

Be it enacted by the Senate and House of Representatives in General
Court assembled, and by the authority of the same, as follows:

SECTION 1. Chapter 670 of the acts of 1970 is hereby amended by
striking out section 8 and inserting in place thereof the following section: —
Section 8. Said chapter 175 is hereby amended by inserting after section 22D the following three sections: —
Section 22E. Every policy of insurance issued by an insurance company to a person who is sixty-five years of age or over which provides coverage against loss or damage to, or loss of use of, a motor vehicle resulting from
collision, fire, lightning, larceny, pilferage, theft, malicious mischief, vandalism or other perils usually insured against, or which insures against legal
liability for loss or damage on account of the bodily injury or death of any
other person or on account of any damages to property of another, arising
out of the ownership, maintenance, control or use of a motor vehicle, including motor vehicle liability policies, as defined in section thirty-four A
of chapter ninety, shall be renewed at the option of the policyholder, so
long as the company is licensed to write such policies in the commonwealth,
except for fraud in the application for insurance or renewal thereof; a guilty
finding for a moving violation; suspension for a period of more than thirty
days of an operator's license; or revocation of such license or a registration;
ineligibility for merit rating discounts due to accident involvement; conviction under the provisions of subdivision (1) (a) of section twenty-four of
said chapter ninety; nonpayment of premiums; or in the case of a particular
insurer a general reduction in volume of automobile insurance in the commonwealth determined by the commissioner not to be an attempt to circumvent the purposes of this section. No insurance company, and no officer
or agent thereof in its behalf, shall refuse to issue, renew or execute as surety
a motor vehicle liability policy or bond, or any other insurance based on the

ownership or operation of a motor vehicle because of age, sex, race, occupation or principal place of garaging of the vehicle.

Any company which is authorized not to issue a renewal policy because of the exceptions contained in this section shall give a thirty day written notice of its intention not to issue a policy for the ensuing policy period, containing a statement of the reasons therefor.

Section 22F. Except for fraud in an application for insurance, or for nonpayment of premiums an insurance company as long as it is licensed to write insurance in the commonwealth shall not refuse to renew the policy or policies under section thirty-four A of chapter ninety to a policyholder who is entitled to the discount provided in section one hundred and thirteen B for two consecutive years which entitles him to a net discount of four percent for such years without any surcharge or the balance thereof assessed against him, except for a general reduction in volume of automobile insurance as provided in section twenty-two E.

Section 22G. An insurance company may refuse to renew the policy or policies of any person under sixty-five years of age, except a person entitled to such renewal under the provisions of section twenty-two F, but if such refusal is due to any cause other than fraud in the application for insurance or renewal thereof, a guilty finding for a moving violation, suspension of an operator's license for a period of more than thirty days or revocation of such license or a registration, ineligibility for merit rating discounts due to accident involvement, conviction under the provisions of subdivision (1) (e) of section twenty-four of chapter ninety, nonpayment of premiums or in the case of a particular insurer a general reduction in volume of automobile insurance in the commonwealth determined by the commissioner not to be an attempt to circumvent the purposes of this section, such company shall be required to accept an additional assigned risk for each such refusal.

Section 22H. If any company refuses to issue motor vehicle liability policies set forth in section thirty-four A of chapter ninety the commissioner may after a public hearing suspend said company's license to issue or sell any other form of insurance within the commonwealth until said company resumes the issuance or renewal of such motor vehicle liability policies in compliance with the laws and rules and regulations prescribed by said commissioner.

The provisions of this section shall not invalidate any insurance policy issued or renewed by an insurance company suspended pursuant to the authorization contained in this section prior to such suspension.

SECTION 2. Said chapter 670 is hereby further amended by striking out section 10 and inserting in place thereof the following section: —

Section 10. Section six of this act shall take effect upon passage; section twenty-two F of chapter one hundred and seventy-five of the General Laws, inserted by section eight of this act, shall take effect on September the first, nineteen hundred and seventy-two; provided, however, that the provisions of said section twenty-two F shall apply to any policyholder during the year nineteen hundred and seventy-two who has been credited with a two percent discount from September the first, nineteen hundred and seventy to September the first, nineteen hundred and seventy-one under the provisions of section one hundred and thirteen B of said chapter one hundred and seventy-five; all other sections of this act shall take effect on January the first, nineteen hundred and seventy-one and for the purpose of the issuance of motor vehicle liability policies or bonds for the calendar year nineteen hundred and seventy-one all things necessary to be done prior to said effective date may be done.

SECTION 3. Every motor vehicle policy and every motor vehicle liability bond, as defined in section thirty-four A of chapter ninety of the General Laws, shall contain a provision approved by the commissioner of insurance, for indemnifying or protecting the insured or any person responsible for the operation of the insured's motor vehicle to the same extent required by said section thirty-four A in effect prior to January one, nineteen hundred and seventy-one in the event that any provisions of chapter six hundred and seventy of the acts of nineteen hundred and seventy providing for the exemption of persons from tort liability or a restriction on the right to recover damages for pain and suffering are held to be unconstitutional.

SECTION 4. Notwithstanding any other provision of law, the commissioner of insurance is hereby authorized with the approval of the governor to adopt regulations, without observance of the requirements of notice and public hearing otherwise applicable, that may remain in effect for the whole or any part of the period commencing on the effective date of this act and ending on February the sixth, nineteen hundred and seventy-one, unless ratified by both the house and the senate before said date, for the purpose of enabling motorists to readily obtain adequate insurance through private enterprise. Any such regulation shall be accompanied by a finding and a brief statement of the reasons for the finding that it is necessary for the above purposes and shall be filed with the state secretary in accordance with the provisions of section two of chapter thirty A of the General Laws which regulate the filing of emergency regulations.

APPENDIX B

THE DELAWARE LAW

APPENDIX B
THE DELAWARE LAW

AN ACT TO AMEND TITLES 18 AND 21, DELAWARE CODE, RELATING TO THE REQUIREMENT OF INSURANCE ON MOTOR VEHICLES; REQUIRING INSURANCE COMPANIES TO OFFER CERTAIN POLICY COVERAGE; REQUIRING ARBITRATION OF CERTAIN CLAIMS AND PROVIDING A PENALTY FOR VIOLATION THEREOF.

BE IT ENACTED BY THE GENERAL ASSEMBLY OF THE STATE OF DELAWARE:

SECTION 1. Amend Subchapter 1, Chapter 21, Title 21, Delaware Code by adding thereto a new section to read as follows:

"Section 2118   Requirement of insurance for all motor vehicles registered in the State of Delaware; penalty

(a)   No owner of a motor vehicle registered in the State of Delaware, other than a self-insurer pursuant to Section 2906, Title 21, Delaware Code, shall operate or authorize any other person to operate such vehicle unless the owner has insurance on such motor vehicle providing the following minimum insurance coverage:

(1)   Indemnity from legal liability for bodily injury, death or property damage arising out of ownership, maintenance or use of the vehicle to the limit, exclusive of interest and costs, of at least $25,000 for any one accident or to the limit of the Financial Responsibility Law of the State of Delaware, whichever is greater.

(2)   Compensation to injured persons for reasonable and necessary for medical, hospital, dental, surgical, medicine, x-ray, ambulance or prosthetic services, professional nursing and funeral services, and for loss of earnings and reasonable and necessary extra expense for personal services which would have been performed by the injured person had he not been injured, arising out of an accident involving such motor vehicle and incurred or medically ascertainable within 12 months of said accident. This compensation shall have minimum limits of $10,000 for any one person and $20,000 for all persons injured in any one accident. The compensation for funeral services pursuant to subsection (a) (2) shall not exceed the sum of $2,000 per person.

A.   The coverage required by subsection (2) shall be applicable to each person occupying such motor vehicle and to any other person injured in an accident involving such motor vehicle, other than an occupant of another motor vehicle.

B.   The owner of a vehicle may elect to have the coverage described in subsection (2) written subject to certain deductibles, waiting periods, sublimits, percentage reductions, excess provisions and similar reductions offered by insurers in accordance with filings made by such insurers with the Department of Insurance, applicable to expenses incurred as a result of injury to the owner of the vehicle or members of his household. This election must be made in writing and signed by the owner of the vehicle; insurers issuing such policies may not require such reductions.

(3)   Compensation for damage to property, in or upon the motor vehicle, and other property damaged in an accident involving the motor vehicle, other than damage to a motor vehicle, with the minimum limits of $5,000 for any one accident.

A.   The owner of the motor vehicle may elect to have coverage described in subsection (3) written to exclude in whole or in part the following:

(i)   Aircraft, water craft, self-propelled mobile equipment and any property in or upon any of the aforementioned.

(ii)   Any property in or upon the vehicle when the owner of said property is not occupying the vehicle.

B.   This election must be made in writing and signed by the owner of the vehicle, and the insurer issuing such policies may not require such reductions. Any reductions shall be in accordance with filings made by the insurer with the Department of Insurance.

(4)   Compensation for damage to the insured motor vehicle, including loss of use of the motor vehicle, not to exceed the actual cash value of the vehicle at the time of the loss and $10.00 per day, with a maximum payment of $300 for loss of use of such motor vehicle.

A.   The owner of the motor vehicle may elect to exclude, in whole or in part, the coverage described in subsection (4) by the use of certain deductibles and exclusions in accordance with filings made by the insurer with the Department of Insurance.

(b)   Only insurance policies validly issued by companies authorized to write in this State all the kinds of insurance embodied in the required coverages shall satisfy the requirements of this section.

(c)   Nothing in this section shall be construed to prohibit the issuance of policies providing coverage more extensive than the minimum coverages required by this section, or to require the segregation of such minimum coverages from other coverages in the same policy.

(d)   Policies purporting to satisfy the requirements of this section shall contain a provision which states that, notwithstanding any of the other terms and conditions of the policy, the coverage afforded shall be at least as extensive as the minimum coverage required by this section.

(e) The coverage described in subsections (a)(1), (a)(2), (a)(3) and (a)(4) may be subject to conditions and exclusions customary to the field of liability, casualty and property insurance and not inconsistent with the requirements of this section.

(f) Insurers providing benefits described in subsections (a)(1), (a)(2), (a)(3) and (a)(4) shall be subrogated to the rights, including claims under any Workmen's Compensation law, of the person for whom benefits are provided, to the extent of the benefits provided.

(g) Any person eligible for benefits described in subsections (a)(2) or (a)(3), other than an insurer in an action brought pursuant to subsection (f), is precluded from pleading or introducing into evidence in an action for damages against a tortfeasor those damages for which compensation is available under subsections (a)(2) or (a)(3) without regard to any elective reductions in such coverage and whether or not such benefits are actually recoverable.

(h) Nothing in this section shall be construed to require an insurer to insure any particular risk. Nothing herein shall limit the insurer's obligations pursuant to Delaware Automobile Plan.

(i) Every insurance policy shall require the insurer to submit to arbitration a claim for damage to a motor vehicle, other than the insured motor vehicle, including loss of use of such vehicle upon the request of the owner of the damaged vehicle. Such request shall be in writing and mailed to the Insurance Commissioner of the State of Delaware within 90 days from the date of the accident causing such damage.

(1) All arbitrations shall be administered by the Insurance Commissioner or his nominee.

(2) The Insurance Commissioner or his nominee shall establish a panel of arbitrators consisting of attorneys authorized to practice law in the State of Delaware and insurance adjusters licensed to act as such in the State of Delaware.

(3) The Insurance Commissioner, or his nominee, shall select three individuals from the panel of arbitrators, at least one of which shall be an attorney authorized to practice law in the State of Delaware, to hear each request for arbitration.

(4) The Insurance Commissioner or his nominee shall promulgate all rules and regulations necessary to implement this arbitration program.

(5) The right to require such arbitration shall be purely optional and neither party shall be held to have waived any of their rights by any act relating to arbitration.

(6) The Insurance Commissioner shall establish a schedule of costs of arbitration; provided however, the arbitrators fee shall not exceed $25.00 per arbitrator for any one arbitration.

(7) The cost of arbitration shall be payable to the State of Delaware, Department of Insurance, and shall be maintained in a special fund identified as the 'Arbitration Fund' which shall be administered by the

Insurance Commissioner. These funds under no circumstances shall revert to the General Fund. All costs of arbitration including administrative expenses of the Insurance Department and the arbitrators fees shall be payable from this fund.

(8) The cost of arbitration shall be borne equally by the parties to the arbitration.

(j) Whoever violates any provisions of this section shall be guilty of a misdemeanor and fined not less than $300 or more than $1,000 and may be imprisoned not more than 6 months.

(k) The Superior Court of the State of Delaware shall have exclusive original jurisdiction of any violation of this section notwithstanding any provision of the Delaware Code to the contrary.

SECTION 2. Amend Section 3902, Chapter 39, Title 18, Delaware Code, by striking subsection (b) in its entirety and adding thereto a new subsection to read as follows:

(b) The amount of coverage to be so provided shall not be less than the maximum limits for bodily injury, death and property damage liability insurance provided for under the motorist financial responsibility laws of this State. The coverage for property damage shall be subject to a $250.00 deductible for property damage arising out of any one accident unless the insurer and the insured agree in writing to a different deductible. Each insured shall be offered the option to purchase additional coverage for personal injury or death up to a limit of $300,000 but not to exceed the limits for personal injury set forth in the basic policy.

(1) As used herein, the term 'property damage' shall include the loss of use of a vehicle.

SECTION 3. Amend Section 3902, Chapter 39, Title 18, Delaware Code, by inserting in subsection (a) after the words and punctuation mark "including death," and before the words "resulting from" the words "or personal property damage".

SECTION 4. If any section, subsection, sentence, phrase or work of this Act shall be declared unconstitutional under the Constitution of the State of Delaware or of the United States or by a State or Federal Court of competent jurisdiction, the remainder of this Act shall be unimpaired and shall continue in full force and effect and prosecutions thereunder shall not be affected.

SECTION 5. This Act shall be effective on January 1, 1972.

APPENDIX C

THE FLORIDA LAW

AN ACT RELATING TO MOTOR VEHICLE INSURANCE; PROVIDING
DEFINITIONS; REQUIRING SECURITY BY MOTOR VEHICLE OWNERS;
REQUIRING MOTOR VEHICLE NO-FAULT REPARATION INSURANCE
AND LIABILITY INSURANCE UP TO CERTAIN LIMITS AND LIMITING
TORT LIABILITY; PROVIDING PENALTIES FOR FAILURE TO SHOW
PROOF OF SECURITY; PROVIDING PERSONAL INJURY PROTECTION
BENEFITS; PROVIDING FOR PRIORITY OF PAYMENT OF BENEFITS;
PROVIDING FOR TORT EXEMPTIONS AND LIMITATION ON DAMAGES;
PROVIDING NO-FAULT PROPERTY PROTECTION; PROVIDING FOR
CERTAIN DEDUCTIBLES; PROVIDING FOR SUBROGATION; PROVID-
ING THAT THE DEPARTMENT SHALL ADOPT RULES AND REGULA-
TIONS NECESSARY TO IMPLEMENT THIS ACT; PROVIDING RIGHTS
OF RESIDENTS; PROVIDING THAT INSURERS FILE PROPOSED MAN-
UAL, RULES, RATES AND RATING PLANS WITH THE DEPARTMENT
FOR APPROVAL; PROVIDING THAT INSURERS SHALL MAKE CER-
TAIN RATE REDUCTIONS; PROVIDING FOR SEVERABILITY; PRO-
VIDING AN EFFECTIVE DATE.

Be It Enacted by the Legislature of the State of Florida:

SECTION 1. Short title — This act may be cited and known as the
"Florida automobile reparations reform act."

SECTION 2. Purpose — The purpose of this act is to require medical,
surgical, funeral and disability insurance benefits to be provided without regard to fault under motor vehicle policies that provide bodily injury and property damage liability insurance, or other security, for motor vehicles registered in this state, and with respect to motor vehicle accidents, a limitation
on the right to claim damages for pain, suffering, mental anguish and inconvenience.

SECTION 3. Definitions — As used in this act:
(1) "Motor vehicle" means a sedan, station wagon or jeep type vehicle
not used as a public livery conveyance for passengers, and includes any other
four-wheel motor vehicle used as a utility automobile and a pickup or panel
truck which is not used primarily in the occupation, profession or business
of the insured.
'(2) "Owner" means a person who holds the legal title to a motor vehicle, or in the event a motor vehicle is the subject of a security agreement or
lease with option to purchase with the debtor or lessee having the right to

possession, then the debtor or lessee shall be deemed the owner for the purposes of this act.

(3) "Named insured" means a person, usually the owner of a vehicle, identified in a policy by name as the insured under the policy.

(4) "Relative residing in the same household" means a relative of any degree by blood or by marriage, who usually makes his home in the same family unit, whether or not temporarily living elsewhere.

SECTION 4. — Required security —

(1) Every owner or registrant of a motor vehicle required to be registered and licensed in this state shall maintain security as required by subsection (3) of this section in effect continuously throughout the registration or licensing period.

(2) Every nonresident owner or registrant of a motor vehicle which, whether operated or not, has been physically present within this state for more than ninety (90) days during the preceding three hundred sixty-five (365) days, shall thereafter maintain security as defined by subsection (3) of this section in effect continuously throughout the period such motor vehicle remains within this state.

(3) Such security shall be provided by one of the following methods:

(a) Security by insurance may be provided with respect to such motor vehicle by an insurance policy delivered or issued for delivery in this state by an authorized or eligible insurer as otherwise defined in this code, which qualifies as evidence of automobile or motor vehicle liability insurance under chapter 324, Florida Statutes, "the financial responsibility law", except as modified to provide the benefits and exemptions contained in this act. Any such policy of liability insurance covering motor vehicles registered or licensed in this state and any policy of insurance represented or sold as providing the security required hereunder for registered and licensed motor vehicles under this act shall be deemed to provide insurance for the payment of such benefits; or

(b) Security may be provided with respect to any motor vehicle by any other method approved by the department of insurance as affording security equivalent to that afforded by a policy of insurance, provided such security is continuously maintained throughout the motor vehicle's registration or licensing period. The person filing such security shall have all of the obligations and rights of an insurer under this act.

(4) An owner of a motor vehicle with respect to which security is required by this act who fails to have such security in effect at the time of an accident shall have no immunity from tort liability, and be personally liable for the payment of benefits under Section 7. With respect to such benefits, such an owner shall have all of the rights and obligations of an insurer under this act.

SECTION 5. Proof of security; security requirements; penalties –

(1) The provisions of chapter 324, Florida Statutes, which pertain to the method of giving and maintaining proof of financial responsibility, and which govern and define a motor vehicle liability policy, shall apply to filing and maintaining proof of security or financial responsibility required by this act. It is intended that the provisions of chapter 324, Florida Statutes, relating to proof of financial responsibility required of each operator and each owner of any motor vehicle, shall continue in full force and effect.

(2) Any person who gives information required in a report or otherwise as provided for in this act, knowing or having reason to believe that such information is false, or who shall forge, or, without authority, sign any evidence of proof of security, or who files or offers for filing any such evidence of proof, knowing or having reason to believe that it is forged or signed without authority, shall, upon conviction, be punished by fine not to exceed one thousand dollars ($1,000) or imprisonment not to exceed one (1) year, or by both such fine and imprisonment.

(3) This act does not apply to any motor vehicle owned by the state or by a political subdivision of the state, nor to any motor vehicle owned by the federal government.

Section 5A. Subsection (2) of section 5 of this act is created to read:

SECTION 5. Proof of security; security requirements; penalties –

(2) Any person who gives information required in a report or otherwise as provided for in this act, knowing or having reason to believe that such information is false or who shall forge, or, without authority, sign any evidence of proof of security, or who files or offers for filing any such evidence of proof, knowing or having reason to believe that it is forged or signed without authority, shall be guilty of a misdemeanor of the first degree, punishable as provided in sections 775.082 or 775.083.

Section 5B. In the event CS for HB 935, introduced in the 1971 regular session of the legislature is enacted into law, subsection (2) of section 5 of this act will stand repealed and be omitted from the Florida Statutes. In the event CS for HB 935 is not enacted into law, section 5A of this act will stand repealed and be omitted from the Florida Statutes.

SECTION 6. Operation of a motor vehicle illegal without security; penalties –

(1) Any owner or registrant of a motor vehicle with respect to which security is required under subsection (1) or (2) of section 4 who operates such motor vehicle or permits it to be operated in this state without having in full force and effect security complying with the terms of said subsection (1) or (2) of section 4 shall have his operator's license and registration revoked.

(2) Any motor vehicle liability insurance policy which provides security required pursuant to subsection (3) of section 4 shall also be deemed to

comply with the applicable limits of liability required under the financial responsibility or compulsory laws of any other state.

SECTION 7. Required personal injury protection benefits; exclusions; priority —

(1) Every insurance policy complying with the security requirements of section 4 shall provide personal injury protection providing for payment of all reasonable expenses incurred for necessary medical, surgical, x-ray, dental and rehabilitative services, including prosthetic devices, necessary ambulance, hospital, nursing services, funeral and disability benefits to the named insured, relatives residing in the same household, persons operating the insured motor vehicle, passengers in such motor vehicle and other persons struck by such motor vehicle and suffering bodily injury while not an occupant of a motor vehicle or motorcycle, all as specifically provided in subsection (2) and paragraph (d) of subsection (4) of this section, to a limit of five thousand dollars ($5,000) for loss sustained by any such person as a result of bodily injury, sickness, disease or death arising out of the ownership, maintenance or use of a motor vehicle as follows:

(a) Medical benefits: all reasonable expenses for necessary medical, surgical, x-ray, dental and rehabilitative services, including prosthetic devices, necessary ambulance, hospital and nursing services. Such benefits shall include also, necessary remedial treatment and services recognized and permitted under the laws of the state for an injured person who relies upon spiritual means through prayer alone for healing in accordance with his religious beliefs.

(b) Disability benefits: one hundred percent (100%) of any loss of gross income and loss of earning capacity per individual, unless such benefits are deemed not includable in gross income for federal income tax purposes, in which event such benefits shall be limited to eighty-five percent (85%), from inability to work proximately caused by the injury sustained by the injured person, plus all expenses reasonably incurred in obtaining from others ordinary and necessary services in lieu of those that, but for the injury, the injured person would have performed without income for the benefit of his household. All disability benefits payable under this provision shall be paid not less than every two weeks.

(c) Funeral, burial or cremation benefits: funeral, burial or cremation expenses in an amount not to exceed one thousand dollars ($1,000) per individual.

(2) Any insurer may exclude benefits:

(a) For injury sustained by the named insured and relatives residing in the same household while occupying another motor vehicle owned by the named insured under the policy, or for injury sustained by any person operating the insured motor vehicle without the express or implied consent of the insured.

(b)   To any injured person, if such person's conduct contributed to his injury under any of the following circumstances:

      1.   Causing injury to himself intentionally;

      2.   Convicted of driving while under the influence of alcohol or narcotic drugs to the extent that his driving faculties are impaired;

      3.   While committing a felony.

  (3)   Insurer's rights of reimbursement and indemnity:

    (a)   No subtraction from personal protection insurance benefits will be made because of the value of a claim in tort based on the same bodily injury, but after recovery is realized upon such a tort claim, a subtraction will be made to the extent of the recovery, exclusive of reasonable attorneys fees and other reasonable expenses incurred in effecting the recovery, but only to the extent that the injured person has recovered said benefits from the tortfeasor or his insurer or insurers. If personal protection insurance benefits have already been received, the claimant shall repay to the insurer or insurers out of the recovery a sum equal to the benefits received, but not more than the recovery exclusive of reasonable attorneys' fees and other reasonable expenses incurred in effecting the recovery, but only to the extent that the injured person has recovered said benefits from the tortfeasor or his insurers or insurer. The insurer or insurers shall have a lien on the recovery to this extent. No recovery by an injured person or his estate for loss suffered by him will be subtracted in calculating benefits due a dependent after the death, and no recovery by a dependent for loss suffered by the dependent after the death will be subtracted in calculating benefits due the injured person except as provided in paragraph (c) of subsection (1) of section 7.

    (b)   The insurer shall be entitled to reimbursement of any payments made under the provisions of subsection (3) of this section based upon such equitable distribution of the amount recovered as the court may determine less the pro rata share of all court costs expended by the plaintiff in the prosecution of the suit to recover such amount against a third-party tortfeasor including a reasonable attorney's fee for the plaintiff's attorney. The proration of the reimbursement shall be made by the judge of a trial court handling the suit to recover damages in the third-party action against the tortfeasor upon application therefor and notice to the carrier.

    (c)   Indemnity from one paying in tort without regard for rights of insurer having reimbursement interest — A personal protection insurer with a right of reimbursement under this section, if suffering loss from inability to collect such reimbursement out of a payment received by a claimant upon a tort claim is entitled to indemnity from one who, with notice of the insurer's interest, made such a payment to the claimant without making the claimant and the insurer joint payees as their interests may appear, or without obtaining the insurer's consent to a different method of payment.

    (d)   In the event an injured party or his legal representative is entitled to bring suit against a third party tortfeasor under the provisions of section 8, and fails to bring such suit against such third party tortfeasor within one year after the last payment of any benefits under subsection (1) of section 7, the insurer of such injured party, upon giving thirty (30) days written notice to such injured party, shall have the right to bring suit against such third party, in its own name or in the name of the injured person or his legal representative, to recover the amount of the benefits paid pursuant to the provisions of section 7 of this act to or for the benefit of such injured person; provided, however, that the prosecution or settlement of such suit without the consent of the injured person or his legal representative shall be without prejudice to such person.

(4)   Benefits due from an insurer under this act shall be primary, except that benefits received under any workmen's compensation law shall be credited against the benefits provided by subsection (1) of section 7, and be due and payable as loss accrues, upon receipt of reasonable proof of such loss and the amount of expenses and loss incurred which are covered by the policy issued under this act.

(a)   An insurer may require written notice to be given as soon as practicable after an accident involving a motor vehicle with respect to which the policy affords the security required by this act.

(b)   Personal injury protection insurance benefits shall be overdue if not paid within thirty (30) days after the insurer is furnished written notice of the fact of a covered loss and of the amount of same. If such written notice is not furnished to the insurer as to the entire claim, any partial amount supported by written notice is overdue if not paid within thirty (30) days after such written notice is furnished to the insurer. Any part of all of the remainder of the claim that is subsequently supported by written notice is overdue if not paid within thirty (30) days after such written notice is furnished to the insurer; provided, however, that any payment shall not be deemed overdue where the insurer has reasonable proof to establish that the insurer is not responsible for the payment, notwithstanding that written notice has been furnished to the insurer. For the purpose of calculating the extent to which any benefits are overdue, payment shall be treated as being made on the date a draft or other valid instrument which is equivalent to payment was placed in the United States mail in a properly addressed, postpaid envelope, or, if not so posted, on the date of delivery.

(c)   All overdue payments shall bear simple interest at the rate of ten percent (10%) per annum.

(d)   The insurer of the owner of a motor vehicle shall pay personal injury protection benefits for:

1.   Accidental bodily injury sustained in this state by the owner while occupying a motor vehicle, or while not an occupant of a motor vehicle or motorcycle if the injury is caused by physical contact with a motor vehicle.

2.   Accidental bodily injury sustained outside this state but within the United States of America, its territories or possessions or Canada by the owner while occupying the owner's motor vehicle.

3.   Accidental bodily injury sustained by a relative of the owner residing in the same household, under the circumstances described in subparagraph 1 or 2 of this paragraph (d), provided the relative at the time of the accident is domiciled in the owner's household and is not himself the owner of a motor vehicle with respect to which security is required under this act.

4.   Accidental bodily injury sustained in this state by any other person while occupying the owner's motor vehicle or, if a resident of this state, while not an occupant of a motor vehicle or motorcycle, if the injury is caused by physical contact with such motor vehicle, provided the injured person is not himself:

a.   The owner of a motor vehicle with respect to which security is required under this act, or

b.   Entitled to personal injury benefits from the insurer of the owner of such a motor vehicle.

(e)   If two or more insurers are liable to pay personal injury protection benefits for the same injury to any one person the maximum payable shall be as specified in subsection (1) of section 7, and any insurer paying the benefits shall be entitled to recover from each of the other insurers an equitable pro rata share of the benefits paid and expenses incurred in processing the claim.

(5)   Charges for treatment of injured persons — Any physician, hospital, clinic, or other person or institution lawfully rendering treatment to an injured person for a bodily injury covered by personal injury protection insurance may charge only a reasonable amount for the products, services, and accommodations rendered. In no event, however, may such a charge be in excess of the amount the person or institution customarily charges for like products, services, and accommodations in cases involving no insurance.

(6)   Discovery of facts about an injured person; disputes —

(a)   Every employer shall, if a request is made by an insurer providing personal injury protection benefits under this act against whom a claim has been made, furnish forthwith, in a form approved by the department of insurance, a sworn statement of the earnings since the time of the bodily injury and for a reasonable period before the injury, of the person upon whose injury the claim is based.

(b)   Every physician, hospital, clinic, or other medical institution providing, before or after bodily injury upon which a claim for personal injury protection insurance benefits is based, any products, services, or accommodations in relation to that or any other injury, or in relation to a condition claimed to be connected with that or any other injury, shall, if requested to do so by the insurer against whom the claim has been made, furnish forthwith a written report of the history, condition, treatment, and dates and costs of such treatment of the injured person, and produce forthwith and permit the inspection and copying of his or its records regarding such history, condition, treatment, and dates and costs of treatment. The person requesting such records shall pay all reasonable costs connected therewith.

(c) In the event of any dispute regarding an insurer's right to discovery of facts about an injured person's earnings or about his history, condition, treatment, and dates and costs of such treatment, the insurer may petition a court of competent jurisdiction to enter an order permitting such discovery. The order may be made only on motion for good cause shown and upon notice to all persons having an interest, and it shall specify the time, place, manner, conditions, and scope of the discovery. Such court may, in order to protect against annoyance, embarrassment, or oppression, as justice requires, enter an order refusing discovery or specifying conditions of discovery and may order payments of costs and expenses of the proceeding, including reasonable fees for the appearance of attorneys at the proceedings, as justice requires.

(d) The injured person shall be furnished upon demand a copy of all information obtained by the insurer under the provisions of this section, and shall pay a reasonable charge, if required by the insurer.

(7) Mental and physical examination of injured person; reports —

(a) Whenever the mental or physical condition of an injured person covered by personal injury protection is material to any claim that has been or may be made for past or future personal injury protection insurance benefits, such person shall, upon request of an insurer, submit to mental or physical examination by a physician or physicians. The costs of any examinations requested by an insurer shall be borne entirely by the insurer. Such examination shall be conducted within the city of residence of the insured. If there is no qualified physician to conduct the examination within the city of residence of the insured, then such examination shall be conducted in an area of the closest proximity to the insured's residence. Personal protection insurers are authorized to include reasonable provisions in personal injury protection insurance policies for mental and physical examination of those claiming personal injury protection insurance benefits.

(b) If requested by the person examined, a party causing an examination to be made shall deliver to him a copy of every written report concerning the examination rendered by an examining physician, at least one of which reports must set out his findings and conclusions in detail. After such request and delivery, the party causing the examination to be made is entitled upon request to receive from the person examined every written report available to him (or his representative) concerning any examination, previously or thereafter made, of the same mental or physical condition. By requesting and obtaining a report of the examination so ordered or by taking the deposition of the examiner, the person examined waives any privilege he may have, in relation to the claim for benefits, regarding the testimony of every other person who has examined or may thereafter examine him in respect of the same mental or physical condition.

(8) With respect to any dispute under the provisions of this act between the insured and the insurer, the provisions of section 627.0127, Florida Statutes, shall apply.

SECTION 8. Tort exemption; limitation on right to damages —

(1) Every owner, registrant, operator or occupant of a motor vehicle with respect to which security has been provided as required by this act, and every person or organization legally responsible for his acts or omissions, is hereby exempted from tort liability for damages because of bodily injury, sickness or disease arising out of the ownership, operations, maintenance or use of such motor vehicle in this state to the extent that the benefits described in subsection (1) of section 7 are payable for such injury, or would be payable but for any exclusion or deductible authorized by this act, under any insurance policy or other method of security complying with the requirements of section 4, or by an owner personally liable under section 4 for the payment of such benefits, unless a person is entitled to maintain an action for pain, suffering, mental anguish and inconvenience for such injury under the provisions of subsection (2) of this section.

(2) In any action of tort brought against the owner, registrant, operator or occupant of a motor vehicle with respect to which security has been provided as required by this act, or against any person or organization legally responsible for his acts or omissions, a plaintiff may recover damages in tort for pain, suffering, mental anguish and inconvenience because of bodily injury, sickness or disease arising out of the ownership, maintenance, operation or use of such motor vehicle only in the event that the benefits which are payable for such injury under paragraph (a) of subsection (1) of section 7 or which would be payable but for any exclusion or deductible authorized by this act exceed one thousand dollars ($1,000), or the injury or disease consists in whole or in part of permanent disfigurement, a fracture to a weight-bearing bone, a compound, comminuted, displaced or compressed fracture, loss of a body member, permanent injury within reasonable medical probability, permanent loss of a bodily function, or death. Any person who is entitled to receive free medical and surgical benefits shall be deemed in compliance with the requirements of this subsection upon a showing that the medical treatment received has an equivalent value of at least one thousand dollars ($1,000). Any person receiving ordinary and necessary services normally performed by a nurse from a relative or a member of his household shall be entitled to include the reasonable value of such services in meeting the requirements of this subsection.

SECTION 9.

(1)   The owner of a motor vehicle as defined in section 3 is not required to maintain security with respect to property damage to his motor vehicle, but may elect to purchase either full or basic coverage for accidental property damage to his motor vehicle.

(2)   Every insurer providing security under this act shall offer the owner either full or basic coverage for accidental property damage to the insured motor vehicle as follows:

(a)   Full coverage shall provide insurance without regard to fault for accidents occurring within the United States of America, its territories or possessions or Canada.

(b)   Basic coverage shall be limited to insurance against damage caused by the fault of another resulting from contact between the insured vehicle and a vehicle with respect to which security is required under this act.

(3)   The insurer may include within the terms and conditions applicable to full or basic coverage such other provisions as it customarily applies to collision coverage for private passenger automobiles in other states, including deductibles without limitation.

(4)   Every owner, registrant, operator or occupant of a motor vehicle with respect to which security has been provided as required by this act, and every other person or organization legally responsible for the acts or omissions of such an owner, registrant, operator or occupant, is hereby exempted from tort liability for damages because of accidental property damage to motor vehicles arising out of the ownership, operation, maintenance or use of such motor vehicle in this state, provided that a person shall not be exempt from such liability if he was operating the motor vehicle without the express or implied consent of its owner or an insured under the owner's policy or if his willful and wanton misconduct was the proximate cause of the accident. This exemption applies only with respect to property damage to motor vehicles subject to this act but shall not be applicable as to a motor vehicle damaging a parked vehicle.

(5)   Notwithstanding paragraph (4) above, an owner who has elected not to purchase insurance with respect to property damage to his motor vehicle may maintain an action of tort therefor against the owner, registrant, operator or occupant of a motor vehicle causing such damage if such damage exceeds five hundred and fifty dollars ($550), and the insurer of an owner who has elected to purchase full or basic collision coverage for his motor vehicle shall have the right, if the damage to such motor vehicle exceeds the above amount, to recover the amount of the benefits it has paid and, in behalf of its insured, any deductible amount from the insurer of the owner, registrant, operator or occupant of a motor vehicle causing such damage. The issues of liability in such a case and the amount of recovery shall be decided on the basis of tort law, and shall be determined by agreement between the insurers involved, or if they fail to agree by arbitration.

SECTION 10. Each insurer providing security as required by this act to any owner shall, at the election of the owner, issue a policy endorsement, approved as to content by the department of insurance and subject to such other reasonable regulations regarding said endorsement as the department may make after appropriate hearing, which endorsement shall provide that there shall be deducted from personal protection benefits that would otherwise be or become due to the policyholder alone or to the policyholder and relatives residing in his household, an amount of either two hundred and fifty dollars ($250), five hundred dollars ($500) or one thousand dollars ($1,000), again as the policyholder elects, said amount to be deducted from the amounts otherwise due each person subject to the deduction. Any person electing such an endorsement or subject to such an endorsement as a result of the policyholder's election shall have no right to claim or to recover any amount so deducted from any owner, registrant, operator or occupant of a motor vehicle or any person or organization legally responsible for any such person's acts or omissions who is made exempt from tort liability by this act.

SECTION 11. Notwithstanding any other provision of this act, the rights of residents of this state to claim damages in tort shall not be diminished when such residents are involved in motor vehicle accidents with persons not required to provide security under this act.

SECTION 12. Implementation of this act —
(1) The department of insurance shall adopt rules and regulations necessary to implement the provisions of this act.
(2) Notwithstanding any other provision of law, all insurers issuing insurance coverage under this act shall comply with the following provisions:
(a) Within sixty (60) days after the effective date of this act, each insurer shall file its proposed manual, rules, rates and rating plans with the department for approval. Rates for required financial responsibility coverage after the effective date of sections 1 through 11 of this act shall be reduced by each insurer by not less than fifteen percent (15%), calculated as a percentage of the combined required financial responsibility rate of such insurer in effect on June 7, 1971, or of the combined required financial responsibility rate of such insurer approved by the comissioner and in effect at the time of the filing of the new rates required herein. There shall be no exception to the requirements of this provision, unless the department shall find that the use of the rates required herein by any insurer will result in rates which are inadequate under Section 627.082, Florida Statutes, to the extent that such rates jeopardize the solvency, as defined in section 631.011, Florida Statutes, of the insurer required to use such rates. Notwithstanding the provisions of Chapter 71-3(B), Laws 1971, no rate for the insurance required by this act shall be increased prior to January 1, 1973, unless the insurer proposing such rate increase shall show that the rates required herein

are inadequate as defined in Section 627.082, Florida Statutes.

(b)   Within sixty (60) days from the date of filing by such insurer, the department may approve or disapprove the filing. If no action is taken by the department within sixty (60) days, the filing shall be deemed approved.

(c)   If the department approves the filing or the filing otherwise becomes effective, the manual, rules, rates and rating plans shall take effect upon the effective date of sections 1 through 11 of this act. If the department disapproves the filing, the insurer shall revert to a rate level for required coverage which shall be lower, by not less than fifteen percent (15%), than the combined premiums for required financial responsibility coverage at the time such proposed new rates were filed.

(d)   Upon complying with this subsection, any insurer appealing an order of disapproval may use the rates set forth in the disapproved filing during the pendency of the appeal, so long as such rates do not exceed its rates for required financial responsibility coverage at the time of its rate filing required herein. As a condition to the use of such disapproved rates, the insurer must enter into a legally binding agreement with the department to secure the repayment to the insurer's policyholders of the difference between the insurer's proposed rate and that rate which would be lower, by not less than fifteen percent (15%), than the combined premiums for required financial responsibility coverage at the time such proposed new rates were filed. In addition to the repayment of the difference in premium, the company shall agree to pay to the insured the legal rate of interest on any money refunded.

(e)   Any private passenger automobile liability policy in force on January 1, 1972 and thereafter, shall reflect by endorsement any reduction in rates for the required coverage under this act as filed by the insurer and such reduction shall be computed on a pro rata basis for the remaining term of said policy. Such endorsement may be issued at the renewal date of the policy or the termination of the policy. Any return premium shall be credited to the renewal policy or if the policy is terminated the return premium shall be refunded to the insured.

(f)   For the purposes of the implementation of this act, rating organizations as defined in chapter 627 shall be permitted until January 1, 1973, to develop and furnish rates and forms to their members or subscribers. Provided, however, that members and subscribers of rating organizations shall not participate in the decisions or deliberations of such organizations in the development of such rates under this act.

SECTION 13.   If any provision of this act, or the application thereof to any person or circumstances is held invalid, such invalidity shall not affect other provisions or applications of this act which can be given effect without the invalid provision or application. To this end the provisions of this act are declared to be severable.

SECTION 14. This act shall become effective July 1, 1971; provided, however, the provisions of sections 1 through 11 of this act shall not become effective until January 1, 1972, and shall not apply to accidents or injuries occurring before said date.

APPENDIX D

THE ILLINOIS LAW

APPENDIX D
THE ILLINOIS LAW

SYNOPSIS:

Adds Article to Illinois Insurance Code providing new requirements for compensation of automobile accident victims. Requires mandatory first party coverages and benefits which will compensate accident victims regardless of fault. Provides for optional excess coverages. Permits certain illegal acts to be excluded from coverage. Provides for periodic payments to be made every 30 days to a person entitled to benefits. Provides that payments made by an insurance company under this Article must offset and be deducted from any verdict or award for damages. Requires inter-company arbitration. Sets guidelines for recovery of damages for pain and suffering. Provides for the Supreme Court to set guidelines for the mandatory arbitration of small claims arising out of an automobile accident.

AN ACT TO ADD ARTICLE XXXV TO THE "ILLINOIS INSURANCE CODE", APPROVED JUNE 29, 1937, AS AMENDED, AND TO REPEAL SECTION 143a OF SAID CODE.

Be It Enacted by the People of the State of Illinois, Represented in the General Assembly:

SECTION 1. Article XXXV is added to the "Illinois Insurance Code", approved June 29, 1937, as amended, the added Article to read as follows:

ARTICLE XXXV.
COMPENSATION OF AUTOMOBILE ACCIDENT VICTIMS

Sec. 600. Mandatory Extension of First Party Coverages and Benefits.

(a)   On and after the effective date of this Article every policy delivered or issued for delivery in this State insuring against loss resulting from liability imposed by law for accidental bodily injury or death suffered by any person arising out of the ownership, maintenance or use of any private passenger automobile registered or principally garaged in this State and insuring 5 or less private passenger automobiles, must provide coverage affording payment of the following minimum benefits to the named insured and members of his family residing in his household when injured in any motor vehicle accident, and to other persons injured while occupying such insured automobile as guest passengers or while using it with the permission of the named insured, and to pedestrians struck by the automobile in accidents occurring within this State:

(1)   Medical, Hospital and Funeral Benefits: Payment of all reasonable and necessary expenses arising from the accident for medical, surgical, x-ray, dental, prosthetic, ambulance, hospital, professional nursing and funeral services and incurred within one year from the date thereof, subject to a limit of $2,000 per person.

(2)   Income Continuation Benefits: Payment of 85% of the income, including but not limited to salary, wages, tips, commissions, fees or other earnings, lost by an income or wage-earner as a result of total disability arising from the accident, subject to a limit of $150 per week for 52 weeks per person.

(3)   Loss of Services Benefits: Where the person injured in the accident was not an income or wage producer at the time of the accident, payments of benefits must be made in reimbursement of necessary and reasonable expenses incurred for essential services ordinarily performed by the injured person for care and maintenance of the family or family household subject to a limit of $12 per day for 365 days per person injured.

(b)   Every company subject to the provisions of paragraph (a) of this Section must also offer, at the option of rejection by the person named in the policy as insured, coverage affording payment of the following minimum excess loss benefits to the named insured and members of his family residing in his household, upon depletion of the medical, income continuation and loss of services benefits provided by the company in the same policy and subject to a total minimum aggregate limit of not less than $50,000 per person and not less than $100,000 per accident:

(1)   Medical, Hospital and Funeral Benefits: Payment of reasonable and necessary expenses arising from the accident for medical, surgical, x-ray, dental, prosthetic, ambulance, hospital, professional nursing and funeral services. However, the benefits payable for funeral services may not exceed $2,000.

(2)   Income Continuation Benefits: Payment of 85% of the income, including but not limited to salary, wages, tips, commissions, fees or other earnings, lost by an income or wage-earner as a result of total disability arising from the accident, subject to a limit of $150 per week for a period of 260 weeks per person.

(3)   Loss of Services Benefits: Where the person injured in the accident was not an income or wage producer at the time of the accident, payments of benefits must be made in reimbursement of necessary and reasonable expenses incurred for essential services ordinarily performed by the injured person for care and maintenance of the family or family household subject to a limit of $12 per day for 260 weeks per person injured.

(4)   Survivor's Benefits: In the event the injured person dies within one year of the date of the accident, a survivor's benefit equal to 85% of the average weekly income the deceased earned during the 52-week period immediately preceding the accident, subject to a limit of $150 per week for a period of 260 weeks, must be paid to a surviving spouse dependent upon the deceased for income, or, in the event there is no surviving spouse, to the surviving children dependent upon the deceased for income. Payments to a dependent surviving spouse may be terminated in the event such surviving spouse dies leaving no surviving dependent children or remarries. Payments to a dependent child may be terminated in the event the child attains majority, marries or becomes otherwise emancipated or dies.

(c)   As used in this Section, the term "private passenger automobile" means a sedan, station wagon or jeep-type automobile not used as a public livery conveyance for passengers, nor rented to others, and includes any other 4 wheel motor vehicle used as a utility automobile, pickup truck, sedan delivery truck or panel truck with a load capacity of 1,500 pounds or less which is not used primarily in the occupation, profession or business of the insured.

(d)   The benefits set forth in this Section must be paid by the company insuring the vehicle to the injured person except:

(1)   Where any person insured under a policy providing such benefits is injured in an automobile accident while occupying or being struck by an automobile not insured for such benefits under another policy, the benefits are payable by the company affording the benefits. However, such benefits may be reduced to the extent of any similar automobile medical, income continuation, loss of services or survivor's benefits coverage available to the injured person under such other automobile policy.

(2)   No person may recover benefits under the coverages prescribed in this Section from more than one policy or company on either a duplicative or supplemental basis.

(e)   The benefits set forth in this Section must be paid regardless of collateral sources, including but not limited to the existence of any wage continuation benefits except:

(1)   Such benefits do not apply to any direct or indirect loss or interest of, or for services or benefits provided or furnished by, the United States of America or any of its agencies coincident to a contract of employment or of military enlistment, duty or service.

(2)   Such benefits must be reduced or eliminated if the injured person is entitled to benefits under any workmen's compensation act of any state or the Federal Government.

(f)   Whenever an insured purchases the excess coverage provided in paragraph (b) of this Section, such insured must be notified by the company of his right to reject the coverage provided for under Section 601 of this Code.

Sec. 601.   Uninsured or Hit-and-Run Motor Vehicle Coverage.

(a)   On and after the effective date of this Article, no policy insuring against loss resulting from liability imposed by law for bodily injury or death suffered by any person arising out of the ownership, maintenance or use of a motor vehicle may be renewed or delivered or issued for delivery in this State with respect to any motor vehicle registered or principally garaged in this State unless coverage is provided therein or supplemental thereto, in limits for bodily injury or death set forth in Section 7-203 of "The Illinois Vehicle Code" for the protection of persons insured thereunder who are legally entitled to recover damages from owners or operators of uninsured motor vehicles and hit-and-run motor vehicles because of bodily injury, sickness or disease, including death, resulting therefrom, except that the named insured has the right to reject such coverage whenever the named insured purchases the excess loss coverage prescribed in Section 600 of this Article.

(b)   For the purpose of this coverage the term "uninsured motor vehicle" includes, subject to the terms and conditions of such coverage, a motor vehicle where on, prior to or after the accident date the liability company thereof is unable to make payment with respect to the legal liability of its insured within the limits specified in the policy because of the entry by a court of competent jurisdiction of an order of rehabilitation or liquidation by reason of insolvency on or after the accident date. A company's extension of coverage, as provided in this paragraph, is applicable to all accidents occuring after the effective date of this Article during a policy period in which its insured's uninsured motor vehicle coverage is in effect. Nothing in this Section may be construed to prevent any company from extending coverage under terms and conditions more favorable to its insureds than is required hereunder.

Sec. 602. Exclusions Permitted.

(a)   The company may exclude benefits to any injured person covered under a policy, where such person's conduct contributed to the injury in any of the following ways:

(1)   Intentionally causing injury to himself;

(2)   While under the influence of intoxicating liquor or narcotic drugs;

(3)   Operating a motor vehicle without a license or after suspension or revocation of a license;

(4)   Operating a motor vehicle upon a bet or wager or in a race;

(5)   While seeking to elude lawful apprehension or arrest by a police officer;

(6)   While operating or riding in a vehicle known to him to be stolen;

(7)   While in the commission of a felony.

(b)   The company may provide such other exclusions as may be approved by the Director of Insurance as consistent with public policy.

Sec. 603. Prompt Payment of Benefits.

(a)   Payment of the benefits set forth under Section 600 of this Article must be made promptly after valid proof of loss has been submitted to the company. The existence of a potential cause of action in tort by any recipient of the benefits prescribed in this Article does not obviate the company's obligation to promptly pay such benefits. However, if prior to timely payment by the company of such benefits, payment in whole or in part of his loss is received by the recipient from a third person who is or may be liable in tort for such loss, or from the agent or company of such third person, either by way of advance payment or settlement of the potential liability of such third person, the recipient must disclose such fact, and may not collect benefits hereunder to the extent that such benefits would produce a duplication of payment or reimbursement of the same loss. In the event of any duplication of payment or reimbursement of the same loss, and to the extent of the amount involved, the company may deduct that amount from any present or future benefits to which the recipient is or may be entitled, in addition to such other remedies as exists for recovery at law.

(b) Payments under the coverages provided under Section 600 of this Article must be made periodically on a monthly basis as expenses are incurred. Benefits for any period are overdue if not paid within 30 days after the company has received reasonable proof of the fact and amount of expenses incurred during that period. If reasonable proof is not supplied as to the entire claim the amount supported by reasonable proof is overdue if not paid within 30 days after such proof is received by the company. Any part or all of the remainder of the claim that is later supported by reasonable proof is overdue if not paid within 30 days after such proof is received by the company. In the event the company fails to pay such benefits when due, the person entitled to such benefits may bring an action in contract to recover them. In the event the company is required by such action to pay any overdue benefits, the company must, in addition to the benefits received, be required to pay the reasonable attorney's fees incurred by the other party. In the event of a wilful refusal of the company to pay such benefits, the company must pay to the other party, in addition to other amounts due the other party, an amount which is three times the amount of unpaid benefits in controversy in the action.

Sec. 604. Offset. If any person receiving or entitled to receive benefits under this Article files an action for damages for bodily injury, sickness, disease or death arising out of the same automobile accident in any court in this State, such benefits must be disclosed to the court, or in the event of arbitration of such action, to the arbitrators, and the value of such benefits must be deducted from any award recovered by such person in such proceeding prior to the entry of a verdict or award and may not be considered a part of the verdict, award or recovery obtained by such person.

Sec. 605. Subrogation and Inter-Company Arbitration.

(a) Except as otherwise provided in this Section, where a company has paid benefits provided under this Article to an injured person, the company paying such benefits is, to the extent of such payments, subrogated to any right of action for damages by the injured person against the alleged wrongdoer.

(b) Every company licensed to write insurance in this State under Class 2 or Class 3 of Section 4 of this Code, is deemed to have agreed, as a condition of doing business in this State or maintaining its license after the effective date of this Article, that (1) where its insured is or would be held legally liable for damages or injuries sustained by any person to whom the benefits provided in paragraph (a) of Section 600 of this Article have been paid by another company, it will reimburse such other company to the extent of such benefits, but not in excess of the amount of damages so recoverable for the types of loss covered by such benefits, or in excess of the limits of its liability under its policy; or (2) where its insured is or would be held legally liable for property damages or destruction sustained by any person to whom payment has been made by another company, it will reimburse such other company to the extent of such payment, but not in excess of the amount of damages so recoverable for the types of loss covered by such insurance or in excess of the limits of its liability under its policy; and (3) that the issue of liability for such reimbursement and the amount thereof must be decided by mandatory, binding inter-company arbitration procedures approved by the Director of Insurance.

(c) Any evidence or decision in the arbitration proceedings is privileged and is not admissible in any action at law or in equity by any party.

Sec. 606. Uninsured Motorists Coverage. All benefits provided under Section 600 of this Article may be deducted by the company from any recovery received by an injured person under Uninsured Motorists Coverage as defined by Section 601 of this Code.

Sec. 607. Advance Payments.

(a) In any claim or action in tort or contract brought against any person as a result of bodily injury, sickness, disease or death caused by accident and arising out of the operation, ownership, maintenance or use of a motor vehicle, the person or company against whom such a claim or suit for benefits or damages is made, or if such person is insured against loss by reason of his liability to pay such damages, the company of such person, may make or offer advance payments to such claimant, or plaintiff, as the case may be.

(b) For the purpose of this Section, the words "advance payment" include but are not limited to the following: Any partial payment, loan or settlement made by any person, corporation or insurer thereof, to another, which is predicated upon possible tort liability or under the contractual obligations of the company to the injured party or on his behalf, including but not limited to medical, surgical, hospital, rehabilitation services, facilities or equipment, loss of earnings, out-of-pocket expenses, death claims, loans, bodily injury or property damage, loss or destruction, and any offer thereof.

(c) This Section applies to any action commenced in this State, regardless of the situs of the accident, location of the property or residence of the parties.

(d) An advance payment does not interrupt the running of the Statute of Limitations. However, any person, including any company, who makes such advance payment, must at the time of the first payment, notify the recipient thereof in writing of the date the applicable Statute of Limitations will expire.

(e) In any action in which the defendant, his company or any other person has made or offered to make an advance payment to or on behalf of any claimant prior to trial, any evidence of or concerning that advance payment is not admissible in evidence or may not be construed as an admission of liability in any action brought by the claimant, his survivors or personal representative, to recover damages for personal injuries or for the wrongful death of another, or for property damage or destruction.

(f)   In the event that such action results in a verdict in favor of the claimant, the defendant must be allowed to introduce evidence of such payments after the verdict has been rendered and the court must then reduce the amount awarded to the claimant by the amount of payments made prior to trial.

(g)   No such payment made under this Section by a company may be construed to be in lieu of or in addition to the limits of liability of the company under any existing policy of insurance. Such sums paid in advance are considered to have been made under the limits of the policy and must be credited to the company's obligation to the insured arising from such policy and must be deducted therefrom.

Sec. 608. General Damages.

(a)   In any action in tort brought as a result of bodily injury, sickness, disease or death caused by accident and arising out of the operation, ownership, maintenance or use of a motor vehicle within this State, such damages as may be recoverable for pain, suffering, mental anguish and inconvenience may not exceed the total of a sum equal to 50 percent of the reasonable medical treatment expenses of the claimant if and to the extent that the total of such reasonable expenses is $500 or less, and a sum equal to the amount of such reasonable expenses if any, in excess of $500.

(b)   For the purpose of this Section medical treatment expenses mean the reasonable and necessary value of services rendered for medical, surgical, x-ray, dental, prosthetic, ambulance, hospital, professional nursing and funeral services.

(c)   The limitations prescribed in paragraph (a) of this Section do not apply in cases of death, dismemberment, permanent total or permanent partial disability and permanent serious disfigurement.

(d)   The court on its own motion or the motion of either party shall designate an impartial medical panel of not more than three licensed physicians, to examine the claimant and testify on the issue of the reasonable value of medical treatment services, or any other issue hereunder to which such expert medical testimony would be relevant.

Sec. 609. Mandatory Arbitration of Small Claims — $3,000.

(a)   In counties with a population of 200,000 or more inhabitants, the Supreme Court of this State shall, by Rules of Court, provide for the arbitration of all cases where the cause of action arose out of the operation, ownership, maintenance or use of a motor vehicle and where the amount in controversy may not exceed $3,000, exclusive of interest and costs.

(b)   In all other counties the Supreme Court of this State may, by Rules of Court, provide for the arbitration of all cases where the cause of action arose out of the operation, ownership, maintenance or use of a motor vehicle and where the amount in controversy may not exceed $3,000, exclusive of interest and costs.

(c)   The Court shall maintain a list of attorneys within its jurisdiction who have agreed in writing to serve as arbitrators, subject to the right of each attorney to refuse to serve in a particular assigned case and subject further to the right of any party to show good cause why an appointed arbitrator should not serve in a particular assigned case. The Court Rules shall provide that the case subject to arbitration must be assigned for hearing to a single arbitrator selected by the Court from the list of arbitrators in reasonable rotation. Any party to arbitration may, upon payment of the additional costs involved therein, request that the arbitration hearing be before a panel of 3 arbitrators selected in the manner as provided. Any such request must be filed, and the required payment made, at such time as the initial complaint or answer is filed with the Court.

(d)   Cases which are not at issue and whether or not suit has been filed may be referred to arbitration by agreement of reference signed by counsel for both sides in the case. The agreement of reference must define the issues involved for determination in the arbitration and may also contain stipulations with respect to agreed facts, issues or defense. In such cases, the agreement of reference must take the place of the pleadings in the case and be filed of record.

(e)   The Rules of the Court may provide for the taking of evidence in the form of reports, statements, intemized bills, or in any other manner without the procedural and evidentiary limitations which obtain in jury trials.

(f)   The arbitration award must be in writing, signed by the arbitrator or by a majority of the arbitrators, if it is heard by a panel of 3, and filed with the Court. The award must be entered by the Court in its record of judgments, and has the effect of a judgment upon the parties unless reversed upon appeal.

(g)   Except as otherwise provided in this Section, either party may appeal from an award of arbitration to the Court in which the case was pending under the following rules:

(1)   The party appellant, his agent or attorney, must make oath or affirmation that "it is not for the purpose of delay such appeal is entered, but because he firmly believes injustice has been done."

(2)   Such party, his agent or attorney must pay all costs that may have accrued in such suit or action.

(3)   Such appeal must be entered, and the costs paid, within 20 days after the day of the entry on the docket of the award of the arbitrator.

(4)   All appeals must be de novo both as to the law and the facts.

(5)   This paragraph is not applicable to those cases of arbitration heard under paragraph (d) of this Section.

(h)   All arbitrators have such power to administer oaths or affirmations, to issue and enforce subpoenas, and to conduct the hearings, as the Rules of Court provide.

(i)   This Section does not apply to arbitration agreements between companies, whether mandatory or voluntary.

Sec. 610. Fraudulent Claims.

(a)   In any claim or action arising out of the operation, ownership, maintenance or use of a motor vehicle, any person who directly or indirectly (1) obtains or attempts to obtain, from any other person or any insurance company in this State, either as a policyholder or a claimant, any money or other thing of value by falsely or fraudulently representing that such person is injured or has sustained an injury or damage to property, for which money may be paid by way of compensation for medical expenses incurred, wage loss sustained, or damages determined to be due as pain, suffering, inconvenience or damages of the same or similar nature or damages to such property, or (2) makes any statement, produces any document or writing or in any other way presents evidence for the purpose of falsely and fraudulently representing any injury or damage to property or exaggerating the nature and extent of such injury or damage, or (3) cooperates, conspires or otherwise acts in concert with persons seeking to falsely and fraudulently represent an injury or damage to property or exaggerate the nature and extent of such injury or damage to property, may, upon conviction, if the sum so obtained or attempted to be obtained is less than $100, be fined not more than $500 or imprisoned in a penal institution other than the penitentiary for not more than one year, or both. If such sum so obtained or attempted to be obtained is $100 or more, such person may, upon conviction, be fined not less than an amount equal to 3 times the sum or sums so obtained or attempted to be obtained or imprisoned for not more than 10 years, or both.

(b)   In those cases where, upon conviction under this Section for obtaining or attempting to obtain a sum of $100 or more, the person so convicted participated in the obtaining or attempt to obtain the sum or sums involved under authority of any license or licenses issued by any unit of State or local government acting pursuant to the Constitution of the State of Illinois, the court must further order the immediate temporary suspension of the license or licenses involved and issued and must mandate an immediate inquiry by the body or bodies charged with the responsibility and duty of issuing or supervising the licenses to determine whether the licenses should be permanently suspended or revoked.

Sec. 611. Medical Disclosure. Any person who claims damages for personal injuries arising out of the operation, maintenance or use of a motor vehicle from another person or benefits therefor under an insurance policy must upon request of the defendant or company from whom recovery is sought, submit to physical examination by a physician or physicians selected by the defendant or company as may reasonably be required and must do all things reasonably necessary to enable the defendant or company to obtain medical reports and other needed information to assist in determining the nature and extent of the claimant's injuries and the medical treatment received by him. If the claimant refuses to cooperate in responding to requests for examination and information as authorized by this Section, evidence relevant to such noncooperation is admissible in any suit or arbitration proceeding filed by the claimant for damages for such personal injuries or for benefits under any insurance policy.

Sec. 612. Authority of the Director of Insurance. The Director of Insurance has the authority to issue and promulgate all rules, regulations and definitions necessary to implement the provisions of Sections 600 trhough 603, 605, 606, 607, and 611 of this Article.. He also has the authority to approve schedules of reasonable maximum benefit payments for specified medical services which companies may incorporate into their policies of basic mandatory or optional excess coverages herein prescribed.

Sec. 613. Severability. If any provision of this Article or the application thereof to any person or circumstance is held invalid, such invalidity does not affect other provisions or applications of this Article which can be given effect without the invalid application or provision, and to this end the provisions of this Article are declared to be severable. However, Section 608, or any part thereof, of this Article is expressly made inseverable.

SECTION 2. Section 143a of the "Illinois Insurance Code", approved June 29, 1937, as amended, is repealed.

SECTION 3. This Amendatory Act of 1971 becomes effective January 1, 1972.

APPENDIX E

EXISTING AND PROPOSED AUTO INSURANCE SYSTEMS

APPENDIX E
EXISTING AND PROPOSED AUTO INSURANCE SYSTEMS

PLAN	STATUS	KIND OF SYSTEM	TYPE OF COVERAGE	BENEFITS UNDER BASIC PLAN — Medical, Funeral
Tort Liability	Existing system in all 50 states.	Third-party fault system, with added first-party accident benefit coverages under insurance.	Personal **Injury**. Damage to Property.	No statutory limits.
Keeton-O'Connell	Proposed.	First-party benefits under insurance. No fault on basic coverage. Tort liability above plan benefits.	Personal Injury. Damage to Property.	Up to $10,000 (including other economic loss).
Complete Personal Protection	Proposed by American Insurance Association.	First-party no-fault system.	Personal Injury. Damage to Property (auto optional).	Medical unlimited. Funeral, $1,000.
Uniform Motor Vehicle Insurance Act	Introduced in U.S. Senate Sept. 14, 1970, by Sen. Philip A. Hart (D-Mich.). Re-introduced on February 24, 1971.	First-party no-fault. Provides for tort liability in catastrophic injury cases and, in death cases, when amounts are in excess of reimbursed economic loss.	Personal Injuries, including death.	Unlimited as to reasonable and necessary medical hospital and rehabilitation costs and incidental expenses.
New York State Insurance Department Plan	Subject to Legislative Committee hearings. Probable introduction next session.	Combines elements of first-party no-fault and strict liability. Compulsory system. Retains tort action in death cases.	Personal Injury. Damage to Non-Automotive Property (auto optional).	No statutory limits, Medical-hospital and rehabilitation not compensated from other sources.
Cotter Plan	Proposed in Connecticut by former Insurance Commissioner William R. Cotter.	Third-party fault; mandatory first-party medical and disability coverages. Mandatory arbitration of small claims (under $3,000).	Personal Injury. Damage to Property.	Up to $2,000 aggregate limit on first-party medical. Third-party recovery same as tort liability.
Massachusetts "Compulsory Personal Injury Protection"	Enacted in 1970, effective January 1, 1971.	Limited first-party no-fault. Optional deductibles of $250, $500, $1,000 or $2,000 on no-fault benefits. Compulsory program.	Personal Injury.	Up to $2,000 medical and hospital expenses.
Saskatchewan	In effect since 1946 in province of Saskatchewan, Canada. Proposed in Manitoba.	First-party no-fault, plus liability coverage and right to sue over basic coverage.	Personal Injury. Damage to Property.	Medical up to $2,000. Permanent impairment, $4,000. Funeral, $3,000.
Puerto Rico	In effect.	First-party no-fault system, Government administered. Tort liability above plan benefits.	Personal Injury.	Unlimited services in Government hospitals. Funeral, $500.
British Columbia "Enriched Accident Benefits"	In effect.	Personal injury accident benefits under fixed schedule with option to sue third party. Does not apply to property damage. System is compulsory	Personal Injury. Full third-party liability for property damage. (Minimum policy limits of $50,000 mandatory.)	Scheduled, including $5,000 death benefit for loss of household head, plus $1,000 for each surviving dependent. Weekly payment scale to surviving spouse. Medical and rehabilitation as accrued. Funeral, $5,000.
Canadian "Accident Benefits Plan"	In effect in 8 provinces.	Limited accident benefits, optional additional third-party liability policy. Voluntary program.	Personal Injury. Does not apply to property.	Up to $5,000 for death, dismemberment or loss of sight, plus $1,000 for each surviving dependent. Medical as accrued; funeral expenses up to amount subscribed by the assured.

BENEFITS UNDER BASIC PLAN

Other Economic Loss	Pain and Suffering	How Payable	Maximum Payment
No statotory limits.	No statutory limits.	Lump sum, except for voluntary advance payments by insurers.	No statutory limits (except death benefits limited in some states).
Up to $10,000 (including medical, etc.).	None. Policyholder may sue for claims over $5,000.	Monthly as accrued.	$10,000 per person, $100,000 per accident.
Unlimited, except wage loss limited to $750 per month.	None	As accrued.	Unlimited.
85% of wage loss or $1,000 up to 30 months; maximum death benefit $30,000.	Recoverable where tort action is provided for.	As accrued.	Unlimited.
Unlimited net income less compensation.	None	As accrued.	Unlimited.
Up to 52 weeks disability benefits on first-party basis, $500 per month maximum. Third-party recovery same as tort liability.	50% of medical expenses up to $500, 100% of medical expenses exceeding $500. Limitations not applicable for death, dismemberment, or where "unconscionable."	As accrued in first-party claims; lump sum in third-party cases.	No statutory limits (except for pain and suffering as indicated). First-party benefits deducted from third-party settlement.
Up to 75% loss of wages and salary.	Barred unless hospital and medical expenses exceed $500, or in cases of death, dismemberment, loss of sight or hearing, serious disfigurement or fracture.	As accrued.	Limited schedules for no-fault benefits.
Schedule for disability, loss of wages, etc. $100,000 max. death benefit.	None under plan benefits. Policyholder can sue.	Weekly payments.	Limited to schedules. No statutory limit for third-party claims.
50% of salary up to $50 per week. Dismemberment, $5,000. Death, $5,000.	None. Policyholder may sue for claims over $1,000.	Weekly payments.	Limited to total of plan benefits. Policyholder may sue for economic loss over $2,000.
Weekly disability indemnity of $50 for up to 4 years. Payments then continue for life if injury is permanent. Rehabilitation benefits up to policy limits of $50,000;	No statutory limits. Dual recovery not permitted.	As accrued.	Limited benefits. No limit on third-party claims.
Up to $35 weekly disability for two years. Two additional years of disability payments if injury proves permanent.	No statutory limits. Dual recovery not permitted.	As accrued.	No maximum on benefits. Third-party liability claims up to policy limit.

PLAN	STATUS	KIND OF SYSTEM	TYPE OF COVERAGE	BENEFITS UNDER BASIC PLAN Medical, Funeral
Defense Research Institute "Responsible Reform Plan"	Proposed.	Retains tort liability; comparative negligence; mandatory arbitration of claims under $3,000 with right of appeal; regulation of contingent fees; admits evidence of collateral benefits.	Personal Injury. Damage to Property.	No statutory limits.
American Bar Association	Proposed	Retains tort liability and collateral source rule. Voluntary arbitration only.	Personal Injury. Damage to Property.	No statutory limits.
Guaranteed Benefits	Tested in parts of New York, Illinois, American Mutual Insurance Alliance.	Third-party fault system, with option to accept benefits or negotiate a liability settlement.	Personal Injury.	Up to $5,000.
Inverse Liability	Proposed	First-party benefits, with option of insured or insurer to sue third party.	Personal Injury.	Unlimited
Dual Protection	Proposed by National Association of Independent Insurers.	Limited first-party no-fault. Preserves right to tort action for damages in excess of policy limits. Provides for subrogation and arbitration in immediate pay cases involving at-fault third party.	Personal Injury.	Up to $2,000 per person for medical, hospital and funeral expenses. Excess limits coverage available as option.
Guaranteed Protection Plan	Proposed by American Mutual Insurance Alliance.	Insurance portion blends liability and no-fault coverages, regulates attorney fees, requires arbitration of claims under $3,000.	Personal Injury. Full third-party liability for property damage.	Mandatory $2,000 minimum for first-party medical. Higher limits optional. Tort action retained for full medical expenses.
Delaware	Enacted in 1971, effective January 1, 1972.	No-fault, with tort liability retained above plan benefits.	Personal injury and property damage, other than motor vehicle.	Medical up to $10,000, including $2,000 funeral. $20,000 limit each accident
Florida Automobile Reparations Reform Act	Enacted in 1971, effective January 1, 1972.	Limited no-fault. Optional deductibles of $250, $500, and $1,000 on first-party benefits. Prohibits property damage suits under $550. Compulsory program.	Personal injury.	Medical up to $5,000. Funeral, $1,000.
Illinois	Enacted in 1971, effective January 1, 1972.	Retains tort liability. Extends first-party coverage.	Personal injury.	$2,000 per person.

BENEFITS UNDER BASIC PLAN

Other Economic Loss	Pain and Suffering	How Payable	Maximum Payment
No statutory limits.	No statutory limits.	Lump sum, except for voluntary advanced payments by insurers. Advance payments legally not admission of liability and non-admissable as evidence to prove fault.	No statutory limits except as some states may limit recovery in death cases.
No statutory limits.	No statutory limits.	Lump sum, except for voluntary payments by insurers.	No statutory limits except as some states may limit recovery in death cases.
Up to $7,500 (together with pain and suffering).	Up to $7,500 (together with other economic loss).	As accrued for medical and basic disability. Lump sum for supplemental and final payments.	$12,500, but not more than limits of policy.
Unlimited.	Unlimited if policyholder sues third party, none under first party.	As accrued, except for final settlement.	Suggested policy limit, $100,000.
Up to $6,000 for wage loss; up to $4,380 for services otherwise performed by an injured non-wage earner. Excess limits coverage available as option.	For non-permanent injuries, up to 50% of medical and hospital expenses of $500 or less; up to 100% of medical and hospital expenses of more than $500. Right to sue preserved in serious injury, death or exceptional cases.	As accrued, subject to two-week waiting period for lost wages and reimbursement for services otherwise performed by an injured non-wage earner.	Limited schedules for no-fault benefits.
Mandatory $6,000 minimum for income loss. Up to $12 a day for non-wage earner. Both retain right to tort action for full economic losses.	Preserves right to tort action in cases of permanent disfigurement, dismemberment, permanent loss of a bodily function. In minor cases, limited to 50% of medical expense up to $500; 100% of medical expense exceeding $500.	As accrued for first-party benefits. Lump sum for liability benefits, subject to deduction of voluntary advance payments by insurers.	No statutory limits, except death benefits limited in some states, and as indicated for pain and suffering. First-party benefits deducted from third-party settlement.
Up to $10,000 (including medical, etc.).	None. Policyholder retains right to sue for claims.	As accrued.	$10,000 per person. $20,000 per accident. $5,000 for property damage.
100% of gross income or 85% if income is not subject to federal tax.	None. Suit barred unless medical expenses exceed $1,000, or in cases of death, permanent injury, disfigurement, loss of function, serious fractures.	As accrued.	Medical and related expenses to $5,000; suit for such expenses over $1,000, otherwise full tort right of recovery.
85% of income, limit of $150 per week for 52 weeks.	None. Tort action limited to 50% of reasonable medical expenses up to $500 and 100% over $500. Limitation is not applicable for death, dismemberment, permanent disability and disfigurement.	As accrued.	No limit, except for pain and suffering.

(Courtesy of Insurance Information Institute, "Existing and Proposed Auto Insurance Systems, Fall, 1970" and Addendum; modified and up-dated).

APPENDIX F

HOW CANADIAN AUTO INSURANCE PLANS COMPARE

APPENDIX F

HOW CANADIAN AUTO INSURANCE PLANS COMPARE*

Type of Insurance Coverage	Ontario (Present Plan)	Ontario Only (New Plan) January 1, 1972	British Columbia	Saskatchewan	Manitoba November 1, 1971
Automobile Accident Coverage	Optional	Mandatory**	Compulsory	Compulsory	Compulsory
Disability Income Benefits	$35.00 per week	80% of Wages Max. $70 weekly	Employed Person 80% Gross Wages Max. $50.00 weekly Min. $40.00 weekly	Employed Person $25.00 per week	Employed Person $50.00 per week
	104 weeks temporary + 104 weeks permanent	Lifetime	104 weeks temporary + lifetime — total and permanent	104 weeks total 104 weeks partial @12.50	Lifetime
	7-day waiting period	First day cover 1st 14 days	7-day waiting period	7-day waiting period	7-day waiting period
	Contributory	Non-contributory 1st 14 days	Contributory	Contributory	Contributory
	Housewife	Unpaid housekeeper	Housewife	Housewife	Housewife
	$12.50 per week Max. 12 weeks	$35.00 per week Max. 12 weeks	$50.00 per week Max. 26 weeks	$25.00 weekly — Total $12.50 weekly — Partial Max. 12 weeks	$25.00 weekly — Total $12.50 weekly — Partial Max. 12 weeks
				Hospitalized $12.50 for 52 weeks	

(ONTARIO PLAN ALSO EFFECTIVE IN NEW-FOUNDLAND, PRINCE EDWARD ISLAND, NOVA SCOTIA, NEW BRUNSWICK, QUEBEC AND ALBERTA)

* Courtesy of the Insurance Bureau of Canada, June 29, 1971.

** Mandatory with third-party liability coverage. Third-party liability coverage not compulsory but 97% of vehicles are insured.

APPENDIX F (Continued)

Type of Insurance Coverage	Ontario (Present Plan)	Ontario Only (New Plan) January 1, 1972	British Columbia	Saskatchewan	Manitoba November 1, 1971
Death Benefits	Various – but $5,000 usual Death within 3 months after accident Married Male Age limits: 10-59 - $5,000 60-69 - 3,000 70+ - 2,000 Plus $1,000 each dependent child No limit Married Female Age limit: 10-59 - $2,500 60-69 - 1,500 70+ - 1,000 Unmarried Person with living parents Scale by age Maximum $2,500	$5,000 Death within 2 years after accident Head of Household Age limits: none Plus $1,000 each dependent beyond first No limit Spouse No age limit: $2,500 Dependent Child Scale by age Maximum $1,000	$5,000 Death within 6 months after accident Head of Household Age limits: 10-64 - $5,000 65-69 - 3,000 70+ - 2,000 Plus $1,000 each dependent beyond first No limit Spouse Age limit: 10-64 - $2,500 65-69 - 1,500 70+ - 1,000 Dependent Child Scale by age Maximum $1,500	$5,000 Death within 2 years after accident Head of Household Age limits: none Plus $1,000 each secondary dependent To limit of 5 Spouse No age limit: $2,000 Equal division to surviving dependents Dependent Child Scale by age Maximum $1,000	$5,000 Death within 2 years after accident Head of Household Age limits: none Plus $1,000 each secondary dependent To limit of 5 Spouse No age limit: $2,000 Equal division to surviving dependents Dependent Child Scale by age Maximum $1,000
Dismemberment Benefits	Scheduled based on 1% of principal sum	Not included as schedule. Becomes part of other recovery	Not included	Scheduled benefits Maximum $4,000	Scheduled benefits Maximum $6,000 but deducted from death benefits

APPENDIX F (Continued)

Type of Insurance Coverage	Ontario (Present Plan)	Ontario Only (New Plan) January 1, 1972	British Columbia	Saskatchewan	Manitoba November 1, 1971
Medical Payments Benefits	$2,000 per person other than Ontario Hospital Ontario Medical	$5,000 per person including rehabilitation	Bodily injury Policy limits for all injured persons excludes Government medical and hospital plans	$2,000 per person discretionary to meet expenses	$2,000 per person as excess over any other cover except auto insurance
	Time limit: 2 years	Time limit: 4 years			
Funeral Expense Benefits	$500 maximum	$500 maximum	$500 maximum	$300 maximum	$500 maximum
Damage to own car (collision and comprehensive) (no fault insurance)	Optional	Optional	Optional	Compulsory $200 deducted for all losses	Compulsory $200 deducted for all losses
(Public Liability and Property Damage) Fault Protection	Minimum $50,000 optional ($25.00 to Motor Vehicle Accident Claims Fund but no Insurance Protection)	Minimum $50,000 optional ($25.00 to Motor Vehicle Accident Claims Fund but no Insurance Protection)	Minimum $50,000 Compulsory	Minimum $35,000 Compulsory	Minimum $50,000 Compulsory
Administration by:	Private Insurors	Private Insurors	Private Insurors	Basic Insurance	Government Monopoly
				For excess – government and private insurors compete	

APPENDIX G

NATIONWIDE'S COMPARISON OF SEVEN PLANS

APPENDIX G

NATIONWIDE'S COMPARISON OF SEVEN PLANS

(The following is taken from NO-FAULT INSURANCE — A READY REFERENCE. Columbus, Ohio: Nationwide Mutual Insurance Company, April, 1971; reprinted by permission).

This is a comparison of seven automobile insurance plans that are being offered to modify — or to replace — the present auto insurance system.

Among the plans examined are those of the country's three largest fire and casualty insurance trade associations — the National Association of Independent Insurers (NAII); the American Mutual Insurance Alliance (AMIA), and the American Insurance Association (AIA).

The review also includes the Massachusetts Plan, which is the only no-fault system now in operation in the United States, and the Keeton-O'Connell Plan, the forerunner of most of the no-fault plans that have come to public attention in recent years.

Another plan is in the form of a bill introduced in the United States Senate by Sen. Philip A. Hart of Michigan. It is known as The Hart-Magnuson Plan and would require a no-fault system of auto insurance that would be uniform among the states and, presumably, would supersede any other plan in effect — or under consideration — in the individual states.

The seventh plan in the review is the Nationwide Insurance Reform Plan, developed by the companies which have prepared this comparison.

All auto insurance systems are complex and this review compares only the major elements of the seven plans selected. It does not attempt to cover all minor technical distinctions among the plans. In addition, sponsors of each plan could make subsequent changes or amendments which would be at variance with the information contained in this review at the time of its completion on April 3, 1971.

BRIEF DESCRIPTION OF PLANS

All seven plans compared in this review offer some compensation, regardless of fault, for personal injuries. The AIA and Nationwide plans are distinct in that they do not limit the amount of compensation, regardless of fault, for medical services, and both would offer some regardless-of-fault payment for property damage. In addition, they would completely eliminate the present liability system for settling auto accident claims. They contain no provision for payments for pain and suffering or other intangibles.

The other five plans offer more limited settlements, regardless of fault, in injury cases. But they would retain what their sponsors consider to be the best features of the present legal liability system.

The Nationwide Plan is a compulsory system that provides compensation for damage to property, personal injury, or death resulting from an automobile accident on a first-party basis without regard to fault. This coverage would eliminate entirely any need to resort to the present legal liability system. A distinguishing feature of the Nationwide Plan is that it is the only plan in which coverage for damage to the insured's auto is a part of the compulsory insurance package.

The AIA Plan provides compulsory coverage for personal injury, death, or damage to property other than automobiles without regard to fault. This plan would eliminate recourse to the present legal liability system. Coverage for the insured's auto is not in the basic compulsory insurance package, but is available as an optional item.

The NAII and AMIA Plans are quite similar. They retain the present legal liability system, except for the first $2,000 of medical expenses and the first $6,000 of lost wages, both of which would be payable on a first-party basis. If negligence were a factor in an auto accident the company making these payments later could make a claim against the negligent person or his insurance company. In addition, a claimant who receives first-party payments would have these amounts deducted from any other recovery he might get later under the liability system.

The Massachusetts Plan retains the present legal liability system except for first-party benefits up to a maximum of $2,000 for both medical expenses and wage loss combined. The plan is compulsory for the first-party benefits for medical expenses and wage loss. Insurance for bodily injury liability continues to be compulsory in Massachusetts as it has been since 1927.

The Keeton-O'Connell Plan retains the present legal liability system in cases where claims for pain and suffering exceed $5,000 or in cases where medical expenses, loss of wages, and other losses exceed $10,000. All other claims for medical expenses, loss of wages and other losses would be paid to a claimant on a first-party basis without regard to fault.

The Hart-Magnuson Plan is a compulsory coverage designed to compensate persons injured in an auto accident for economic losses resulting from personal injury. The coverage is not compulsory for property damage liability, or for first-party coverage for damage to property. Claims for damage to property would be made under the legal liability system. Access to the liability system is also prescribed in cases in which an accident victim suffers what the plan calls "catastrophic harm."

MAXIMUM BENEFITS FOR MEDICAL EXPENSES

(Regardless of Fault)

NATIONWIDE:

- No limit on reasonable and necessary medical expenses, including costs of rehabilitation, for as long as necessary.

- Reasonable costs for services the insured normally would perform for himself but has had to hire someone to do because of his injury.

NAII AND AMIA:

- Up to $2,000 for medical expenses.

- Up to $4,500 to disabled persons who are non-wage earners to pay for substitute help hired to perform services the injured person would have performed. (NAII only.)

AIA:

- No limit on reasonable and necessary medical expenses, including cost of rehabilitation.

- Expenses reasonably incurred for services in lieu of those the injured person would have performed without income.

MASSACHUSETTS:

- Will pay limited medical expenses. Could be as much as $2,000 (but not more) only if no loss of wages is involved.

KEETON-O'CONNELL:

- Will pay medical expenses and other out-of-pocket costs to a limit of $10,000 per person and a limit of $100,000 per accident. The limits include whatever is paid for loss of wages.

HART-MAGNUSON:

- Will pay all reasonable and necessary costs for medical expenses, including costs of rehabilitation.

- All other expenses reasonably and necessarily incurred as the result of injury or death in an auto accident.

SURVIVORS' BENEFITS IN FATAL ACCIDENTS

NATIONWIDE:

. Up to $30,000 in survivors' benefits payable in installments, regardless of fault.

NAII AND AMIA:

. Retains the present liability system for survivors' loss.

AIA:

. Survivors' benefits consist of "contributions of tangible things of economic value" and expenses for ordinary and necessary services that the deceased would have performed for the survivors.

MASSACHUSETTS:

. Retains the present liability system for survivors' benefits.

KEETON-O'CONNELL:

. Survivors' benefits consist of "contribution of tangible things of economic value" and expenses for ordinary and necessary services that the deceased would have performed for the survivors.

HART-MAGNUSON:

. Up to $30,000 for survivors' benefits. Liability claims can be made for damages in excess of the amount paid regardless of fault.

MAXIMUM BENEFITS FOR LOSS OF WAGES

(Regardless of Fault)

NATIONWIDE:

. Will compensate for loss of wages at a rate of 85 per cent of the injured party's salary up to a limit of 200 per cent of the average weekly salary prevailing in the state in which he resides. Payments will be made as long as the disability persists, but not beyond age 65.

NAII AND AMIA:

. Up to $6,000 (at a maximum of $750 per month) for lost wages.

AIA:

. Will compensate for loss of wages at a rate of 85 per cent of the injured party's salary as long as the disability persists.

MASSACHUSETTS:

. Will compensate for loss of wages up to 75 per cent of the annual salary the injured party received during the previous year. Could be as much as $2,000 (but not more) only if no medical expenses are claimed.

KEETON-O'CONNELL:

. Will compensate for loss of wages at a rate of 85 per cent of the injured party's weekly wage to a limit of $750 per month up to a limit of $10,000 per person and $100,000 per accident.

HART-MAGNUSON:

. Loss of wages will be compensated up to a maximum of $1,000 per month for 30 months immediately following injury.

BENEFITS FOR PROPERTY DAMAGE

NATIONWIDE:

. The compulsory first-party coverage includes damage to the insured's car (up to actual cash value of the vehicle) and damage to another's property other than his automobile (up to $5,000) without regard to fault.

. Eliminates the present system of liability for damage to property.

NAII AND AMIA:

Retains the present system of first-party collision coverage and third-party property damage liability coverage without change.

AIA:

. The compulsory first-party coverage includes damage to another's property other than his automobile without regard to fault.

. The purchase of collision coverage for damage to the insured's car is optional to the individual.

. Eliminates the present system of liability for damage to property.

MASSACHUSETTS:

. Retains the present system of first-party collision coverage and property damage liability coverage without change.

KEETON-O'CONNELL:

. Retains the present system of first-party collision coverage and property damage liability coverage with some modifications.

HART-MAGNUSON:

. Retains the present system of first-party collision coverages and property damage liability without change.

COLLISION AND COMPREHENSIVE

(As defined under the present system)

NATIONWIDE:

.   Collision is part of the compulsory coverage since the insurance company would repair an insured's car up to the actual cash value of the car, less deductibles. Comprehensive would continue to be an optional coverage at extra cost.

NAII AND AMIA:

.   Under both plans, collision and comprehensive coverage both would be optional and at extra cost, as in the present system.

AIA:

.   Both collision and comprehensive would be optional and at extra cost. Eliminates present system of liability for damage to property.

MASSACHUSETTS:

.   Both collision and comprehensive are optional and at extra cost as in the present system.

KEETON-O'CONNELL:

.   Comprehensive would be optional and at extra cost. Collision would also be optional and at extra cost but with a choice for the policyholder. He could (1) get coverage comparable to the present collision coverage except that the insurance company would not have the right to recover by making a claim against the driver of the other car even if the other driver caused the accident, or (2) get coverage that would protect him only if the other driver was at fault. Again his insurance company couldn't make a claim against the other driver.

HART-MAGNUSON:

.   Both collision and comprehensive would be optional and at extra cost.

ACCESS TO LIABILITY SYSTEM AND SUBROGATION

NATIONWIDE:

- None. Claims of all kinds, including personal injury and damage to property, would be settled without determining fault. All payments would be made to the policyholder by his own insurance company.

- Subrogation would not be authorized.

NAII AND AMIA:

Claims can be pursued under the liability system:

- If medical expenses exceed the $2,000 limit on first-party payments.

- If loss of wages exceeds the $6,000 limit on first-party payments.

- For pain and suffering. Damages would be limited to 50 per cent of the first $500 of medical expenses and 100 per cent of such expenses over $500. The limitation would not apply in the event of death, permanent disability, dismemberment, disfigurement, and certain other serious injuries.

- Subrogation would be authorized to the extent of first-party payments.

AIA:

- None. Claims of all kinds would be settled without determining fault.

- Subrogation would not be authorized.

MASSACHUSETTS:

- Claims can be pursued under the liability system if economic loss exceeds the $2,000 limit payable regardless of fault for medical expenses and loss of wages. Also when an accident causes death, loss of hearing or sight, loss of a limb, permanent and serious disfigurement, or a fracture. Third-party claims for pain and suffering may be made if medical and hospital expenses exceed $500.

- Subrogation would be authorized for first-party injury benefits.

KEETON-O'CONNELL:

- A claim could be pursued under the liability system if the victim claimed more than $10,000 for all damages including medical expenses, loss of wages, and other out-of-pocket expenses — or if he claimed more than $5,000 for pain and suffering (inconvenience, scars, disability, etc.). Under the pain and suffering provision, however, the claimant would only receive that part of an award that is in excess of $5,000.

- Subrogation would not be authorized, for first-party injury benefits.

HART-MAGNUSON:

Access to the liability system is provided:

- In cases involving property damage first-party coverage without regard to fault applies to bodily injury but not property damage.

- In cases in which an auto accident results in "catastrophic harm" to an individual. This is defined as "a permanent partial or total loss of, or loss of use of, a bodily member or a bodily function." The definition also includes death or permanent disfigurement.

- Subrogation would be allowed only in cases where the vehicle operator was intoxicated, under the influence of drugs, committing or attempting to commit a felony, or intended to cause damage or injury or was using the vehicle for a purpose other than the one for which he had the owner's permission.

PAYMENT FOR PAIN AND SUFFERING

NATIONWIDE:

- None. The plan will compensate only for measurable economic loss. Optional insurance for pain and suffering on a first-party basis may be offered as supplementary insurance.

NAII AND AMIA:

- Payments for pain and suffering would be made only on a third-party basis. But even under the liability system, payments for pain and suffering would be limited to 50 percent of the first $500 of medical and hospital expenses and 100 percent of hospital and medical expenses in excess of $500. The limitation would not apply in cases in which an auto accident caused death, loss of a limb, permanent and serious disfigurement, loss of sight or hearing, or a fracture.

AIA:

- None. The plan would compensate only for measurable economic loss.

MASSACHUSETTS:

- Payments for pain and suffering could be claimed but only under the liability system and only in cases in which medical expenses exceed $500 or which involve death, loss of a limb, permanent and serious disfigurement, loss of sight or hearing, or a fracture.

KEETON-O'CONNELL:

- No payments for pain and suffering unless the claim for pain and suffering amounts to $5,000 or more, and then only the amount in excess of $5,000 would be paid.

HART-MAGNUSON:

- Payments for pain and suffering only under the legal liability system and only in cases in which an accident victim has suffered "catastrophic harm." This is defined as death, a permanent partial, or total loss of or loss of use of a bodily member or bodily function, or permanent disfigurement.

IS IT COMPULSORY?

NATIONWIDE:

- Yes. It would be compulsory for both personal injury and damage to property. Only comprehensive coverage is optional.

NAII AND AMIA:

- No. It would not be compulsory in either plan. The originators of the NAII Plan hope that the basic first-party coverage would be a mandatory part of every policy sold in a given state. But they are content to allow the various state legislatures to decide whether the coverage should be mandatory. The AMIA Plan would require that the basic first-party coverage be offered by insurance companies to every applicant for an auto policy, but acceptance would not be compulsory.

AIA:

- Yes, it would be compulsory for personal injury and damage to property, other than damage to the policyholder's auto or its contents.

MASSACHUSETTS:

- Yes, it is compulsory for first-party personal injury coverage and for third-party bodily injury liability coverage.

KEETON-O'CONNELL:

- Yes, it would be compulsory for the basic first-party protection. But the plan's authors recently have proposed that the plan be tried on an optional basis.

HART-MAGNUSON:

- Yes, the basic first-party protection for personal injury only would be compulsory.

SUPPLEMENTAL INSURANCE

(Specifically named in a given plan)

NATIONWIDE:

- Additional coverage, beyond the basic plan, would be available on an optional basis, at extra cost. This would include such things as higher limits for loss of wages, additional survivors' benefits, loss-of-use coverage (under damage to property), and possibly first-party payments for pain and suffering.

NAII AND AMIA:

- "Catastrophe" coverage would be available under the NAII Plan at extra cost which would pay benefits up to $100,000 per person for medical expenses and loss of wages. It also would pay survivors' benefits up to $25,000. No supplemental insurance is specified in the AMIA Plan.

AIA:

- Optional coverages available at extra cost. Would include higher limits on payments to compensate for loss of wages, as well as collision coverages.

MASSACHUSETTS:

- None.

KEETON-O'CONNELL:

- Additional coverage for pain and suffering and for higher limits on payments to compensate for loss of income would be available on an optional, extra cost basis.

- Catastrophe protection coverage, which provides benefits up to $100,000 in addition to basic benefits, would be available on an optional, extra cost basis.

HART-MAGNUSON:

- Third-party liability insurance of at least $50,000 per individual and $300,000 per accident would be available on an optional, extra cost basis.

SPECIAL FEATURES

NATIONWIDE:

- No applicant for insurance could be rejected. Each applicant is entitled to be insured by the company of his choice.

- Establishes fund to compensate accident victims who are not member of a car-owning family and who are injured in an accident involving an uninsured vehicle.

- Establishes mechanism to spread the burden of insuring high-risk drivers through reinsurance.

- Pays for expenses of rehabilitation and provides incentives for the individual to participate in rehabilitation procedures.

- Establishes incentives to encourage injured parties to return to productive work.

- Compulsory collision coverage.

NAII:

- First-party "catastrophe" coverage at extra cost.

- Court supervision of attorney fees.

- Crackdown on claim fraud.

- Fast disposition of disputed liability claims under $3,000 by arbitration.

AIA:

- Establishes mechanism for compensating uninsured accident victims.

- Pays for expenses of rehabilitation.

MASSACHUSETTS:

- Establishes by law a merit system which penalizes poor drivers and rewards good ones through rate differentials.

MASSACHUSETTS: (Continued)

- Insurers may exclude from benefits those whose conduct contributes to the injury; e.g., under the influence of alcohol or a narcotic drug, committing a felony, or intending to cause injury or damage.

KEETON-O'CONNELL:

- To eliminate duplicate claims payments the auto insurance coverage will pay only after other insurance and wage continuation plans have been exhausted.

- Mandatory arbitration of disputed liability claims under $3,000.

- Court regulation of attorney fees.

- Adoption of comparative negligence laws. Most states now have contributory negligence laws.

- Stronger drunk driving and drivers' licensing laws.

HART-MAGNUSON:

- The insurer will be required to offer third-party liability insurance coverage of at least $50,000 for injury to one person and $300,000 for all persons injured in one accident. The policyholder doesn't have to buy it, but the company must offer it.

- No applicant for the basic economic protection insurance may be rejected and no policy cancelled except for suspension or revocation of license or failure to pay the premium.

- Any first-party benefits for loss of wages or medical expenses collected by an insured under his own first-party policy would be deducted from any settlement or court award he might get later under the liability system.

- The operator or user would be liable to reimburse the insurer for benefits payable if such operator or user was intoxicated, under the influence of drugs, committing or attempting to commit a felony, or intended to cause damage or injury, or was using a vehicle for a purpose other than the one for which he had the permission of the owner.

APPENDIX H

CALIFORNIA NO-FAULT PLAN
(The Fenton Bill)

APPENDIX H

THE CALIFORNIA NO-FAULT PLAN
(The Fenton Bill)

As this book went to press, the State of California was considering the passage of a limited system of compensation without regard to fault for injuries caused by automobile accidents. The bill, AB 1505, was introduced by State Assemblyman Jack R. Fenton, Chairman of the Assembly Committee on Finance and Insurance. Authored by Mr. Fenton, the proposal passed the California State Assembly on July 27, 1971. The bill was then assigned to the Senate Judiciary Committee which, on September 28, voted to send the bill to the Rules Committee for further study. Observers feel that this action virtually killed the bill — at least for the present time.

Features of the Bill

Assembly Bill 1505, designated as the "Motor Vehicle Basic Loss Insurance Act," provides for the following features of coverage:

1.   A mandatory requirement for proof of security covering Basic Loss Insurance benefits as a prerequisite for motor vehicle registration. The law does not apply to commercial vehicles or to motorcycles.

2.   Persons covered include the named insured, his spouse and members of his household, guests in the car, and pedestrians.

3.   Pedestrians have coverage under their own insurance if they have the coverage. If not, pedestrians are covered under the insurance of the owner of the involved vehicle. Where no insurance is applicable, guest passengers or pedestrians look to the assigned claims plan.

4.   An assigned claims plan is established, funded by all automobile insurance companies and from which a claim of an otherwise uninsured injured person may be assigned to an insurance company. Insurers accept such assignments in proportion to the amount of automobile insurance business written in the State of California. Cost of the coverage is borne in the rating structure by all Basic Loss Insurance policyholders.

5.   Benefits under Basic Loss Insurance are in the maximum amount of $10,000, covering medical and related expenses, including rehabilitation; work loss, reduced by a tax savings of 15 percent or less, and limited to $750 per month; scheduled benefits for disfigurement and dismemberment; funeral expenses limited to $1,000; and expenses paid to others in lieu of services that the injured party would have performed had he not been injured.

6.   Property loss is not covered under the basic coverage.

7.   Amounts provided under the basic coverage are reduced by workmens' compensation and Social Security disability benefits.

8.   Excluded from benefits are persons injured while converting a vehicle, while committing a felony, while under the influence of drugs or alcohol, while intentionally causing injuries, while driving without effective security in violation of the law, and non-residents, be they operators or occupants,

if they do not have the required insurance.

9.   Additional coverages are provided on an optional basis to extend the basic compensation.

10.   Mandatory optional coverage includes standard collision coverage and first party pain and suffering insurance.

11.   Optional coverage which may be offered includes additional coverage for dismemberment and bodily impairment, catastrophic loss coverage, additional hospital room benefits, additional work loss benefits, and anything the insurer may wish to market.

12.   Payments are payable monthly as the loss accrues. By agreement, however, the insured may receive a lump sum award, discharging the insurer.

13.   The bill provides interest on overdue payments, awards for future benefits, and attorneys' fees for insurers and insureds in proper cases.

Alteration of Tort System

The plan limits recovery under tort liability in claims for damages for pain and suffering to those cases where (1) expenses for medical and related costs exceed $1,000, (2) the injury consists of the loss of a body member or a serious impairment of a bodily function, (3) the injury consists of permanent disfigurement, or (4) the injury results in death. Once the right to sue for pain and suffering is established, there is no limit on recovery.

There is an exemption in tort liability to the extent that the injured party is entitled to receive benefits under the Basic Loss Insurance. There is no exemption for property damage.

Arbitration

The bill requires that all cases in which claims for damages are less than $10,000 must be arbitrated. The judge of the court before which a case is brought is permitted to make a preliminary determination of the value of the case to ascertain whether it is to be ordered to the arbitration process.

Bill is Presented In This Appendix

A copy of AB 1505 follows for the information of the reader. In the event that the Fenton Bill is enacted into law, it will represent a significant national development, since California residents reportedly purchase 12 percent of all automobile insurance written in the United States.

AB 1505

MOTOR VEHICLE BASIC LOSS INSURANCE ACT

Article 1. General Provisions and Definitions

11890. This chapter is known and may be cited as the "Motor Vehicle Basic Loss Insurance Act."

11891. The purpose of this chapter is to provide a means of prompt and equitable compensation to persons for losses from accidental bodily injury arising from the ownership, operation, or use of motor vehicles, in lieu of tort liability.

11892. As used in this chapter:

(a) "Bureau" means assigned claims bureau.

(b) "Commissioner" means the Insurance Commissioner.

(c) "Injured person" means a natural person suffering accidental bodily injury.

(d) "Motor vehicle" means any vehicle required to be registered under the Vehicle Code.

(e) "Passenger vehicle" means all motor vehicles used primarily for the transportation of passengers but not primarily used for the transportation of persons for hire, compensation, or profit; or not designed, used, or maintained primarily for the transportation of property as defined in Section 260 of the Vehicle Code. "Passenger vehicle" does not include any motor vehicle described in Section 400 or 405 of the Vehicle Code.

(f) "Nonresident" means a person who is not a resident of this state.

(g) "Operator" means every person who drives or is in physical control of a motor vehicle.

(h) "Owner" means a person who holds legal title to a motor vehicle, or, in the event the motor vehicle is subject to a security interest or lease with option to purchase with the debtor or lessee having the right to possession, the debtor or lessee shall be deemed the owner for the purposes of this chapter.

(i) A "relative residing in the same household" means a relative of any degree by blood or marriage who usually makes his home in the same family unit, whether or not temporarily living elsewhere.

(j) "Survivors" means (1) a spouse living with the deceased person at the time of death, (2) any unemancipated minor legally residing in the same household or otherwise receiving financial support at the time of death, or (3) any other person receiving regular financial support from the deceased at the time of death.

11893. As used in this chapter:

(a) "Basic loss insurance" is required insurance with terms and conditions consistent with the provisions of Article 3 (commencing with Section 11900) of this chapter.

(b) "Basic loss insurance benefits" are payable under basic loss insurance.

11894. The Motor Vehicle Basic Loss Insurance Act shall be operative on January 1, 1973.

Article 2. Financial Security for the Operation of a Passenger Vehicle

11895. The owner or registrant of a passenger vehicle required to be registered in this state shall not operate or permit the vehicle to be operated on any public highway in this state at any time on or after the effective date of this chapter unless security for the payment of basic loss insurance benefits in accordance with the terms of this chapter is in effect continuously throughout the registration period.

11896. (a) Security is required for the payment of basic loss insurance benefits under this chapter and for the payment of tort judgments as required in Section 16023 of the Vehicle Code.

(b) Security for the payment of the benefits provided in this chapter may be provided by the owner or registrant by a policy issued by an insurer authorized to transact business in this state which affords insurance for payment of basic loss insurance benefits consistent with the provisions of this chapter applicable to injuries arising out of the ownership, maintenance, or use of the motor vehicle.

(c) Security for the payment of basic loss insurance benefits may be provided by the owner or registrant by any other method approved by the Department of Motor Vehicles as affording security equivalent to that afforded by a policy of insurance which meets the requirements of this chapter.

11897. A nonresident owner of a motor vehicle not registered in this state shall not operate or permit such vehicle to be operated in this state for an aggregate of more than 30 days in any calendar year unless he has in effect security for payment of basic loss insurance benefits in accordance with the terms of this chapter and for tort judgments as required in Section 16023 of the Vehicle Code.

11898. The Director of Motor Vehicles may promulgate and from time to time amend reasonable regulations to provide effective administration and enforcement of the provisions of this article in accordance with their purpose.

11899. The Department of Motor Vehicles may require insurers to notify it of the termination of insurance policies, and may require insurers to furnish the registration numbers of vehicles that they insure. The Department of Motor Vehicles shall require proof of security for payment of basic loss insurance benefits of the owner of a vehicle if that owner is convicted of violating any provision of this chapter. The Department of Motor Vehicles may require proof of such security under other circumstances at its discretion pursuant to regulations promulgated pursuant to Section 11898.

Article 3. Terms and Conditions of Basic Loss Insurance

11900. (a) Basic loss insurance shall be applicable to accidental bodily injuries, sickness, or disease arising out of the ownership, maintenance, or use of a motor vehicle. Use of a motor vehicle includes loading and unloading, but does not include conduct within the course of a business of repairing, servicing, or otherwise maintaining vehicles, unless the conduct occurs outside the business premises.

(b) Basic loss insurance benefits are due under the provisions of this chapter without regard to fault.

11901. Basic loss insurance benefits are payable for allowable expenses, work loss, funeral and burial expenses, disfigurement and impairment of bodily functions, necessary payments to others, and survivors benefits.

(a) Allowable expenses consist of all reasonable charges incurred for reasonably necessary products, drugs, services, and accommodations for an injured person's diagnosis, cure, recovery, or rehabilitation. Allowable expenses within basic loss insurance coverage shall not include charges for a hospital room in excess of a reasonable and customary charge for semi-private accommodations, except when the injured person requires special or intensive care.

(b) Work loss consists of (1) loss of income that an injured person would have earned had he not been injured, including loss of pension and social security benefit entitlements and reduction in earning capacity. However, work loss does not include any loss after the date on which the injured person dies. Because the benefits received from basic loss insurance for loss of income are not taxable income, the benefits payable for loss of income will be reduced 15 percent unless the claimant presents to the insurer, in support of his claim, reasonable proof of a lower value of the income tax advantage in his case, in which event the lower value shall apply. The benefits payable for work loss sustained in any 30-day period, and the income earned by an injured person for work during the same period, reduced by the income tax advantage provided in this section, shall together not exceed seven hundred fifty dollars ($750), this maximum to apply pro rata to any lesser period of work loss.

(c) Funeral and burial expenses consist of expenses of all types in any way related to funeral and burial not to exceed the amount of one thousand dollars ($1,000).

(d) Disfigurement and impairment of bodily function payments shall be made in accordance with a schedule of benefits established by the commissioner pursuant to Section 11903.

(e) Necessary payments to others consist of payments in fact made to others, not members of the insured person's household, and reasonably incurred in obtaining from those others ordinary and necessary services in lieu of those that, had he not been injured, the injured person would have performed not for income but for the benefits of himself or members of his household.

(f) Survivors benefits consist of (1) expenses, after the date on which the deceased died, of contribution of tangible things of economic value, including wages or salary limited as provided in subdivision (b), including services that survivors would have received from the deceased had he not suffered the injury causing death, and (2) expenses reasonably incurred by such survivors after the date on which the deceased died in obtaining ordinary and necessary services in lieu of those that, had he not suffered the injury causing death, would have performed for the benefit of himself or the members of his household.

(g) Pain, suffering, and inconvenience are not loss compensable under basic loss insurance benefits, but economic detriment, such as loss of wages arising from the interference of pain, and suffering with work, is loss compensable as work loss.

11902. Subject to the limitations of this chapter, recovery for all basic loss insurance benefits shall not exceed ten thousand dollars ($10,000) per person per accident.

11903. The Insurance Commissioner shall, after notice and hearing as provided by Chapter 4.5 (commencing with Section 11371) of Part 1 of Division 3 of Title 2 of the Government Code, establish a schedule of benefits as a measure of compensation for disfigurement and impairment of bodily functions resulting from accidents involving motor vehicles. Such schedule shall constitute the minimum amounts of benefits for basic loss insurance coverage. The amounts provided in such schedule shall be applicable to disfigurement, loss of members and to complete loss of function of the member. If function is partially lost, the benefit amount shall be an appropriate percentage of the benefit for complete loss of function. The commissioner shall annually review such schedule to determine whether it represents realistic benefits in light of then current living standards.

11904. Basic loss insurance benefits are payable for accidental bodily injury suffered in an accident occurring out of the state, if the accident occurs within the United States, its territories and possessions, or in Canada, and the person whose injury is the basis of the claim was at the time of the accident either:

(a) A named insured under a basic loss insurance policy;

(b) Or additional insureds, including:

(1) The spouse of the insured;

(2) A relative of either the insured or his spouse who is residing in the same household;

(3) Occupants of a vehicle involved in the accident, the owner or registrant of which is insured under a basic loss insurance policy, or has provided security approved by the department under subdivision (b) of Section 11896.

(4) Persons not occupying any vehicle but injured by one or all vehicles involved in the accident.

11905. Injuries received in an out-of-state accident by one who is a named insured under a basic loss insurance policy, or a relative residing in the same household as a named insured, or an occupant of a vehicle covered by basic loss insurance are covered to the same extent as if the injury had occurred within this state.

11906. (a) Basic loss insurance benefits are payable to or for the benefit of the injured person, or, in the event of his death, to or for the benefit of his survivors as defined in subdivision (j) of Section 11891.

(b) If an insurer in good faith pays the basic loss insurance benefits required by this chapter to or for the benefit of a person who it believes is entitled to those benefits, the payment shall discharge such insurer's liability to the extent of the payments made, unless the insurer has been notified in writing of the claim of another person.

(c) If there is doubt as to the proper person to receive the benefits or the proper apportionment among the persons entitled to them, the insurer, the claimant, or any other interested person, may apply to the superior court having jurisdiction over the matter for an appropriate order. The superior court may designate the payees and make an equitable apportionment, taking into account the relationship of the payees to the injured person and other factors the court considers appropriate.

(d) In the absence of a court order directing otherwise the insurer may pay the following:

(1) To the dependents of the injured person, the basic loss insurance benefits accrued before his death without the appointment of an administrator or executor.

(2) To the surviving spouse, the basic loss insurance benefits due any dependent children living with the spouse.

11907. A person is not entitled to be paid basic loss insurance benefits for accidental bodily injury if at the time of the accident either:

(a) The person was using a motor vehicle which he had converted, unless his use was in the good-faith belief that he was entitled to take and use the vehicle.

(b) The person was the owner or registrant of a motor vehicle involved in the accident with respect to which the security required under this chapter was not in effect.

(c) The person was not a resident of the state, and was an occupant of a motor vehicle not registered in the state and not insured by an insurer issuing insurance in accordance with the provisions of this chapter.

(d) The person was in the process of committing a felony.

(e) The person was an operator and was under the influence of drugs or alcohol.

(f) The person operated a motor vehicle with the intent of causing bodily injury or property damage.

11908. (a) Except as provided in subdivisions (b) and (c), each basic loss insurance policy shall apply to accidental bodily injury to the person named in the policy, his spouse, and any relative of either residing in the same household. When basic loss insurance benefits are payable to or for the benefit of an injured person under his own policy, and would also be payable under the policy of his spouse, relative, or relative's spouse, the injured person's insurer shall pay all of the benefits, and is not entitled to recoupment from the other insurer.

(b) A person suffering accidental bodily injury while he is an operator or a passenger of a motor vehicle operated in the business of transporting passengers shall receive the basic loss insurance benefits to which he is entitled from the insurer of such motor vehicle.

(c) An employee, his spouse, or any relative of either residing in the same household, who suffers accidental bodily injury while an occupant of a motor vehicle owned or registered by the employer of the employee shall receive basic loss insurance benefits to which he is entitled from the insurer of the furnished behicle.

(d) Except as provided in subdivisions (a), (b) and (c), a person suffering accidental bodily injury while an occupant of a motor vehicle shall claim basic loss insurance benefits from insurers in the following order of priority:

(1) The insurer of the owner or registrant of the vehicle occupied.

(2) The insurer of the operator of the vehicle occupied.

(3) The insurer of the injured occupant if he has basic loss insurance coverage.

(e) The following applies to persons not occupying any vehicle:

(1) Except as provided in subdivision (a) of this section, a person suffering accidental bolidy injury while not an occupant of a motor vehicle shall claim basic loss insurance benefits from insurers in the following order of priority:

(i) Insurers of the injured person if he has basic loss insurance coverage.

(ii) Insurers of owners or registrants of motor vehicles involved in the accident.

(iii) Insurers of operators of motor vehicles involved in the accident.

(2) When two or more insurers are, in the same order of priority, required to provide basic loss insurance benefits, an insurer paying benefits due is entitled to partial contribution from the other insurer or insurers in the same order of priority, together with a reasonable amount of partial contribution of the expense of processing the claim, in order to accomplish equitable distribution of the loss among the insurers.

(f) Any limitation upon the amount of basic loss insurance benefits available because of accidental bolidy injury to one person arising from one motor vehicle accident shall be determined without regard to the number of policies applicable to the accident.

11909. Except for the owner of a motor vehicle involved in the accident who knowingly failed to maintain security as required by Section 11895, each person suffering loss because of an injury arising out of an accident may obtain benefits through the assigned claims plan established pursuant to Article 9 (commencing with Section 11965) of this chapter when:

(a) No basic loss insurance is applicable to the injury.

(b) No basic loss insurance applicable to the injury can be identified.

(c) The basic loss insurance applicable to the injury is, because of financial inability of an insurer to fulfill its obligations, inadequate to provide the benefits contracted for.

11910. The amount of all disability benefits an injured person, otherwise entitled to basic loss insurance benefits, receives or is entitled to under any workman's compensation plan or similar statutory plan or under the Social Security Act because of accidental bolidy injury shall be deducted from the basic loss insurance benefits otherwise payable for the injury;

Article 4. Basic Loss Insurers

11920. A policy of insurance issued by an insurer authorized to transact business in this state represented or sold as providing security required in Sections 11895 and 11897 shall be considered as providing security for the payment of basic loss insurance as required by this chapter.

11921. Every insurer offering basic loss insurance shall also offer to the insured:

(a) Basic tort liability insurance with coverage at least equal to the financial responsibility requirements specified in Section 16059 of the Vehicle Code.

(b) Insurance for accidental loss of, or damage to, motor vehicles owned by the insured regardless of fault, subject to any deductible stated on the face of the policy and to a limit not less than the actual cash value of the vehicle, or subject to, any exclusion as to damage caused otherwise than by collision or upset.

(c) Additional loss insurance under which the insurer agrees to pay to an injured person who is the named insured or a relative residing in the same household as the named insured, during any period of complete inability to work in his occupation of at least one week in duration, benefits for pain and inconvenience in a specified amount per week or month, at a rate chosen by the insured (from an offering including rates of benefits of one hundred dollars ($100), two hundred dollars ($200), three hundred dollars ($300), four hundred dollars ($400), and five hundred dollars ($500) per month), and, during any period of partial inability to work in his occupation, a percentage of such rate proportioned to the degree of partial inability. This form of coverage is subject to an overall limit of liability for all pain and inconvenience sustained by one injured person from injuries occurring in one accident, during periods of complete and periods of partial inability to work combined, in an amount 25 times that stated as the monthly benefit for complete inability of one to work in his occupation. "Complete inability to work in his occupation," as used in relation to this coverage, means inability to perform, on even a part-time basis, even part of the duties of his occupation (or if unemployed at the time of injury, of the occupation or occupations for which he was qualified). One who is able to perform part of the duties of his occupation on a part-time basis is not completely unable to work in his occupation. For purposes of this pain and inconvenience coverage, a person 16 years of age or over has an occupation if he is a full-time student or is in full-time domestic service, whether as a member of a household or as an employee. Partial inability of one to work in his occupation is any degree of inability other than complete.

(d) Additional loss insurance covering disfigurement and impairment of bodily function in higher amounts than those established by the Insurance Commissioner pursuant to Section 11903.

11922. Every insurer offering basic loss insurance may also offer:

(a) A provision under which it agrees to pay to the named insured only, or to the named insured and one or more other persons, benefits in compensation for pain or inconvenience, or both, under other terms and conditions than those specified in subdivision (c) of Section 11921.

(b) Catastrophe loss coverage under which the insurer agrees to pay to the named insured only, or the named insured and one or more other persons, benefits in reimbursement of net losses that are not within applicable basic loss coverage because in excess of the limits of that coverage. Catastrophe loss coverage may be offered with no deductible or with any stated deductible not in excess of 30 percent of all loss. If coverage is to qualify as catastrophe loss coverage its limits of liability must be not lower than one hundred thousand dollars ($100,000) because of injury (including death resulting therefrom) to one person in one accident and, subject to the limit for one person, three hundred thousand dollars ($300,000) because of injury to more than one person in one accident.

(c) Any form of additional basic loss insurance, including, but not limited to, additional hospital room coverage and additional work loss coverage.

Article 5. Examination, Treatment, and Rehabilitation of Injured Persons; Discovery

11930. Whenever the mental or physical condition of a person is material to any claim that has been or may be made for past or future basic loss insurance benefits, a court of competent jurisdiction may order the person to submit to mental or physical examination by a physician or physicians. The order may be made only on motion for good cause shown and upon notice to the person to be examined and to all other persons having an interest and shall specify the time, place, manner, conditions, and scope of the examination and the person or persons by whom it is to be made.

11931. If requested by the person examined, a party causing an examination to be made shall deliver to him a copy of every written report concerning the examination rendered by an examining physician, at least one of which reports must set out his findings and conclusions in detail. After such request and delivery, the party causing the examination to be made is entitled upon request to receive from the person examined every written report available to him (or his representative) concerning any examination, previously or thereafter made, of the same mental or physical condition. By requesting and obtaining a report of the examination so ordered or by taking the deposition of the examiner, the person examined waives any privilege he may have, in relation to the claim for basic loss insurance benefits, regarding the testimony of every other person who has examined or may thereafter examine him in respect of the same mental or physical condition.

11932. If any person refuses to comply with an order entered pursuant to Sections 11930 and 11931, the court may make such orders in regard to the refusal as are just, except that no order shall be entered directing the arrest of any person for disobeying an order to submit to a physical or mental examination. The orders that may be made in regard to such a refusal include, but are not limited to, the following: (1) an order that the mental or physical condition of the disobedient person shall be taken to be established for the purposes of the claim in accordance with the contention of the party obtaining the order; (2) an order refusing to allow the disobedient person to support or oppose designated claims or defenses, or prohibiting him from introducing evidence of mental or physical condition; (3) an order rendering judgment by default against the disobedient person as to his entire claim or a designated part of it; (4) an order requiring the disobedient person to reimburse the insurer for reasonable attorneys' fees and expenses incurred in defense against the claim; (5) an order requiring delivery of a report, in conformity with Section 11931 on such terms as are just, and if a physician fails or refuses to make such a report a court may exclude his testimony if offered at trial.

11933. (a) After a hearing upon application by any interested person and reasonable notice to all other interested persons, and upon findings supported by evidence, a court of competent jurisdiction may enter an order determining that an insurer of basic loss insurance applicable to an injury is responsible, subject to the limits and other terms and conditions of the coverage, for the cost of a specified procedure or treatment for rehabilitation to which the injured person has submitted or does thereafter submit.

(b) The findings required to support such an order are (1) that the specified course of procedure or treatment, whether or not involving surgery, is recognized and acceptable medically or is acceptable nonmedical remedial

Christian Science treatment and care, (2) that it has contributed or will contribute substantially to rehabilitation, and (3) that the cost of such procedure or treatment is reasonable in relation to its probable rehabilitative effects.

11934. (a) After a hearing upon application by any interested person and reasonable notice to all other interested persons, and upon findings supported by evidence, a court of competent jurisdiction may enter an order determining that an insurer of basic loss insurance applicable to an injury is responsible, subject to the limits and other terms and conditions of the coverage, for the cost of a specified course of rehabilitative occupational training that the injured person has taken or does thereafter take.

(b) The findings required to support such an order are (1) that the specified course of occupational training is a recognized form of training and is reasonable and appropriate for the particular case, (2) that it has contributed or will contribute substantially to rehabilitation, and (3) that the cost of such training is reasonable in relation to its probable rehabilitative effects.

11935. (a) After a hearing upon application by any interested person and reasonable notice to all other interested persons, and upon findings, supported by evidence, as stated in Section 11933 or in Section 11934, and further findings (1) that the injured person has refused or has by his conduct caused the insurer reasonably to believe that he may refuse to submit to such procedure, treatment, or training, and (2) that he does not have reasonable grounds to continue such refusal, a court of competent jurisdiction may enter an order invoking reasonable sanctions against the injured person and others whose claims are based on his injury.

(b) In determining whether an injured person has reasonable grounds for continuing refusal to submit to the specified procedure, treatment, or training, the court shall take into account, among all other relevant factors, the extent of the probable benefit, the attendant risks, the extent to which the procedure, treatment, or training is or is not recognized as standard and customary, and whether the imposition of sanctions because of the injured person's refusal would abridge his right to the free exercise of his religion.

(c) The sanctions that may be invoked in such an order include, but are not limited to, the following: (1) an order that benefits be reduced or terminated at such time as necessary to limit recovery of benefits to an amount equal to the benefits that in reasonable probability would have been due had the injured person submitted to such rehabilitative procedure, treatment, or training; (2) an order that the physical or mental condition of the injured person shall be taken to be established for the purposes of the claim in accordance with the contention of the insurer; (3) an order that, if the insurer elects to pay a specified lump sum (found to be fair and reasonable compensation in lieu of benefits that in reasonable probability would be due if the injured person submitted to the specified procedure, treatment, or training) it shall be fully discharged from all liability arising from the injury.

11936. Any physician, hospital, clinic, or other person or institution lawfully rendering treatment to an injured person for an injury covered by basic loss insurance, and any person or institution providing rehabilitative occupational training following such an injury, may charge a reasonable amount for the products, services, and accommodations rendered. In no event, however, may such a charge be in excess of the amount the person or institution customarily charges for like products, services, and accommodations in cases involving no insurance.

11937. (a) Every employer shall, if a request is made by a basic loss insurer against whom a claim has been made, furnished forthwith, in a form approved by the commissioner, a sworn statement of earnings, since injury and for a reasonable period before injury, of the person upon whose injury the claim is based.

(b) Every physician, hospital, clinic, or other medical institution providing, before or after an injury upon which a claim for basic or added protection benefits is based, any products, services, or accommodations in relation to that or any other injury, or in relation to a condition claimed to be connected with that or any other injury, shall, if requested to do so by the insurer against whom the claim has been made, subject to conditions approved by the commissioner, (1) furnish forthwith a written report of the history, condition, treatment, and dates and costs of such treatment of the injured person and (2) produce forthwith and permit the inspection and copying of his or its records regarding such history, condition, treatment, and dates and costs of treatment.

(c) An employer, physician, hospital, clinic, or other person or institution providing information in response to a request under the terms of this section may charge a reasonable amount in reimbursement for the time and cost of providing the information.

(d) In the event of any dispute regarding an insurer's right to discovery of facts about an injured person's earnings or about his history, condition, treatment, and dates and costs of such treatment, a court of competent jurisdiction may enter an order for such discovery. The order may be made only on motion for good cause shown and upon notice to all persons having an interest, and it shall specify the time, place, manner, conditions, and scope of the discovery. A court may, in order to protect against annoyance, embarrassment, or oppression, as justice requires, enter an order refusing discovery or specifying conditions of discovery and may order payments of costs and expenses of the proceeding, including reasonable fees for the appearance of attorneys at the proceedings, as justice requires.

Article 6. Claims and Actions

11940. (a) Basic loss benefits are payable monthly as loss accrues.

(b) Benefits other than for disfigurement and impairment of bodily functions for any period are overdue if not paid within 30 days after the insurer receives reasonable proof of the fact and amount of net loss realized during that period. If reasonable proof is not supplied as to the entire claim, the amount supported by reasonable proof is overdue if not paid within 30 days after such proof is received by the insurer. Any part or all of the remainder of the claim that is later supported by reasonable proof is overdue if not paid within 30 days after such proof is received by the insurer. The requirement of partial payment of a claim of which only part is supported by reasonable proof does not apply, however, if the part duly supported is for an amount less than one hundred dollars ($100).

11941. An agreement for assignment of any rights to benefits payable in the future is unenforceable.

11942. (a) A lump-sum award or settlement is an award or settlement for full and final discharge of all liability of the insurer to a claimant on account of a specified accident upon payment of a single sum of money.

(b) An installment award or settlement is an award or settlement for full and final discharge of all liability an insurer might otherwise have to a claimant on account of a specified accident in return for an obligation to pay a specified sum in installments.

(c) An insurer or a claimant may require a lump-sum award or an installment award in an action for basic loss insurance benefits that would come due after the date of award, but only upon a finding that the present value of all future benefits to come due does not exceed one thousand dollars ($1,000) or a finding supported by medical evidence that a final settlement will contribute substantially to the health and rehabilitation of the injured person.

(d) Rights and obligations arising under basic loss insurance, either with respect to a claim for a limited period of time or with respect to a full claim inclusive of all future loss arising from an injury, may be discharged by settlement, but only by (1) installment settlement for payments of not more than one thousand dollars ($1,000) per month, (2) lump-sum settlement for an amount not exceeding one thousand dollars ($1,000), or (3) settlement for larger installments or for a larger lump sum with judicial approval upon a finding that the form of the settlement, in larger installments or a larger lump sum, is in the best interests of the claimant.

11943. All overdue payments bear simple interest at the rate of 7 percent per annum.

11944. Payment of benefits may be made by a valid draft payable to the order of the person suffering loss or to his authorized representative and honored when presented for payment. For the purpose of calculating either the extent to which any benefits were overdue or the termination of any period of limitation of actions, payment by such a draft shall be treated as made on the date it was placed in the United States mail in a properly addressed, postpaid envelope, or, if not so posted, on the date of delivery.

11945. If no basic loss insurance benefits are paid to any survivor for loss arising from a death, no action for basic loss insurance benefits for loss suffered by survivors shall be commenced later than one year after the death or two years after the motor vehicle accident from which the death arises, whichever is earlier. If no basic loss insurance benefits are paid because of loss arising out of the ownership, maintenance or use of a motor vehicle, no action for recovery of such benefits shall be commenced later than two years after the accident or one year after an aggregate net loss in excess of two hundred dollars ($200) is suffered by the claimant, whichever is earlier. If basic or loss insurance benefits are paid, no action for recovery of further benefits by the same or another claimant because of loss arising from the injury shall be commenced later than one year after the last payment of benefits, except that when benefits have been paid for loss suffered by an injured person before his death arising from the injury, survivors may commence an action not later than one year after the death or two years after the last payment of benefits, whichever is earlier.

11946. (a) Upon arbitration or trial of an action for benefits, an award or judgment shall be entered as to all benefits to come due thereafter during such periods as to which the court finds that a reasonably certain determination of future loss can be made in the light of the evidence.

(b) A judgment awarding benefits to come due more than five years after the date of judgment is binding as to the period beyond five years unless set aside upon application of an interested party presented for hearing not sooner than five years after the date of judgment. Such an application shall be filed not later than six years after the date of the judgment or one year after the date the last payment of benefits was made, whichever is later. Upon such application, the only issue to be tried is the amount of any unpaid benefits coming due beyond five years after the date of such previous judgment and not more than one year before the date of the application, and that issue shall be tried de novo.

(c) A judgment awarding future benefits for a period less than five years beyond the date of the judgment is binding as to the period it covers, and an application for unpaid benefits falling due after the conclusion of that period shall be filed in the same court and proceeding within one year after the conclusion of that period, or one year after the last payment of benefits was made, whichever is later.

(d) A judgment determining that no benefits have become due or will become due after a past or future date specified in the judgment is binding and is not subject to being set aside under the special procedures for retrial prescribed in this section. It can be vacated, revised, or modified only in accordance with the laws and procedures of this state applicable to judgments generally.

11947. (a) An attorney is entitled to a reasonable fee for advising and representing a claimant on a claim or action for basic loss insurance benefits.

(b) If overdue benefits are involved, the attorney's fee shall be a charge against the insurer in addition to benefits recovered, except that, first, there shall be no such charge against the insurer unless some overdue benefits have been recovered in the judgment or paid after receipt by the insurer of notice of the attorney's representation of the claimant, and, second, in the discretion of the court part or all of this fee may be charged against the benefits due the claimant because his claim was fraudulent or so excessive as to have no reasonable foundation. The provisions of this subdivision are applicable to settlement of a disputed claim before or after commencement of an action, as well as to arbitration and actions tried, but the extent to which the claim was disputed and the question whether the action was heard in arbitration or tried are factors among others that may be taken into account in determining what amount of fee will be permitted and how much if any of it will be charged against benefits.

(c) If no overdue benefits are involved, an attorney, to be entitled to payment of a fee by an insurer, must give the insurer reasonable notice of his representation of his client with respect to the claimed benefits before payment of such benefits has been made. After such notice, the insurer shall pay the fee directly to the attorney. Half of such a fee is a charge against benefits otherwise due the claimant and is chargeable against limits of liability as benefits paid. The other half is a charge against the insurer in addition to the benefits due, and it is not chargeable against limits of liability.

(d) Whenever the claimant, his attorney, and the insurer agree upon a fee to be awarded and upon the manner in which it is to be charged, no judicial approval of the fee is required; in the absence of such agreement, either as to a settled claim or an action tried, a controversy over an attorney's fee may be submitted at the instance of any interested party for determination by the court in which the action was pending or, if no action was pending, in a court competent to accept jurisdiction over the claim for benefits.

11948. Within the discretion of a court, an insurer may be allowed an award of a reasonable sum against a claimant as an attorney's fee for the insurer's attorney in defense against a claim that was fraudulent or so excessive as to have no reasonable foundation. To the extent that **any** benefits are then due or thereafter come due to the claimant because of loss resulting from the injury on which the claim is based, such a fee may be treated as an offset against such benefits; also, judgment may be entered against the claimant for any amount of a fee awarded against him and not offset in this way or otherwise paid.

11949. The insured shall be informed in writing by the insurer of the reason for any increase in his premium rates.

Article 7. Tort and Related Actions

11950. Basic loss insurance provided by this chapter because of injury suffered in an accident occurring in this state is granted in lieu of damages in tort to the extent indicated in Sections 11951, 11952, and 11953. These sections do not apply to injury suffered in an out-of-state accident.

11951. (a) In any action in tort brought as a result of bodily injury arising out of the ownership, maintenance or use of a motor vehicle, damages for pain, suffering, and inconvenience may be recovered only if:

(1) The reasonable and necessary expenses incurred in the diagnosis, care, recovery, or rehabilitation of such bodily injury for necessary medical, surgical, and dental services, including prosthetic devices, and necessary ambulance, hospital, and professional nursing expenses are determined to be in excess of one thousand dollars ($1,000); or

(2) The injury consists in whole or in part of a loss of a body member or a serious impairment of a bodily function; or

(3) The injury consists in whole or in part of permanent disfigurement.

(4) The injury results in death.

(b) Every person (whether a natural person or any other legal entity) who is a basic loss insured (whether named or otherwise) with respect to an injury arising out of the ownership, maintenance, or use of a motor vehicle as a motor vehicle is entitled to an exemption from tort liability due to the injury. The exemption exists to reduce tort liability to the extent that the injured party is entitled to receive benefits under basic loss insurance.

(c) The exemption shall not exceed ten thousand dollars ($10,000) or the policy limits, whichever is the greater.

(d) This section shall apply when the law of this state is controlling in determining tort liability.

(e) Whenever one is entitled to an exemption under the terms of this section, he is nevertheless subject to liability for damage to property caused under circumstances such that he would be liable to pay damages in tort in the absence of this exemption.

11952. (a) Whenever one is held liable in tort, otherwise than under subdivision (b) of Section 11951 for an injury as to which he is a basic loss insured (whether named or additional), he is entitled to an exemption reducing his tort liability to the extent provided in this section.

(b) In each case to which this section applies, the fact-finder in the tort action shall state separately the amount found for all elements of recovery.

(c) Whenever a claimant recovers a judgment in tort against any person or persons who, apart from this chapter, would, after discharging their liability, be entitled to contribution or indemnity from one who is a basic loss insured (whether named or additional) with respect to the injury, rights and liabilities of the claimant and all other interested persons are to be calculated as if amounts equal to those specified in Section 11951 had been paid by the insured to the claimant in partial satisfaction of the tort claim.

(d) If two or more basic loss insureds are liable in tort because of an injury, the exemption provided in this section is allowed only once, for their combined benefit. Whenever for any purpose (including the purpose of calculating amounts due by way of contribution or indemnity) the benefit or burden of the exemption provided in this section is distributed among several interested persons, such distribution is to be made on the basis considered by the court to be most equitable.

11953. (a) Rights to and liabilities for contribution or indemnity that would have existed apart from this chapter are affected by this chapter only as stated in this section.

(b) In the calculation of liabilities of a basic loss insured (whether named or additional) for payment of any sum in contribution or indemnity, the insured is entitled to an exemption as provided in Sections 11951 and 11952.

(c) Except as stated in Section 11954 and in this subdivision, no insurer or insured is entitled to contribution or indemnity on account of basic loss insurance benefits paid. This chapter does not bar any right of one who is a basic loss insured with respect to an injury (or of his tort liability insurer, as his subrogee) to recover contribution or indemnity on account of payments made in disposition of a tort claim against him based on the injury. In such cases, rights to contribution or indemnity are calculated as if an amount equal to the exemption provided in Section 11952 had been paid on the tort claim.

11954. (a) An insurer paying benefits due under the terms of basic loss insurance because of an injury caused intentionally, or because of an injury caused by a converter under circumstances such that he cannot qualify as an insured under Section 11907, is entitled to indemnity from the person or persons so causing injury, for all the outlay incurred on account of such injury, including the net amount of benefits paid, costs of processing claims for benefits, and reasonable attorneys' fees and other expenses of enforcement of this right of indemnity.

(b) A basic loss insurer with a right of reimbursement under subdivision (a), if suffering loss from inability to collect the reimbursement out of a payment received by a claimant on a tort claim, is entitled to indemnity from one who, with notice of the insurer's interest, made a payment to the claimant without making the claimant and the insurer joint payees as their interests may appear, or without obtaining the insurer's consent to a different method of payment.

(c) The right of an insurer of subrogation to recover basic loss insurance benefits paid to its insureds exists only as provided in this subdivision. Any insurer paying benefits in accordance with the provisions of this chapter shall be subrogated, to that extent, to the rights of the insured or other beneficiary under the policy to whom such claim was paid, against any person causing such injury or death to the extent that payment was made.

When the person causing such injury or death is insured by a motor vehicle liability insurance policy, the determination as to whether the insurer paying such claim shall be legally entitled to recover any payments to which it has a right of subrogation under this subdivision, and if so entitled, the amount thereof, shall be by intercompany arbitration and in the event of disagreement the arbitration shall be conducted by a single neutral arbitrator, without right of judicial review.

11955. (a) All civil actions for damages arising out of personal injury, death, or property damage arising out of the ownership, maintenance, or use of a motor vehicle, where the total value of the claim does not exceed ten thousand dollars ($10,000), exclusive of interest, attorney's fees, and costs shall be submitted to arbitration pursuant to Title 9 (commencing with Section 1280) of Part 3 of the Code of Civil Procedure.

(b) There is a right to jury trial with respect to claims for basic loss insurance and general tort liability or both only if the total value of the claim is at least ten thousand dollars ($10,000), exclusive of interest, attorney's fees, and costs.

(c) All civil actions referred to in this section in which the total value of the claim exceeds ten thousand dollars ($10,000), exclusive of interest, attorney's fees and costs, may be ordered to arbitration provided for in this section by the superior court if in its sound discretion the actual value of the claim will not exceed ten thousand dollars ($10,000). The order of the superior court sending a claim or cause of action to arbitration is reviewable.

(d) The award made in arbitration is not limited to the jurisdictional limit of ten thousand dollars ($10,000).

Article 8. Appeal or Other Review

11960. A judgment, order, finding, or award is ripe for appeal or any other form of review permitted under the laws of this state if it is one of the following, and not otherwise: (1) a judgment, order, finding, or award of any amount of benefits due, or that no benefits are due, entered pursuant to the terms of Section 11946; (2) a judgment, order, or finding under the terms of Section 11942 granting or refusing lump-sum payment; or (3) an order pursuant to Section 11955.

11961. (a) Except as otherwise provided in Section 11946, a judgment, order, finding, or award that is ripe for appeal or review under the terms of Section 11960 is subject to appeal, review, vacation, revision or modification only in accordance with the laws and procedures of this state applicable respectively to judgments, orders, findings, or awards generally.

(b) Any order, finding, or award that is not ripe for appeal or other form of review under the terms of Section 11960 is subject to revision at any time before there is entered in the same case a judgment or some other order, finding, or award that is ripe for appeal or other form of review and, while the action is still pending, continues to be subject to revision if not within the scope of matters determined on appeal or other form of review.

Article 9. Assigned Claims Plan

11965. Insurers authorized to write basic loss insurance in this state are authorized, subject to approval and regulation by the commissioner, to organize and maintain an assigned claims bureau and an assigned claims plan and to formulate and from time to time amend rules and regulations for their operation and for the assessment of costs on a fair and equitable basis, consistent with the provisions of this chapter. In default of the organization and continued maintenance of an assigned claims bureau and assigned claims plan in a manner considered by the Insurance Commissioner to be consistent with the terms of this chapter, the Insurance Commissioner shall organize and maintain such a bureau and plan.

11966. Costs incurred in the operation of the bureau shall be assessed against insurers according to rules and regulations that assure fair allocation among insurers writing basic loss insurance in the state, on a basis reasonably related to the volume of basic loss insurance they write.

11967. Every insurer writing basic loss insurance in this state is required to participate in the assigned claims bureau and the assigned claims plan.

11968. Each person suffering loss because of an injury arising out of the ownership, maintenance, or use of a motor vehicle in this state may obtain basic loss insurance benefits through the assigned claims plan established pursuant to this chapter. If (1) no basic loss insurance is applicable to the injury, or (2) no basic loss insurance applicable to the injury can be identified, or (3) the only identifiable basic loss insurance applicable to the injury is, because of multiple claims against it or because of financial inability of one or more insurers to fulfill their obligations, inadequate to provide benefits up to the maximum prescribed in Section 11901 (in which last case all unpaid benefits due or coming due are subject to being collected under the assigned claims plan, and the insurer to which the claim is assigned, or the bureau of assigned claims if the claim is assigned to it, is entitled to reimbursement from the defaulting insurers to the extent of their financial responsibility). Subject to the maximum prescribed in Section 11902 for basic loss benefits from all sources, persons entitled to claim through the assigned claims plan are entitled to recover from the insurer to which the claim is assigned (or from the bureau if the claim is assigned to it) the benefits due under standard provisions for basic loss insurance as prescribed in Sections 11901 and 11902.

11969. The claim or claims arising from injury to one person sustained in one accident and brought through the assigned claims plan shall be assigned to one insurer, or to the bureau, which after such assignment shall have rights and obligations as if having issued a policy of basic loss insurance, of standard provisions, applicable to the injury.

11970. The assignment of claims shall be made according to rules and regulations that assure fair allocation of the burden of assigned claims among insurers doing business in the state on a basis reasonably related to the volume of basic loss insurance they write.

11971. A person claiming through the assigned claims plan shall notify the bureau of his claim within the time that would have been allowed for filing an action for basic loss benefits had there been in effect identifiable coverage applicable to the claim. The bureau shall promptly assign the claim and notify the claimant of the identity and address of the insurer to which the claim is assigned (or of the bureau if the claim is assigned to it). No action by the claimant against the insurer to which his claim is assigned (or against the bureau, if the claim is assigned to it) shall be commenced later than 30 days after receipt of notice of the assignment or the last date on which the action might have been commenced had it been against the insurer of identifiable coverage applicable to the claim, whichever is later.

11972. All reasonable costs incurred in the handling and disposition of assigned claims (including amounts paid pursuant to assessments under Section 11966 as well as other amounts reasonably expended in the handling and disposition of assigned claims) shall be taken into account in making and regulating rates for basic loss insurance.

Article 10. Assigned Risks

11975. Agreements may be made among insurers with respect to the equitable apportionment among them of basic loss insurance which may be afforded to applicants who are required by this act to provide security for the payment of tort judgments and basic loss benefits who are unable to procure such security through ordinary methods. The insurers may agree among themselves on the use of reasonable rate modifications for that insurance. Agreements and rate modifications are subject to the approval of the commissioner of insurance. In the event of the failure of insurers to reach an agreement consistent with this section or their failure to agree on rates, the commissioner of insurance shall by regulation establish a plan for equitable apportionment of coverage among insurers and the rates therefor.

Article 11. Uninsured Motorists

11980. The insurer obligated to pay basic loss insurance benefits for accidental bodily injury to a person occupying a motor vehicle, the owner of which is uninsured pursuant to this chapter, or to the spouse or relative resident in the household of the owner or registrant of such motor vehicle, shall be entitled to recover all the benefits paid and appropriate loss adjustment costs incurred from the owner or registrant of such motor vehicle or from his estate. The failure of the person to make payment within 30 days shall be grounds for suspension or revocation of his motor vehicle registration and operator's license.

Article 12. Penalties

11985. Any owner of a passenger vehicle, for which the existence of security for basic loss insurance and tort liability insurance is a requirement for its legal operation upon the public highways of this state, under either Section 11895 or 11897 or Section 4030 of the Vehicle Code who operates such motor vehicle or permits it to be operated upon a public highway in this state without having in full force and effect security complying with the terms of Section 11896 is guilty of a misdemeanor. And any other person who operates such a motor vehicle upon a public highway in this state with the knowledge that the owner does not have such security in full force and effect is guilty of a misdemeanor. And each person convicted of a misdemeanor under the terms of this section may be fined not less than one hundred dollars ($100) or more than five hundred dollars ($500) or may be imprisoned for not more than six months or both.

11986. Any person who charges, demands, receives, or collects for hospital or medical products, services, or accommodations rendered in the treatment of an injured person, or for rehabilitative occupational training, or for legal services rendered in connection with a claim for basic loss insurance benefits, any amount in excess of that authorized by this chapter with awareness that the charge is in excess of that authorized is guilty of a misdemeanor and upon conviction may be fined not less than one hundred dollars ($100) or more than five hundred dollars ($500) or may be imprisoned for not more than six months or both.

Sec. 2. Article 1.5 (commencing with Section 4030) is added to Chapter 1 of Division 3 of the Vehicle Code, to read:

Article 1.5. Financial Security for Tort Judgments

4030. The owner of a motor vehicle required to be registered in the state shall not operate or permit the vehicle to be operated on any public highway in this state at any time on or after the effective date of this chapter unless Section 16059 is in effect continuously throughout the registration period.

4031. (a) Proof of security meeting the financial responsibility requirements may be provided by the owner of the vehicle, with respect to any motor vehicle, by filing with the Department of Motor Vehicles a certificate of insurance evidencing the issuance, by or on behalf of an insurer duly authorized to transact business in this state, of a policy including coverage required under the financial responsibility provisions, applicable to injuries arising out of the ownership, maintenance, or use of the vehicle.

(b) Proof of security for meeting the financial responsibility requirements may be provided, with respect to any motor vehicle, by any other method approved by the Department of Motor Vehicles as affording security substantially equivalent to that afforded by a certificate of insurance.

4032. Each insurer duly authorized to transact business in this state may be required to notify the department in writing of the cancellation of any insurance policy provided for in this article. Such notification shall be made at least 30 days prior to cancellation or other termination.

BIBLIOGRAPHY

BIBLIOGRAPHY

1. "Actuary Disputes Savings Claimed for N.Y. No-Fault," The National Underwriter, (May 8, 1970), 1.

2. Adams, John F. "Law, Insurance, and the Automobile Accident Victim – Social and Economic Aspects," The Journal of Risk and Insurance, (December, 1962).

3. "Administration's National No-Fault Plan Hailed, Hit," Insurance Advocate, (March 27, 1971), 5, 24.

4. "Advocated for N.J. Modified No-Fault By Agents Group," Insurance Magazine, (April 1, 1971), 31.

5. "Aetna's Watkins Urges No-Fault," The National Underwriter, (November 13, 1970), 13.

6. "Agents, AIA Debate No-Fault Before N.Y. Legislative Session," The National Underwriter, (April 2, 1971), 1, 29.

7. "Ahead: A New System of Auto Insurance? " U.S. News & World Report, (April 28, 1969), 54-56.

8. "Ahead: Auto-Insurance Crisis," U.S. News & World Report, (April 17, 1967), 68-71.

9. "AIA Executive Urges State Officials to Move Promptly on No-Fault," The Weekly Underwriter, (April 10, 1971), 6.

10. "AIA Looks At New Insurance Era; No-Fault Auto Gets Close Scrutiny," The National Underwriter, (May 23, 1969), 1, 51.

11. "AIA No-Fault Compared With N.Y. Dept. Proposal," Insurance Advocate, (March 7, 1970), 5.

12. "AIA No-Fault Plan Called Better Than Mass. Version," The National Underwriter, (November 27, 1970).

13. "AIA Tells Federal Probers Of Need For A No-Fault System," The National Underwriter, (January 2, 1970), 20.

14. Aksen. "Arbitration of Automobile Accident Cases," 1 Conn. L. Rev. 70 (1968).

15. "Alleged Savings Under Keeton Plan Disputed," The Defense Research Institute, (December, 1967), 73-75.

16. American Bar Association. Report of the Special Committee on Automobile Accident Reparations 104 (1969).

17. "American Insurance Association Endorses No-Fault Programs Of Other Industry Groups," Insurance Magazine, (March 1, 1971), 32.

18. "American Insurance Association Proposes No-Fault Auto Coverage," Best's Insurance News, (December, 1968), 10-11-12, 74-81.

19. American Insurance Association. Report of Special Committee to Study and Evaluate the Keeton-O'Connell Basic Protection Plan and Automobile Accident Reparations. (1968).

20. American Mutual Insurance Alliance. Actuarial Committee, Report on the Adequacy of the Costing of the American Insurance Association's "Complete Personal Protection Automobile Insurance Plan," (1969).

21. "American Mutual Insurance Alliance Gives Endrosement to Cotter Plan on Auto Claims," The Weekly Underwriter, (February 22, 1969), 5, 12.

22. American Mutual Insurance Alliance. Statement on Automobile Accident Law and Automobile Insurance 10, (November 21, 1969).

23. "Americans Favor No-Fault Auto Plan, Public Opinion Survey Indicates," The Weekly Underwriter, (February 8, 1969), 5, 16.

24. "An Aid To Motorists — Insurance Changes Ahead," U.S. News & World Report, (March 15, 1971), 26-28.

25. "An Initial Proposal Relating to No-Fault Automobile Legislation," The Insur-Law Journal, (April, 1971), 198.

26. "Arbitration: The Philadelphia Story," Journal of American Insurance, (September-October, 1969).

27. "ASIM Officers Endorse Federal Standards for No-Fault Plans," Business Insurance (April 26, 1971), 1.

28. "ASIM Officials Back Federal No-Fault Standards," Insurance Advocate, (April 24, 1971), 9, 25.

29. "Attorney Pans Keeton-O'Connell Program," The National Underwriter, (August 4, 1967).

30. "Attorneys and Adjuster View No-Fault in U.S., Puerto Rico," The National Underwriter, (March 21, 1971).

31. "Authors of P.R. 'No-Fault' Law Hit Administration On Lack of Implementation," Insurance Advocate, (March 22, 1969), 5, 17.

32. "Auto Accident Reform Plans, Including the No-Fault Concept, Offered by NAII and AMIA," Insurance Magazine, (February 1, 1971).

33. "Auto Insurance: Big Blow-up Ahead," Changing Times, (February, 1967), 7-12.

34. "Auto Insurance Has No Friends," Life, LXIII, (November 17, 1967), editorial.

35. "Auto Insurance Reform: Approaching the Fork in the Road," Journal of American Insurance, (May-June, 1970), 6-8.

36. "Auto Insurance Reform Plan Goes to Congress," Lorain Journal, (March 18, 1971), 8.

37. "The Auto-Insurance Tangle — Federal Controls On The Way," U.S. News & World Report, (February 12, 1968), 102-104.

38. "Automobile Insurance," Washington Insurance Newsletter, Inc., Vol. XXII, No. 21, (May 5, 1971).

39. Barker, Donald B. "Report of the Liaison Committee," Insurance Counsel Journal, VOL. XXXV, No. 2, (April, 1968), 218.

40. "Basic Protection for the Traffic Victim — Keeton-O'Connell Plan," F.C. & S. Bulletins (Cincinnati: The National Underwriter Company, January, 1968), Frlc-1 to 8.

41. "A Basic Reform of Automobile Liability Insurance," Part 6, 27 Consumer Reports, (1962), 404.

42. "Better Car Insurance Coming," U.S. News & World Report, (July 8, 1968), 60-62.

43. "W.S. Biggs of Kemper Discusses No-Fault," The National Underwriter, (May 16, 1969), 21.

44. Bjorklund, Richard. "ASIM Officers Endorse Federal Standards For No-Fault Plans," Business Insurance, (April 26, 1971), 1-2.

45. Blum and Kalven. "The Empty Cabinet of Dr. Calabresi," 34 U. Chi. L. Rev. 239, (1967).

46. Blum, W. and Kalven, H. Public Law Perspectives on a Private Law Problem: Auto Compensation Plans 34-36, (1965).

47. "Blum Explains NAIA Stance On No-Fault," The National Underwriter, (November 20, 1970).

48. Body. "Comparative Negligence: The Views of a Trial Lawyer," 44 A.B.A.J. 346, (1958).

49. "Boyd Tells Senate Unit DOT Study Would Seek Out Facts," Insurance Advocate, (March 16, 1968), 3, 5.

50. Brainard, Calvin H. "An Analysis of the Provisions of The Massachusetts No-Fault Law," Best's Review, (December, 1970), 42, 44.

51. Brainard, Calvin H. "Implications of DOT Auto Insurance Study for the Tort Liability System," The Insurance Law Journal, (October, 1970), 575-82.

52. British Columbia. 1 British Columbia, Royal Commission on Automobile Insurance, Report of the Commissioners 404, (1968).

53. "Broader Reform Than No-Fault? Two Professors Split On Issue," The National Underwriter, (March 20, 1970).

54. "Bronx Bar Association Unit Suggests More Study," Insurance Advocate, (December 13, 1969), 6.

55. Burger, Warren. "The Courts on Trial — A Call for Action Against Delay," 44 A.B.A.J. 739, (1958).

56. Burridge, John. "Auto Compensation Plans Up To Date," Best's Insurance News, (December, 1965), 21-24.

57. "The Business With 103 Million Unsatisfied Customers," Time, (January 26, 1968), 20-21.

58. Calabresi, G. "The Decision for Accidents: An Approach to Non-Fault Allocation of Costs," 78 Harv. L. Rev., (1965), 713, 719-20.

59. Calabresi, G. "Does the Fault System Optimally Control Primary Accident Costs?" 33 Law & Contemp. Prob., (1968), 429, 441-44

60. State of California Department of Motor Vehicles. Compensation Plan Report by the Financial Responsibility Study Committee, March, 1967.

61. "Canadian Insurers Speed Payouts," Business Week, (November 9, 1968), 58.

62. "Car Insurance: Should Accident Policies be Changed?," Good Housekeeping, (January, 1971), 130.

63. "Car Renters Endorse No-Fault Insurance," Omaha World Herald, (May 4, 1971).

64. "The Case For/Against No-Fault," Popular Science, (January, 1971), 56-57, 120.

65. Cass, Ronald. "Auto Insurance — A Rough Road Ahead," The Spectator, (December, 1967), 38-39.

66. "Caution Asked in Assessing Massachusetts No-Fault Law 'Success'," Insurance Advocate, (March 13, 1971), 8.

67. "Cautious Reaction Is Urged To Early BI Claim Drop Under Mass. No-Fault," The National Underwriter, (March 19, 1971), 1, 7.

68. "Changes Ahead For Auto Insurance?" U.S. News & World Report, (October 2, 1967), 49-51.

69. "Changes Coming In Auto Insurance," U.S. News & World Report, (June 23, 1969), 40-41.

70. Chapin, Hugh M. "Don't Be Anti-Keeton-O'Connell, You May Be Selling Something Like It — Soon!" Weekly Underwriter, (December 9 and December 16, 1967).

71. "Chrisman Explains NAIA Opposition To Auto No-Fault," The National Underwriter, (November 30, 1970), 37.

72. Cole, Robert J. "Why the High Cost of Auto Insurance; No-Fault: Will It Work?" New York Times, (April 4, 1971), 34.

73. Commonwealth of Pennsylvania, Insurance Department. "Denenberg Assails 'Lawyers Committee For Public Education' For Misrepresenting No-Fault Laws," News, (May 11, 1971).

74. "Company Man Against Pay Without Fault," The National Underwriter, (March 3, 1967).

75. "Compensation Without Fault For Auto? — NAII Hears Pros and Cons From Panel of Four University Professors — Morris, Bickley, Keeton, and Heins," National Underwriter, (November 23, 1964).

76. "Compulsory Auto Compensation Plans May Not Be Bad Solutions, Ehre Says," The National Underwriter, (October 7, 1966), 2, 38.

77. "Compulsory Auto Fund In Saskatchewan Has Continuing Bad Losses," The National Underwriter, (November 1, 1963), 24.

78. Conard, A., J. Morgan, R. Pratt, C. Voltz & R. Bombaugh. Automobile Accident Costs and Payments: Studies in the Economics of Injury Reparation. Michigan: 1964, 147-149.

79. Conard, Alfred, et al. Automobile Accidents Costs and Payments (Ann Arbor, Michigan: University of Michigan Press, 1964).

80. Conard and Jacobs. "New Hope for Consensus in the Automobile Injury Impasse," 52 A.B.A.J. 533, (1966).

81. "Connecticut Industry Almost Unified Behind AFL-CIO No-Fault Bill," Insurance Advocate, (April 3, 1971), 5, 23.

82. Connecticut State Insurance Department. A Program for Automobile Insurance and Accident Benefits Reform 14-16, (1969).

83. Connor, Michael J. "No-Fault Insurance Proposal in New York Alarms Many Lawyers," Wall Street Journal, (March 15, 1971), 8.

84. "Consumer-Oriented Auto Policy Needs New Criteria," Insurance Advocate, (March 14, 1970), 6.

85. Consumers Union. "How Good Is Your Automobile Insurance?" 27 Consumer Reports 204, (1962).

86. Corstvet. "The Uncompensated Accident and Its Consequences," 3 Law & Contemp. Prob., (1936), 466, 468.

87. "The Cost of Casualties," Time, (June 2, 1967), 63.

88. "The Cotter Plan For Automobile Reparations Introduced In Connecticut Deserves Your Consideration," Insurance Counsel Journal, (April, 1969).

89. "Cotter Plan Wins Support At Joint Hearing; Strong Opposition Also Voiced by Bar Unit," Insurance Advocate, (April 12, 1969), 5, 20-21, 36.

90. "Counsel Refutes Basic Program Proposed For Traffic Victims," The National Underwriter, (November 18, 1966), 2, 58.

91. Cowie, E.A. "Pay As You Go for Auto Accident Victims," The Commercial and Financial Chronicle, (August 31, 1967).

92. Cox, Charles K. "What Is Needed to Clear Up Auto Insurance Problems," Insurance Magazine, (January 1, 1970), 29-31, 46.

93. Crane, Frederick G. "Auto Liability Compensation: The System and Its Critics," Underwriters Review, (May, 1967), 18-19.

94. "Crisis in Auto Insurance — What Can Be Done About It," U.S. News & World Report, (June 14, 1965), 112-114.

95. "CU Supports a Plan for Auto Insurance Reform," Consumer Reports, (January, 1968), 9-15.

96. Dammann, George H. "New All-Industry Auto Safety Group Takes First Steps," National Underwriter, (January 26, 1968), 1, 20-21.

97. Dammann, George H. "New Auto Plans Keep Appearing: None Takes Hold," The National Underwriter, (May 3, 1968), 47-49.

98. "Danger on the Highways," U.S. News & World Report, (October 16, 1967), 66-69

99. Davis, E.N. "Socialized Insurance: A Tiger by the Tail," The Journal of Insurance Information, XXVII, (November-December, 1966), 25-31.

100. "DRI Asks Legislators to Improve Present Auto Reparations Method," Insurance Magazine, (January 15, 1970), 41.

101. "DRI Ghirardi Hits Entire Premise of Keeton-O'Connell Basic Protection Plan," Insurance Advocate, (June, 1967), 26.

102. "DRI Official Against Keeton-O'Connell Basic Protection for Traffic Victims," The National Underwriter, (June 23, 1967), 2, 51.

103. "DRI Sees Increase in Highway Blood Bath If Plans on No-Fault Concept is Adopted," Insurance Magazine, (January 1, 1970), 45.

104. Defense Research Institute. An Analysis and Critique of an Automobile Insurance Proposal Prepared for Study and Comment by the American Insurance Association. Milwaukee, Wisconsin, 1969.

105. Defense Research Institute. "Auto Compensation Plans Change — At Any Cost?" For the Defense, (December, 1967).

106. Defense Research Institute. "Basic Protection — Diminished Justice at High Cost," For the Defense, Vol. 8, No. 10, (December, 1967), 73-80.

107. Defense Research Institute. "Directed Verdicts and Judgments N.O.V. — New Test for Prima Facie Case," For the Defense, Vol. 8, No. 10, (December, 1967).

108. Defense Research Institute, International Association of Insurance Counsel, Federation of Insurance Counsel, Association of Insurance Attorneys. Justice in Court After the Accident. A special report, (January, 1968), 26.

109. Defense Research Institute. "The Keeton-O'Connell Plan — Some Questions and Answers," For the Defense, Vol. 9, No. 4, (April, 1968), 25-29.

110. Defense Research Institute. Responsible Reform: A Program to Improve the Liability Reparation System, (1969).

111. "Delaware Agents Unveil Their Own No-Fault Program," The National Underwriter, (April 16, 1971).

112. Denenberg, Herbert S. "The Automobile Insurance Problem: Issues and Choices," The Insurance Law Journal, (August, 1970), 455-63.

113. Denenberg, Herbert S. Commonwealth of Pennsylvania, Insurance Department, "The Automobile Insurance and Reparations System: A Legalized Racket," News, (April 27, 1971).

114. Denenberg, Herbert S. "Legal Reform for Our Automobile Insurance and Reparations System," Insurance Field, (October 15, 1970), 14.

115. Denenberg, Herbert S. "The 1970's — The Decade of No-Fault and the Year of the Dog," Best's Review, (Prop./Liab. ed.), March, 1971), 30, 32, 34, 36.

116. Denenberg, Herbert S. "What's Wrong With the AIA No-Fault Plan," Independent Agent, (May, 1969), 28-31.

117. Department of Transportation. Automobile Insurance and Compensation Study: An Analysis of Complaints in Selected Automobile Insurance Markets. Advisory Report to the Division of Industry Analysis, Bureau of Economics, Federal Trade Commission for the Department of Transportation, (July, 1970). By Douglas G. Olson, Ph.D.

118. Department of Transportation. Automobile Insurance and Compensation Study: Automobile Accident Litigation. A Report of the Federal Judicial Center to the Department of Transportation, (April, 1970).

119. Department of Transportation. Automobile Insurance and Compensation Study: Automobile Personal Injury Claims, Vols. I & II, (July, 1970).

120. Department of Transportation. Automobile Insurance and Compensation Study: Causation, Culpability and Deterrence in Highway Crashes, (July, 1970). By David Klein and Julian A. Waller, M.D.

121. Department of Transportation. Automobile Insurance and Compensation Study: Comparative Studies in Automobile Accident Compensation, (April, 1970).

122. Department of Transportation. Automobile Insurance and Compensation Study: Constitutional Problems in Automobile Accident Compensation Reform, (April, 1970).

123. Department of Transportation. Automobile Insurance and Compensation Study: Compensation for Motor Vehicle Accident Losses in the Metropolitan Area of Washington, D.C., (December, 1970).

124. Department of Transportation. Automobile Insurance and Compensation Study: Driver Behavior and Accident Involvement: Implications for Tort Liability, (October, 1970).

125. Department of Transportation. Automobile Insurance and Compensation Study: Economic Consequences of Automobile Accident Injuries, Vols. I & II, (April, 1970).

126. Department of Transportation. Automobile Insurance and Compensation Study: Economic Regulation of Insurance in the United States, (July, 1970). By John G. Day.

127. Department of Transportation. Automobile Insurance and Compensation Study: Insolvencies Among Automobile Insurers. Advisory Report to the Division of Industry Analysis, Bureau of Economics, Federal Trade Commission for the Department of Transportation, (July, 1970). By Douglas G. Olson, Ph.D.

128. Department of Transportation. Automobile Insurance and Compensation Study: Insurance Accessibility for the Hard-To-Place Driver. Report of the Division of Industry Analysis, Bureau of Economics, Federal Trade Commission to the Department of Transportation, (May, 1970).

129. Department of Transportation. Automobile Insurance and Compensation Study: Mass Marketing of Property and Liability Insurance, (June, 1970). By Spencer Kimball and Herbert Denenberg.

130. Department of Transportation. Automobile Insurance and Compensation Study: Motor Vehicle Assigned Risk Plans. Report of the Division of Industry Analysis, Bureau of Economics, Federal Trade Commission to the Department of Transportation, (August, 1970). By William T. Hold.

131. Department of Transportation. Automobile Insurance and Compensation Study: Motor Vehicle Crash Losses and Their Compensation in the United States. A Report to the Congress and the President, (March, 1971). By John A. Volpe, Secretary of Transportation.

132. Department of Transportation. Automobile Insurance and Compensation Study: The Origin and Development of the Negligence Action. Studies in the Role of Fault in Automobile Accident Compensation Law, (March, 1970).

133. Department of Transportation. Automobile Insurance and Compensation Study: The Price and Availability of Automobile Liability Insurance in the Non-standard Market. Advisory Report to the Division of Industry Analysis, Bureau of Economics, Federal Trade Commission to the Department of Transportation, (January, 1971). By Douglas G. Olson, Ph.D.

134. Department of Transportation. Automobile Insurance and Compensation Study: Price Variability in the Automobile Insurance Market. Report of the Division of Industry Analysis, Bureau of Economics, Federal Trade Commission to the Department of Transportation, (August, 1970). By Calvin H. Brainard and Stephen A. Carbine.

135. Department of Transportation. Automobile Insurance and Compensation Study: Public Attitudes Supplement to the Economic Consequences of Automobile Accident Injuries, (September, 1970).

136. Department of Transportation. Automobile Insurance and Compensation Study: Public Attitudes Toward Auto Insurance. A Report of the Survey Research Center, Institute for Social Research, The University of Michigan to the Department of Transportation, (March, 1970).

137. Department of Transportation. Automobile Insurance and Compensation Study: Quantitative Models for Automobile Accidents and Insurance, (September, 1970). By Joseph Ferreira, Jr.

138. Department of Transportation. Automobile Insurance and Compensation Study: Rehabilitation of Auto Accident Victims, (August, 1970). By John Henle.

139. Department of Transportation. Automobile Insurance and Compensation Study: Structural Trends and Conditions in the Automobile Insurance Industry. Report of the Division of Industry Analysis, Bureau of Economics, Federal Trade Commission to the Department of Transportation, (April, 1970).

140. Department of Transportation. Automobile Insurance and Compensation Study: A Study of Assigned Risk Plans. Report of the Division of Industry Analysis, Bureau of Economics, Federal Trade Commission to the Department of Transportation, (August, 1970). By Dennis F. Reinmuth and Gary K. Stone.

141. Diamond, Joseph. "Auto Insurers Eye Need to Change Focus of Coverage," National Underwriter, (October 20, 1967).

142. Diamond, Joseph. "Uniformity Vital if No-Fault Idea is Adopted: ASIM," The National Underwriter, (April 23, 1971), 1, 16.

143. "Dodd Introduces Legislation to Avert Auto Insolvencies," National Underwriter, (October 21, 1966).

144. Donahue, Richard J. "Prompt-Pay, Limited No-Fault Proposed by Illinois Director," The National Underwriter, (April 9, 1971), 4.

145. "DOT's Auto Probe Indicates Informed Public for No-Fault," The National Underwriter, (April 3, 1970), 1, 35.

146. "DOT Report Favors Action by States," NAII News Memo (Chicago), (March 29, 1971).

147. "DOT Report Urging No-Fault is Ready," The National Underwriter, (March 17, 1971), 1, 32.

148. "DOT Staff Report Nearing Final Stage; Soon Will be Made Public," Insurance Advocate, (August 29, 1970), 5.

149. "DOT Survey Disappointing, Hints at More No-Fault Favor; Lemmon," The National Underwriter, (May 15, 1970), 18.

150. "DOT's $2 Million Study of Auto Insurance Problem Says There is One," Business Insurance, (March 29, 1971), 4.

151. Downey, Eugene G. "Pre-Settlement Help for Accident Victims," Journal of Insurance Information, XXVII, No. 2, (March-April, 1966), 35-40.

152. Duff, J. Kenneth. "Debate Keeton Plan at University of Illinois Meeting," The National Underwriter, (October 20, 1967), 2, 20-21.

153. Dukakis, Michael. "Focus on Basic Protection Insurance," Best's Fire & Casualty News, (November, 1967), 11-12, 89.

154. Dunlop. "Why Your Car Insurance Costs So Much," Traffic Safety, (October, 1958).

155. "Editor Supports No-Fault System," The Weekly Underwriter, (May 24, 1969), 8, 16.

156. "Editorials – New Plan," The Weekly Underwriter, (July 6, 1968), 3.

157. Ehrenzweig, Albert A. "Full Aid Insurance for the Traffic Victim – A Voluntary Compensation Plan," 43 Calif. L. Rev. 1, (1955).

158. "Fair Treatment, Not No-Fault Sought by Public, Harvin Says," The National Underwriter, (November 24, 1969), 7.

159. "Farnam Ecstatic Over Early Results of Massachusetts No-Fault Program," Business Insurance, (April 26, 1971), 10.

160. "Farnam Predicts Repeal of Mass. 40-Year Compulsory Auto Law," Insurance Advocate, (November 4, 1967), 6.

161. Findlay, Gordon S. "No-Fault Compensation for Auto Accidents," Best's Insurance News, (December, 1968), 64-66.

162. "First Returns on 'No-Fault'," Omaha World Herald, (April 26, 1971).

163. "Focus on Basic Protection," Best's Insurance News, LXVIII, (November, 1967), 10, 64-65.

164. Fournier, Frank W. "No-Fault System: Social Protection Insurance: A New Approach to an Old Problem," Insurance Counsel Journal, (January, 1971), 139-45.

165. Fournier, Frank W. "Social Protection Insurance — A New Approach to an Old Problem," Best's Review, (Prop./Liab. ed.), (February, 1971), 18, 20.

166. Franklin, Chanin & Mark, "Accidents, Money and the Law: A Study of the Economics of Personal Injury Litigation," 61 Colum L. Rev., (1961), 1, 34.

167. Fuchsberg. "Lawyers View Proposed Changes," 1967 U. Ill. L. For. 565.

168. Gallup, George. "The Gallup Poll: No-Fault Car Insurance Wins Favor Initially," The Kansas City Star, (April 22, 1971), 15.

169. Gallup, George. "Gallup Poll: Reaction Favorable to No-Fault Plan," Omaha World Herald, (April 22, 1971), 13.

170. "Getting the Answer to the Auto Problem Will Take Time, Study, Careful Analysis," The Weekly Underwriter, (December 2, 1967), 19.

171. Ghiardi, James D. "Automobile Insurance: The Rockefeller-Stewart Plan," Insurance Counsel Journal, (July, 1970), 324-33.

172. Ghiardi, James D. "Report of the Defense Research Institute," Insurance Counsel Journal, (January, 1971), 27-29.

173. Gilkenson, Stephen. "First No-Fault Plan Did Produce That 'Windfall'," Business Insurance, (April 26, 1971), 1-2.

174. "Gilmore Reaffirms Merits of Auto No-Fault Program," The National Underwriter, (June 5, 1970), 5.

175. "Glens Falls Prepared to 'Aggressively Pursue' Evolutionary or Revolutionary Steps to Correct Auto Insurance Situation," Insurance Advocate, LXXVIII, November 25, 1967).

176. "Glens Falls Supports INA on Keeton-O'Connell Type Approach," Insurance Advocate, LXXVIII, (October 28, 1967).

177. "Gordon Cites Flaws in Auto Tort System, But Hits Total No-Fault," Insurance Advocate, (January 23, 1971), 5, 23.

178. "Govt. Approach to No-Fault is Debate Trigger," The National Underwriter, (March 26, 1971), 1, 37.

179. Grad, Frank B. "Recent Developments in Automobile Accident Compensation," Columbia Law Review, (March, 1950).

180. Green, John. "Automobile Accident Insurance Legislation in the Province of Saskatchewan," Journal of Comparative Legislation and International Law, Vol. XXXI, (1949).

181. Griffith, Robert W. "Some Observations on 10 Years of Experience with Compensation Without Fault Auto Coverage," Best's Fire and Casualty News. (January, 1968), 21-24.

182. "Guaranteed Benefits: An Experiment in Reform," Journal of American Insurance, (January-February, 1968), 2-5.

183. "Guaranteed Benefits for Auto Victims," Underwriters Review, (November, 1967), 19.

184. "Guaranteed Benefits in Auto Accidents Urged," National Observer, (November 20, 1967), 6.

185. " 'Guaranteed Benefits' Plan for Compensating Auto Accident Victims Unveiled by Mutual Organization," Insurance Advocate, (November 18, 1967), 16-17.

186. Haase, Robert D. "The High Price of Highway Tragedy," The Journal of Insurance Information, (July-August, 1967), 33-35.

187. Harkavy. "Comparative Negligence: The Reflections of a Skeptic," 43 A.B.A.J.1115, (1957).

188. "Hartford Group Sends No-Fault Brochure to Policyholders in Mass.," Insurance Magazine, (March 15, 1971), 49.

189. "Hart-Magnuson No-Fault Bill Introduced in U.S. Senate," Insurance Advocate, (February 27, 1971), 3, 14.

190. Harwayne, Frank. "Insurance Cost of Automobile Basic Protection Plan in Relation to Automobile Bodily Injury Liability Costs," 53 Cas. Actuarial Society Proceedings 122, (1966).

191. Harwayne, Frank. "Insurance Costs of Basic Protection Plan in Michigan," 1967 U. Ill. L. For. 479.

192. Hashmi, Sajjad A. "The Problem of the Uninsured Motorist: A Proposed Solution," The Journal of Risk and Insurance, XXXIV, No. 3, (September, 1967), 363-370.

193. Haywood, Egbert L. "Evolution, Not Revolution," Insurance Law Journal, (November, 1967), 670-678.

194. Hodosh, Frederick R. "Auto Compensation Plans and the Claim Man," (Bryn Mawr, Pennsylvania: American Institute for Property and Liability Underwriters, March 13, 1968).

195. Hofstadter and Pesner. "A National Compensation Plan for Automobile Accident Cases," 22 Record of N.Y.C.B.A. 615, 618, (1967).

196. Hold, William T. "Critique of Basic Protection for the Traffic Victim – The Keeton-O'Connell Proposal," The Insurance Law Journal, (February, 1968), 73-83.

197. Hold, William T. "DOT's Study is a Mixed Bag of Research Findings, Hold Says," The National Underwriter, (November 30, 1970), 1.

198. "House and Senate Units Vie for No-Fault Spotlight," Insurance Advocate, (April 17, 1971).

199. "House Unit Calls Auto Insurance 'Slow, Incomplete and Expensive'," Business Insurance, (October 30, 1967), 6.

200. "How Auto Repairs Inflate Your Insurance Bill," Journal American Insurance, (November-December, 1969).

201. "How 18 Leading Auto Insurers Answered the Celler Committee," Best's Fire and Casualty News, (December, 1967), 10-14.

202. "How to Waste $2 Million," Business Insurance, (April 12, 1971), 16.

203. "Howell Suggests American Companies 'Look at Canadian Auto Plan as Possible Answer' to Auto Assigned Risk Plans' Problems," The Weekly Underwriter, (November 2, 1968), 5, 12.

204. "Hubbs Strongly Backs No-Fault," The National Underwriter, (June 12, 1970), 32.

205. "Illinois Auto Insurance Reform Plan Unveiled; Fast Payment a Part," Wall Street Journal, (April 7, 1971), 8.

206. "Illinois Limited No-Fault Proposal Called 'Acute Disappointment'," The National Underwriter, (April 16, 1971), 4, 5.

207. "Illinois Unveils Reform of Auto Reparations Payments," Insurance Advocate, (April 17, 1971), 6, 26.

208. "INA Asks Auto Claim Plan Like Keeton-O'Connell," National Underwriter, (October 13, 1967), 29.

209. "INA Issues Call to Action to Change Present System of Auto Insurance," The Weekly Underwriter, (October 14, 1967), 5, 8.

210. "INA No-Fault Plan Explained; Company Sees it as 'Best Solution'," Insurance Advocate, (April 10, 1971), 10.

211. "Injury Claims Down 50% Under Mass. No-Fault," The National Underwriter, (February 12, 1971), 1, 35.

212. Institute of Judicial Administration. Calendar Status Study – 1969, State Trial Courts of General Jurisdiction, Personal Injury Jury Cases, vi-vii, (1969).

213. "Insurance: A Timid Step Toward Reform," Time, (March 29, 1971), 82, 84.

214. "Insurance and the Automobile – An Analysis of an Explosive Situation," The Journal of Insurance Information, (January-February, 1968), 18-32.

215. "Insurance Claims In 'No-Fault' Drop," New York Times, (April 24, 1971).

216. "Insurance Commissioners 99th Meeting: Hogerty of Maine Authorized to Form Task Force to Set Up Auto Insurance Reform Plan," Insurance Magazine, (January, 1971), 36.

217. "The Insurance Crisis: Risks Without Takers," Newsweek, (March 22, 1971), 80, 82, 87-88.

218. "Insurance: Finding Fault With 'No-Fault' Rates," Business Week, (August 29, 1970), 24.

219. Insurance Information Institute. Awareness of and Attitude Toward a New Kind of Automobile Insurance – Research Findings Prepared for the Insurance Information Institute on Behalf of the American Insurance Association (ORC Caravan Surveys, Inc., November, 1968).

220. "Ins. Lawyers Hear of NAII Auto Plan; Discuss Oil Field Liability," The National Underwriter, (February 26, 1971), 4, 5.

221. "Insurance: Politics at Fault," Time, (August 31, 1970), 66.

222. "Insurance: The Road to Reform," Consumer Reports, (April, 1971), 223-26.

223. "Insurers, Govt. Seen Responding to Key Auto Ills," The National Underwriter, (November 17, 1967), 1, 32.

224. "Iowa Department Approves 'No-Fault' Filing by Preferred Risk Mutual: First in Nation," Insurance Advocate, (April 5, 1969), 6.

225. "Is Auto Insurance Meeting the Public's Need?" Journal of Insurance Information, XXVI, No. 2, (March-April, 1965), 18-23.

226. Jaffe. "Damages for Personal Injury: The Impact of Insurance," 118 Law & Contemp. Prob. 219, (1953).

227. Jaffe, Alfred I. "Points and Viewpoints: Closing Ranks — And Compromises," Insurance Magazine, (February 1, 1971), 28.

228. James. "An Evaluation of the Fault Concept," 32 Tenn. L. Rev., (1964-65), 394, 397.

229. James and Law. "Compensation for Auto Accident Victims: A Story of Too Little and Too Late," 26 Conn. B. J. 70, 79-80, (1952).

230. Jeffrey, Walter P. "Is Automobile Insurance Doing the Job?" Underwriters Review, (November, 1967), 16-18.

231. Johnson, H. Clay. "Problems of Automobile Claims Administration," Best's Insurance News, Vol. 67, No. 5, (September, 1966), 32.

232. "Jones Hails Canadian Switch to No-Fault Auto Insurance," The Weekly Underwriter, (November 23, 1968), 13.

233. Jones, T. Lawrence. " 'No-Fault' Auto Insurance: Reply to Critics," Wall Street Journal, (December 24, 1968).

234. Jones, T. Lawrence. "Proposed: A New Auto Insurance System," Journal of Insurance Information, (January-February, 1969).

235. Jones, T. Lawrence and Paul S. Wise. "Two Views on No-Fault Compensation," Independent Agent, (March, 1969), 40-42.

236. ,Jordan, Chandler C. "Hearings Examine 'No-Fault' Auto Reparations Plan Proponents: 'Cuts Premiums'; Critics: 'Un-American'," Insurance Advocate, (May 9, 1970), 3, 13, 33.

237. Jordan, Leo. "Dramatic Changes in Property and Auto Fields are Coming. Will the Industry Lead the Way?," Insurance Magazine: Redbook, Vol. 72, No. 3, (1971), 13.

238. "K-O Type Liability Bill Introduced in New York," Insurance Advocate, LXXIX, (February 17, 1968), 10.

239. "Keeton Calls Auto Compensation System a 'Dismal Failure'; Execs Refute His Views," The Weekly Underwriter, (October 21, 1967), 14-15.

240. Keeton, R. Compensation Systems: The Search for a Viable Alternative to Negligence Law 43-44. (1969 Supplement to Seavey, Keeton and Keeton's Cases and Materials on Torts (2d ed. 1964) and to Keeton's Basic Insurance Law, (1960).

241. "Keeton-O'Connell Basic Protection Insurance Plan: What's It All About?" Mutual Review, (November, 1967), 14-15.

242. "Keeton-O'Connell Bill Watched with Close Attention," The National Underwriter, (September 1, 1967), 1, 29.

243. "Keeton-O'Connell Not Best Nor Only Auto Dilemma Alternative, Connecticut Committee is Told," Insurance Advocate, (February 3, 1968), 12, 34.

244. "Keeton-O'Connell Plan Fares Very Poorly When Scrutinized by Panel," The National Underwriter, (November 6, 1967), 34.

245. "Keeton-O'Connell Plan Seen As Academic Exercise: Assumptions About Claims, Claimants Are Disputed," Insurance Advocate, (September 23, 1967), 10, 26.

246. "Keeton-O'Connell Plan Won't Be Accepted, Counsel Predicts," Underwriters Review, (June, 1967), 12.

247. "Keeton-O'Connell 'Reform' Plan Presented to the Boston Board," Insurance Advocate, (January 21, 1967), 10, 19.

248. "Keeton-O'Connell 'Significant Reform' Challenged," Insurance Advocate, (October 7, 1967), 4, 26-27.

249. "Keeton Outlines Proposal for Reforming Auto Insurance," The National Underwriter, (December 16, 1966), 2, 22-23.

250. "Keeton Plan is Myth Compounded by Academicians, Jeffrey Says," The National Underwriter, (October 13, 1967).

251. Keeton, Robert E. "Automobile Insurance Reform," Best's Fire and Casualty News, (December, 1966), 34-36.

252. Keeton, Robert E. and Jeffrey O'Connell. After Cars Crash. (New York: Dow Jones-Irwin, Inc., 1967).

253. Keeton, Robert E. and Jeffrey O'Connell. "Auto Insurance: Crack-Up Ahead," The Nation, (April 17, 1967), 498-500.

254. Keeton, Robert E. and Jeffrey O'Connell. "Automobile Insurance Underwriting Through the Perspective of the Basic Protection Plan," Best's Fire and Casualty News, (May, 1967), 22-23, 79-85.

255. Keeton, Robert E. and Jeffrey O'Connell. "Basic Protection — A New Plan of Automobile Insurance," Journal of Risk and Insurance, (October, 1967), 539-548.

256. Keeton, Robert E. and Jeffrey O'Connell. "Basic Protection for Traffic Accident Victims," The Annals of the Society of C.P.C.U., (Spring, 1967), 219-232.

257. Keeton, Robert E. and Jeffrey O'Connell. Basic Protection for the Traffic Victim: A Blueprint for Reforming Automobile Insurance. (Boston: Little, Brown and Company, 1965).

258. Keeton, Robert E. "Pro: Basic Insurance Protection," The American Agency Bulletin, (November, 1967), 16, 28, 30-31.

259. "Keeton, Sargent Present Opposing Views of Proposed Basic Auto Protection Plan," National Underwriter, (October 13, 1967), 51-52.

260. "Keeton, Sargent Present Opposing Views of Proposed Basic Auto Protection Plan," National Underwriter, (October 13, 1967), 51-52.

261. Kemper, James S., Jr. "Automobile Insurance: The Criteria for Survival," 1968 Ins. L. J. 264.

262. Kemper, James S., Jr. "Automobile Insurance: A National Approach," Kemper Insurance Reports. Address before the National Association of Mutual Insurance Agents, Washington, D.C., October 22, 1969.

263. "Kemper Exec Rejects Keeton-O'Connell Plan as Panacea for All Auto Insurance Problems," Weekly Underwriter, (March 23, 1968), 29.

264. Kemper, James S., Jr. Automobile Insurance: The Politics of Surrender. A special report published by Lumbermen's Mutual Casualty Company. Address presented before the Northern California C.P.C.U. Chapter, San Francisco, November 1, 1968.

265. Kemper, James S., Jr. "The Keeton-O'Connell Basic Protection Plan: Is It Reform or Regression?", The Weekly Underwriter, Three-part article, (October 21, 1967), 27-28; (October 28, 1967), 31-32; (November 4, 1967), 31-32.

266. Kemper, James S., Jr. "The Keeton-O'Connell Basic Protection Plan: Is It Reform or Regression?", The Weekly Underwriter, Three-part Article, (October 21, 1967), 27-28; (October 28, 1967), 31-32; (November 4, 1967), 31-32. Also published as a Kemper Insurance Report — address before the Auto Claims National Conference, University of Illinois, College of Law, Champaign, October 2, 1967.

267. "Kemper President Refutes Claimed Benefits of Keeton-O'Connell Auto Comp. Program," The Weekly Underwriter, (October 14, 1967), 5, 8.

268. "Key Legislators Cool to Rockefeller 'No-Fault' Auto Plan; Industry Reaction is Mixed, Criticism Sharp," Insurance Advocate, (February 21, 1970), 5, 26-27.

269. Kimball. "Automobile Accident Compensation Systems — Objectives and Perspectives," U. Ill. L. For., (1967), 370, 373-74.

270. Klein. "A Consumer Looks at the Complete Personal Protection Plan for Automobile Insurance," Address before the American Insurance Association, (May 20, 1969).

271. Kluwin, John A. "Analysis of Criticisms of the Fault System," Insurance Law Journal, (July, 1967), 389-394.

272. Knowlton. "Insure the Driver Plan," 3 Federation Insurance Counsel Q. 77, (1953).

273. Kobler, Jay. "Consumer Surveys Show Scant Support for 'No-Fault' Concept, N.Y. Hearing is Told," The Weekly Underwriter, (June 27, 1970), 5, 12-13.

274. La Brum. "Quo Vadis," A.B.A. Ins. Negl. & Comp. L. Sect. Proceedings 87, (1961).

275. "The Law," Time, LXXXVIII, (August 25, 1967), p. 48.

276. "Lawmakers Await Word on Insurance," Omaha World Herald, (March 18, 1971), 25.

277. "Lawyer Criticizes Non-Fault Theory for Auto Insurance," The National Underwriter, (August 4, 1967), 15.

278. "Lemmon Predicts 'No-Fault' Auto Comp System Will Not Be Adopted in U.S.," The Weekly Underwriter, (November 16, 1968).

279. "Lemmon Predicts No-Fault Concept Won't Be Adopted," The National Underwriter, (April 2, 1971), 1, 16.

280. "Lemmon Sees No Valid Case for Change of Entire System," The National Underwriter, (November 6, 1967), 1, 32-33.

281. Leslie, E.C. "The Saskatchewan Automobile Insurance Act," Journal of the American Judicature Society, (June, 1960).

282. Levin, A. and Woolley, E. Dispatch and Delay: A Field Study of Judicial Administration in Pennsylvania, (1961).

283. Levinson, Charles F. "Business Insurance/Perspective: Keeton-O'Connell is Not the Answer," Business Insurance, (December 11, 1967), 19-20.

284. Levit, Victor B. "The Legal Climate for Insurance," The Insurance Law Journal, (November, 1970), 623-27.

285. Linden, A. Report of the Osgoode Hall Study on Compensation for Victims of Automobile Accidents. Chs. III, IV, and IX. Ontario: 1965.

286. Logan, Ben H. "Insure the Driver," (Kansas City, Missouri: an undated paper, about 1967).

287. Lyons, John F. "Insurance Innovation: A Canadian Province Finds a Way to Slash Auto Crash Litigation," Wall Street Journal, (November 7, 1967).

288. Mackey. "The Automobile Insurance and Law Problem in 1968: As Viewed by an Official of Government," A.B.A. Ins. Negl. & Comp. Sect. Proceedings 657, (1968).

289. MacKay, James R. "An Overview of Possible Solutions to the Ever Growing Problem of the Automobile," Weekly Underwriter, (December 2, December 9 and December 16, 1967). Also appears in a special pamphlet published by Fireman's Fund American Insurance Companies, address before Oregon Association of Insurance Agents, September 15, 1967.

290. "MAIIA&B Supports Personal Injury Protection Plan Based on 'No-Fault' and Compulsory Medical Payment," Insurance Advocate, (January 24, 1968), 6, 27.

291. Maisonpierre, Andre. "DOT Automobile Reparations Study," Best's Review, (January, 1971), 24, 26, 56-58.

292. "Major Mass. Producers Endorse 'No-Fault' Auto Plan," Insurance Advocate, (March 15, 1969), 8, 29.

293. Mann, Guy E. "Compensating Auto Accident Victims," Best's Insurance News, (December, 1965), 18.

294. Marryott, Franklin J. "Report of the Subcommittee on Automobile Claims Compensation Proposals," Insurance Counsel Journal, Vol. XXXV, No. 2 (April, 1968), 202.

295. Marryott, Franklin J. "A Response to the Critics of the Automobile Insurance-Tort System: New Concepts to Protect Traffic Victims," Insurance Law Journal, (June, 1967), 350-356.

296. Marryott, Franklin J. "The Tort System and Automobile Claims: Evaluating the Keeton-O'Connell Proposal," 52 A.B.A.J. 639, (1966).

297. Marshall. "Arbitration: A Report of First Impression," 22 Shingle (publication of of the Philadelphia Bar Association) 21, (1959).

298. "Mass. Gets No-Fault Law – and Boycott Continues," The National Underwriter, (August 21, 1970), 1, 49.

299. "Massachusetts House Passes Keeton-O'Connell Plan," Insurance Advocate, (August 19, 1967), 5.

300. "Mass. Insurers Urge 'Guarded Optimism' in Early Drop in 'No-Fault' Claims," The Weekly Underwriter, (March 20, 1971), 8.

301. "Mass. No-Fault Bill Changes Prompt Cos. To Stop Writing," The National Underwriter, (August 14, 1970), 1, 4.

302. "Massachusetts 'No-Fault' Perpetual Renewal Provision is Modified," Insurance Advocate, (August 29, 1970), 6, 17.

303. "Mass. Producers Offer Own Auto No-Fault Program," The National Underwriter, (May 21, 1971), 1, 39.

304. "Massachusetts Supreme Court Rules 'Freeze' on Compulsory Auto Rates 'Unconstitutional'," Insurance Advocate, (January 2, 1971), 8.

305. McCormick, Roy C. "Non-Fault Auto Insurance: Essential Features Explained," Rough Notes, (November, 1967), 16-17, 98.

306. McCrae, William. "Legal Aspects of Automobile Compensation," Journal of Insurance, (June, 1962), 185-197.

307. McCullogh, Roy C. "The Automobile Underwriter and No-Fault," Best's Review, (Prop./Liab. ed.), (May, 1970), 36, 38, 40, 42.

308. McNary, Herbert L. "Basic Protection," Insurance Advocate, (September 9, 1967), 3.

309. Miley, Frank R. "A Simple Reform System for Automobile Insurance," Underwriters Review, (February, 1968), 9-11, 20-21.

310. Morris, John D. "Congress to Spur Bill on Insurance," New York Times, (April 18, 1971).

311. Morris. "Liability for Pain and Suffering," 59 Colum. L. Rev. 476, (1959).

312. Morris, John D. "Volpe Backs a 'No-Fault' Compromise," New York Times, (April, 21, 1971).

313. Morris and Paul. "The Financial Impact of Automobile Accidents," 110 U. Pa. L. Rev. 13, (1962).

314. Moynihan, Daniel Patrick. "Next: A New Auto Insurance Policy," New York Times Magazine, (August 27, 1967), 76, 82-83.

315. Moynihan, Daniel P. "The Soulless City," American Heritage, Volume XX, No. 2, (February, 1969).

316. Mumey, Glen. "Auto Insurance Reform," Journal of Risk & Insurance, (June, 1970), 185-90.

317. Murray, J.B.M. "Inverse Liability Auto Accident Insurance," Best's Fire and Casualty News, (October, 1967), 76-88.

318. "Mutual Agent Leader Calls for NAIC Panel to Make Impartial Analysis of Mass. Auto Rates," Insurance Magazine, (September, 1970), 6, 17.

319. "Mutual Agents Warned of 'Hell Breaking Loose'," The National Underwriter, (March 12, 1971), 1, 6.

320. "Mutual Companies Propose Guaranteed Benefits for Auto Victims," Underwriters Review, (November, 1967), 19.

321. "NACSA Asks 'Common Sense' Auto Liability Reform, Study of Keeton-O'Connell Plan," Insurance Advocate, (December 2, 1967), 16, 32.

322. National Association of Independent Insurers Proceedings of 22nd Annual Meeting Held at the Americana Hotel, Bal Harbour, Florida, October 30-November 2, 1967.

323. National Association of Independent Insurers. "NAII Auto Insurance Principles in Brief," News, (December 1, 1967).

324. National Association of Independent Insurers. Special News Release. News, (December 7, 1967).

325. National Association of Independent Insurers. Statement of Policy. Chicago, November, 1967.

326. National Association of Insurance Commissioners. Automobile Insurance Study Background Memorandum in Report of the Special Committee on Automobile Insurance Problems 106, (1969).

327. "NAIA Adopts Action Programs to 'Guide' Changes in Insurance," The Weekly Underwriter, (February 27,   ), 14.

328. "NAIA, Company Associations Meet on Auto Reform," Insurance Advocate, (January 23, 1971), 4, 19.

329. "NAIA Endorses State-by-State Reform of Auto Insurance System," The Weekly Underwriter, (March 27, 1971), 8.

330. "NAIA National Board of State Directors Says 'No' to AIA's No-Fault Auto Plan," The Weekly Underwriter, (February 15, 1969), 5, 16.

331. "NAIA Reaffirms Opposition to 'No-Fault'," Insurance Advocate, (February 8, 1969), 5, 29.

332. "NAIA Supports Modified No-Fault Auto System," Insurance Advocate, (January 30, 1971), 5, 12.

333. "NAIA Survey Finds Public Favors 'No-Fault' Concept," Insurance Advocate, (February 8, 1969), 5, 22.

334. "NAIA and Three Industry Organizations Exchange Ideas on Auto Insurance Reform," Insurance Magazine, (February 15, 1971), 26.

335. "NAIB Favors Limited Auto Reform, Unlimited Safety Emphasis," The Weekly Underwriter, (April 3, 1971), 10.

336. "NAII, AMIA Both Submit New Auto Insurance Plans," The National Underwriter, (December 18, 1970), 1.

337. "NAII Speakers Hit Failure of Auto System Critics to Make Valid Case, Provide Suitable Alternatives," Insurance Advocate, (November 4, 1967), 6, 26-27.

338. "New AMIA Acturial Study Contends 'No-Fault' Not Real Cost Saver," Insurance Advocate, (July, 1969), 12, 27.

339. "New Form of Coverage Designed to Meet Auto Problems Described," The National Underwriter, (August 25, 1967).

340. "New Look in Auto Coverage," Business Week, (April 20, 1968), 87-90.

341. "New Plan for Auto Insurance," U.S. News & World Report, (November 4, 1968), 10-11.

342. "N.Y. Auto Plan Held Unfair to the Careful," The National Underwriter, (October 16, 1970), 21.

343. "N.Y. Bar Assn. Has Taken No 'Stand' on Keeton-O'Connell, " Insurance Advocate, LXXVIII, (October 28, 1967).

344. New York City Bar Association. Report of the Committee on State Courts of Superior Jurisdiction, Partial Elimination of Jury Trials in Civil Cases — New York Simplified Procedure Versus the Pennsylvania System, 18 Record of N.Y.C.B.A., (1963).

345. New York City Bar Association. Report of the Committee on State Courts of Superior Jurisdiction, Variations on the Pennsylvania System: Partial Elimination of Jury Trials in Civil Cases Through Compulsory Arbitration Before Panels of Lawyers, 22 Record of N.Y.C.B.A. 638, (1967).

346. "N.Y. Lawyers Unit Assails No-Fault Auto Cover Plans," The National Underwriter, (February 14, 1969).

347. "N.Y. No-Fault Reform Bills 'Far Short' of Need," Insurance Advocate, (April 3, 1971), 6, 15.

348. "N.Y. Senate Insurance Committee Reports Gordon No-Fault Bill," Insurance Advocate, (April 10, 1971), 8, 22.

349. New York State. Committee on Automobile Accident Reparations, Report to the Executive Committee of the New York State Bar Association, (1970).

350. New York State Independent Mutual Insurance Agents. Report of the Auto Insurance Study Committee, (September 18, 1968).

351. New York State Insurance Department. Automobile Insurance . . . For Whose Benefit? A report to Governor Nelson A. Rockefeller (New York: State of New York Insurance Department, 1970). The "Stewart Plan."

352. New York State. Meeting of New York Governor's Committee on Compensating Victims of Automobile Accidents, Transcript, 82, 84 (February 29, 1968).

353. New York State. Meeting of New York Governor's Committee on Compensating Victims of Automobile Accidents, Transcript, 143-46, (April 16, 1968).

354. "N.Y. Times Accused of Bias in No-Fault Plan Coverage," The National Underwriter, (May 1, 1970), 8.

355. "Nixon Asking States Revise Car Insurance," Omaha World Herald, (March 18, 1971), 1.

356. "Nixon to Ask Delay on Auto Insurance Reform by Congress," Wall Street Journal, (March 18, 1971), 12.

357. "No-Fault Auto, DOT Study are Viewed by NAII," The National Underwriter, (November 30, 1970), 1, 24, 26, 28.

358. "No-Fault Auto Hearing Covers Familiar Ground," The National Underwriter, (May 7, 1971), 1, 37-38.

359. " 'No-Fault' Characterized as 'No-Justice' Plan," Insurance Advocate, (May 2, 1970), 5, 33.

360. "No-Fault Comp in Auto Claims Being Tested," Insurance Adjuster, (April, 1968), 7.

361. "No-Fault Criticized by Texas Attorney," The National Underwriter, (June 5, 1970), 5.

362. "No-Fault, Group Auto Legislation Introduced by Hart," Insurance Advocate, (September 19, 1970), 5, 26-28.

363. " 'No-Fault' Insurance," Aide, Vol. 2, No. 1, (Winter, 1971), 11-13.

364. "No-Fault Insurance Cuts Claims 36 Percent," Omaha World Herald, (April 23, 1971).

365. "No-Fault Insurance Reaction Mixed," Omaha World Herald, (March 18, 1971), 34.

366. "No-Fault Law Reduced Claims," Omaha World Herald, (May 3, 1971).

367. "No-Fault Legislation Cropping Up Everywhere; Gordon Filing Bill," Insurance Advocate, (February 27, 1971), 6, 14.

368. "No-Fault Plan in Illinois Exempts Fleet Vehicles," Business Insurance, (April 12, 1971), 1-2.

369. "No-Fault Programs Gain Momentum in Countrywide Action," The National Underwriter, (April 9, 1971), 1.

370. "No-Fault Seen as Threat to Established Insurance Values," The National Underwriter, (May 30, 1969), 2, 24.

371. " 'No-Fault' System Lauded in Statement by Jones to Senate Antitrust Unit; Public Sentiment is Viewed," Insurance Advocate, (January 3, 1970), 6, 21.

372. "No-Fault System Opposed in Canada," Insurance Advocate, (February 8, 1969), 22.

373. "No-Fault 'Unsound', Public Will Balk, NY Brokers Charge," The National Underwriter, (May 1, 1970), 22.

374. North Dakota State. Report on Automobile Liability Insurance by Legislative Research Committee of North Dakota, (North Dakota: Bismarck, 1950).

375. Nova Scotia. Report of the Nova Scotia Royal Commission on Automobile Insurance, 2 vols. (Halifax, Nova Scotia: The Queen's Printer, September 30, 1957).

376. O'Connell, Jeffrey. "Basic Protection for the Traffic Victim — A Blueprint for Reforming Automobile Insurance." (Address given at Mutual Claims Conference, Sheraton Hotel, Philadelphia, Pennsylvania, May 8, 1967).

377. O'Connell, Jeffrey. "Crisis in Car Insurance Cause & Cure," (Remarks at the Fall Seminar of the Iowa Association of Mutual Insurance Agents, at the Hotel Roosevelt, Cedar Rapids, Iowa, on September 30, 1967).

378. O'Connell, Jeffrey. "Is it Really Immoral to Pay Regardless of Fault?" Trial Magazine, (October-November, 1967), 18-20.

379. O'Connell, Jeffrey. "A New Approach to Auto Insurance," America, (June 10, 1967), 830-831, 834.

380. O'Connell, Jeffrey and Wallace Wilson. "Public Opinion Polls on the Fault System: State Farm versus Other Surveys," The Insurance Law Journal, (May, 1970), 261-75.

356

381. O'Malley, Thomas D. No Fault: Facts and Fallacies. (Florida, May 7, 1971). Author: Florida State Insurance Commissioner.

382. "Partial 'No-Fault' Auto Insurance System to be Proposed by Nixon Administration," Wall Street Journal, (March 15, 1971), 8.

383. Paulson, Morton C. "Automobile-Insurance Reform to Get a Shove," National Observer, (March 15, 1971), 8.

384. "Plaintiff Attorney Eyes the Situation," The National Underwriter, (March 17, 1967).

385. "A Plan for Auto Insurance Reform," 33 Consumer Reports, (1968), 10.

386. "The Plans Proliferate," Independent Agent, (March, 1969), 32-34.

387. Plant. "Damages for Pain and Suffering," 19 Ohio St. L. J. 200, (1953).

388. "Poll Finds No-Fault Insurance Backed When it is Understood," New York Times, (April 22, 1971).

389. Pollard, Robert S. W. "Compensation for Road Injuries," The Plain View, (London: Stanton Coit House, 13 Prince of Wales Terrace, Winter, 1957).

390. Popa, Robert A. "Auto Unsurance," Detroit (Mich.) News, (February 27, 1969).

391. Powers, Samuel J., Jr. "Report of the Automobile Compensation Committee of the Defense Research Institute," Insurance Counsel Journal, Vol. XXXV, No. 2, (April, 1968), 208.

392. "Preferred Risk Mut. Reports on Partial Answer to Auto Problem," The National Underwriter, (September 4, 1970), 1, 31.

393. "President's Special Message to Congress – The American Consumer," February 6, 1968, 114 Cong. Rec. H. 810 (H. Doc. No. 248, 90th Cong., 2d Sess., 1968).

394. Proceedings of the meeting of the American Mutual Insurance Alliance – Mutual Claims Conference, held at the Sheraton Hotel, Philadelphia, Pennsylvania, on May 8-10, 1967.

395. "Prof. O'Connell Continues Blasting Auto Insurance System: NAII Rep Refutes Him," Property Insurance, (November 11, 1967), 5, 17.

396. "The Prospects for Reform," Consumer Reports, (June, 1970), 342-43.

397. "Regulators Cook Up Their Own No-Fault Plans," Business Insurance, (April 26, 1971), 3.

398. "Regulatory Climate in 'Some' States Major Obstacle for Auto Insurance," Insurance Advocate, (November 18, 1967), 17.

399. Reinmuth, Dennis F. "Automobile Insurance in the 1970's: Decade of Change," Michigan Business Review, (May, 1971), 23-26.

400. Rennie, Robert A. "An Experiment in Limited Absolute Liability," Journal of Insurance, (June, 1962), 177-184.

401. "Results of A.S.I.M.'s Attitude Survey RE: The Automobile Insurance Problem," Risk Management, (March, 1971), 49-50.

402. "Retention of Liability System Seen," Journal of Commerce, (March 29, 1968).

403. "Rhode Island Governor Says Auto Insurance System is 'Intolerable'; Seeks K/O'C Type Plan," The Weekly Underwriter, (January 13, 1968), 75.

404. Ridgeway, James. "Auto Insurance: No Risks Preferred," New Republic, (February 22, 1969), 18-21.

405. Ridgeway, James. "Underground War on Auto Insurance," The New Republic, (December 3, 1966), 19.

406. "Robert T. Richie Explains Results of No-Fault Study," National Underwriter, (November 3, 1970).

407. "The Road to Auto Insurance Reform," Journal of American Insurance, (May-June, 1969), 11-13.

408. Roberts, A. Addison. "Casualty Insurance: Which Way is it Turning?" Journal of Insurance Information, XXVIII, No. 2 (March-April, 1967), 20-22.

409. "Rockefeller No-Fault Proposal Introduced in N.Y.," Insurance Advocate, (March 6, 1971).

410. Rokes, Willis Park. Automobile Indemnification Proposals — A Compendium. (University of Nebraska at Omaha, 1968).

411. Rokes, Willis Park. Human Relations in Handling Insurance Claims. (Homewood, Illinois: Richard D. Irwin, Inc., 1967).

412. Rokes, Willis Park. "Whatever Became of the DOT Study?" Insurance Field, Vol. 100, No. 2, (February, 1971), 12.

413. Rokes, Willis P. "The Saskatchewan Plan," The Journal of Insurance, XXIX, No. 3, (September, 1962).

414. Rokes, Willis Park. "Saskatchewan Plan Analyzed in Terms of Philosophy, Changes, Performance," The National Underwriter, 66th year, No. 42, (October 19, 1962), 32-36.

415. Rokes, Willis Park. "The Saskatchewan Plan," Best's Insurance News, (fire and casualty edition), Vol. 63, No. 10, (February, 1963), 57-63, 86-88.

416. Rosenberg. "Comparative Negligence in Arkansas; A 'Before and After' Survey," 13 Ark. L. Rev. 89, (1959).

417. Rosenberg. "Court Congestion: Status, Causes and Proposed Remedies," The American Assembly, the Courts, the Public, and the Law Explosion, (1965).

418. Rosenberg and Schubin. "Trial by Lawyer: Compulsory Arbitration of Small Claims in Pennsylvania," 74 Harv. L. Rev. 448, (1961).

419. Rosenberg & Sovern. "Delay and the Dynamics of Personal Injury Litigation," 59 Colum. L. Rev., (1959), 1115.

420. Ross, H. Laurence. "A Review Article on Basic Protection for the Traffic Victim," The Journal of Risk and Insurance, XXXIV, No. 4, (December, 1967), 647-652.

421. Ross, H. Laurence. Settled Out of Court: The Social Process of Insurance Claims Adjustment (Chicago: Aldine Publishing Company, 1970).

422. "The Row Over 'No-Fault' Auto Insurance," The Kiplinger Magazine, (May, 1969), 7-11.

423. Sargent, David J. "Con: Basic Insurance Protection," The American Agency Bulletin, (November, 1967), 17, 33-36.

424. Saskatchewan Government Insurance Office. Saskatchewan's Automobile Accident Insurance Act Explained, (1965 Revised Edition).

425. "Second 'No-Fault' Compulsory Auto Bill Filed in Wisconsin," Insurance Advocate, (March 1, 1969).

426. "Sen. Hart Submits Bill for No-Fault Auto, Group Sales," The National Underwriter, (September 18, 1970), 1, 57.

427. "Settling the Claim Without the Blame," Business Week, (November 11, 1967).

428. Shaw, Bruno. "No-Fault Merits Seen as Proven Under Limited British Version," The National Underwriter, (June 12, 1970), 1, 26, 27.

429. Sheehan, Robert. "A New Road for Auto Insurance," Fortune, (November, 1967), 170-172, 218, 221-222.

430. "Should Victims of Auto Accidents be Paid Irrespective of Blame?" The National Observer, (October 28, 1968).

431. Slattery, Thomas J. "AIA Exec. Scores Industry Critics of Auto Proposal," The National Underwriter, (December 27, 1968), 1, 4.

432. "Social Protection Plan in P.R. Is K-O'C and Then Some: No Policies, No Underwriting and No Commissions," The Weekly Underwriter, (July 6, 1968), 50.

433. "Special Report on the Industry's No. 1 Problem — Auto Claims," Insurance Management Review, (July 3, 1965), 23-30.

434. Slattery, Thomas J. "Trial Lawyer, Agent Clash on Keeton-O'Connell Plan," The National Underwriter, (March, 1968), 1, 41.

435. Smith, Bradford, Jr., and A. Addison Roberts. "Two Chief Executives Urge Reevaluation of Industry Positions on Auto Insurance," Best's Insurance News, Vol. 67, No. 8, (December, 1966), 10-12.

436. "State Farm Releases Results of Policyholders Poll; Heavy Majority for 'Negligence' Concept Retention," Insurance Advocate, (December 13, 1969).

437. "Stewart 'No-Fault' Proposal Attacked at Hearing; Feeling Mixed on Need for Revolutionary Change," Insurance Advocate, (March 14, 1970), 5, 33-34.

438. "Stringfellow Says Action by State Groups Key to Auto Compensation," Insurance Magazine, (January 1, 1970), 40.

439. "Study Needed on Auto Accidents and Compensation of Victims," Motorland — The California State Automobile Association News Journal, (June, 1967), 2.

440. "Suggest Regional Approach to Auto Ills," The National Underwriter, (November 20, 1970), 27.

360

441. "Suit Filed in Massachusetts on January 2 Accident to Test 'No-Fault' Constitutionality," Insurance Advocate, (January 16, 1971), 3.

442. "Surprising Amount of Interest Seen in New Auto Plans," The National Underwriter, (August 25, 1967), 1, 17.

443. "Ten Companies to Experiment with Guaranteed Benefits Auto Plan," The National Underwriter, (February 23, 1968), 1.

444. "Text of Rockefeller Sponsored 'No-Fault' Proposal," Insurance Advocate, (March 14, 1970), 31.

445. "Trade Groups Split Over Conn. Proposal for No-Fault Auto," The National Underwriter, (April 9, 1971), 43.

446. "Trailblazing Value of Keeton-O'Connell Compensation Plan Emphasized at Forum," The Weekly Underwriter, (May 20, 1967), 16.

447. "Trial Lawyers Plan to Bar Reform in Auto Insurance," The Omaha World Herald, (May 6, 1971).

448. U.S. Congressional Record, 91st Cong., 2nd Sess., 1970, Vol. 116, No. 159.

449. U.S. Congressional Record, 92nd Cong., 1st Sess., 1971, Vol. 117, No. 22.

450. U.S. Department of Health, Education and Welfare. Report of the Secretary's Advisory Committee on Traffic Safety, 4, 1968.

451. U.S. House of Representatives, Subcommittee on Commerce and Finance, Comm. on Interstate and Foreign Commerce. Hearings on H.J. Res. 958, 90th Cong., 2nd Sess., 1968, ser. 90-30.

452. U.S. House of Representatives, Staff of Antitrust Subcommittee, Comm. on the Judiciary. Automobile Insurance Study, 90th Cong., 1st Sess., 1967, 76-87.

453. U.S. Senate, Subcommittee on Antitrust and Monopoly, Comm. on the Judiciary. Hearings on S. Res. 233, 90th Cong., 2nd Sess., 1968, 714-18. Testimony of Pennsylvania Insurance Commissioner, David Maxwell.

454. "Unreason in the Law of Damages: The Collateral Source Rule," 77 Harv. L. Rev. 741, (1964).

455. "An Unusual System for Insuring Autos," U.S. News & World Report, (October 2, 1967), 51.

456. Varnum. "Comparative Negligence in Automobile Cases," 24 Insurance Counsel Journal 60, (1957).

457. Velie, Lester. "Why Insurance is So Hard to Get," Reader's Digest, (April, 1971), 83-88.

458. "Vestal Urges State Solution to Auto Reparations Problem," NAII News Memo, (May 11, 1971), 1, 7.

459. "Viewpoint on Keeton-O'Connell Proposal," The Cooperator, (February, 1968).

460. "Volpe Proposal for State Reform of Auto Reparations Endorsed by Two Associations," Insurance Magazine, (April 15, 1971), 44.

461. Wallace, Hugh D. "Communications: A Proposed Solution to the Problem of Compensating Automobile Accident Victims," Journal of Risk & Insurance, Vol. 35, (1968), 141-46.

462. Warne. "Let's Hear From the Insurance Consumer," 36 Ins. Couns. J. 494, (1969).

463. "Warns Keeton-O'Connell Plan Would Clog Courts, Induce Fraud," National Underwriter, (February 9, 1968).

464. Warren, Earl. "The Problem of Delay: A Task for Bench and Bar Alike," 44 A.B.A.J. 1043, (1958).

465. "Washington News Letter: No-Fault Insurance Still has Everyone in Capital Intrigued," Insurance Magazine, (April 15, 1971), 58.

466. "What the Public Thinks About Auto Insurance," Journal of American Insurance, (November-December, 1969).

467. "What They're Saying About the Keeton-O'Connell 'Basic Protection Plan'," Mid-America Insurance, (December, 1967), 31-34.

468. "Why Auto Insurance Costs More and More," U.S. News & World Report, (September 12, 1966), 60-63.

469. "Widespread No-Fault Inevitable, Niggeman Tells Chicago Press," The National Underwriter, (November 13, 1970).

470. Wise, Paul S. "Automobile Insurance: An Experiment in Reform," (Speech made before the Mutual Insurance Technical Conference, Chicago, November 13, 1967).

471. Wise, Paul S. "Automobile Insurance: Which Road Toward Reform?" American Mutual Insurance Alliance. Address at the Mutual Insurance Technical Conference, Hotel Roosevelt, New York City, November 20, 1968.

472. Wise, Paul S. "The Federal Government's Increasing Role in Insurance and Risk," American Mutual Insurance Alliance. Address before the American Management Association Insurance Conference, Drake Hotel, Chicago, Illinois, November 11, 1970.

473. Wise, Paul S. "The Guaranteed Benefits Program: Experiment in Auto Insurance Claims Paying Reform," Weekly Underwriter, (March 9, 1968), 35-36.

474. Zeisel, H., H. Kalven and B. Buchholz. Delay in the Court, 1959.

475. Zelermyer. "Damages for Pain and Suffering," 6 Syr. L. Rev. 27, (1954).

476. Chastain, James J. An Evaluation of Group Property Insurance (doctoral dissertation, University of Illinois, 1962).

477. Chastain, James J. "Group Property and Liability Insurance," Group Insurance Handbook, ed. Davis W. Gregg (Homewood, Illinois: Richard D. Irwin, 1965), 732.

478. "Clashing Views Mark the Senate Auto Hearings," The National Underwriter, (May 21, 1971), 1, 44-46.

479. Columbia University. Council for Research in the Social Sciences, Report by the Committee to Study Compensation for Automobile Accidents, (Columbia University, 1932).

480. "Connecticut Independent Agents Introduce Modified No-Fault Auto Insurance Measure," The Weekly Underwriter, (February 13, 1971).

481. "Connecticut Stock Agents Back Cotter's Auto Plan," The Weekly Underwriter, (February 15, 1969), 5, 16.

482. "Consumers Union, Others Call for Federal No-Fault," The National Underwriter, (April 30, 1971), 1, 24.

483. Coombs, Eugene G., Jr., and Davis, Phillip M. "Massachusetts No-Fault Law," Insurance Adjuster, (July, 1971), 16-18.

484. Corrado, Janet. "WIS Agents on No-Fault — 'No Comment'," The National Underwriter, (May 28, 1971), 1, 34-35.

485. "Cotter Auto Plan Rejected in Conn.," The National Underwriter, (May 30, 1969), 2.

486. Crowell, Fred C., Jr. The Insurance Field Newsgram, (June 11, 1971), 1.

487. "Delaware to be Second State with No-Fault Insurance," New York Times, (May 30, 1971).

488. DeWolf, George E., Jr. "NAII's Dual Protection Plan," Underwriters Review, (June, 1971), 25.

489. "Drive for Cheaper Auto Insurance," U.S. News & World Report, (July 26, 1971), 22.

490. Ehrenzweig, Albert A. "Full Aid" Insurance for the Traffic Victim — A Voluntary Compensation Plan, (Berkeley: University of California Press, 1954).

491. Farnam, C. Eugene. "Massachusetts — Cradle of 'No Fault'," Weekly Underwriter, (January 23, 1971), 31.

492. "Faulty No-Fault?", The Weekly Underwriter, (December 5, 1970).

493. "Few States Expected to Act This Year on Proposals for No-Fault Insurance," New York Times, (May 9, 1971), 60.

494. "Florida No Fault Auto Enactment Becomes Law; Governor Seeks Test Case," Insurance Adjuster, (July, 1971), 7.

495. Gibson, William S. "Real No-Fault," Underwriters Review, (June, 1971), 24.

496. Graham, Fred P. "High Court Curbs Penalties for Uninsured Drivers," New York Times, (May 25, 1971).

497. Green, Leon. Traffic Victims — Tort Law and Insurance (Evanston, Illinois: North-western University Press, 1958).

498. Hall, Ira D. "Massachusetts No-Fault and Its Impact on Claims Handling," Proceedings — NAII 17th Annual Workshop, (April 19-21, 1971), 98-105.

499. "Hart Urges National Compulsory Auto Insurance," Weekly Underwriter, (July 3, 1971), 14.

500. "Illinois Adopts Modified Fault Plan; Vestal Calls It An 'Historic' Step," NAII News Memo, (July 12, 1971).

501. "Illinois Auto Insurance Reform Plan Unveiled; Fast Payment a Part," The Wall Street Journal, (April 7, 1971), 8.

502. "Illinois Study Unit Moves to Forestall Federal Insurance Takeover," The Insurance Advocate, (March 27, 1971), 5.

503. "Industry Critical, Press Applauds AIA Auto Plan," Best's Insurance News, (December, 1968), 10, 74-78.

504. "Insurance Bill Passed by Illinois Legislature Includes 'No-Fault' Plan," The Wall Street Journal, (July 1, 1971).

505. "Is Fault Outmoded?" Journal of American Insurance, (January-February, 1969).

506. Jennings, John P. "Federal No-Fault Has Good Chance in '71, Says AIA's Gilmore," The National Underwriter, (May 21, 1971), 1, 28-29.

507. "Jones Labels Auto Insurance System Slow, Unfair, Too Costly," Weekly Underwriter, (December 5, 1970), 10.

508. Joost, Robert H. "No-Fault Insurance: Yes," New York Times, (May 29, 1971).

509. Julien, Alfred S. "No-Fault Insurance: No," New York Times (May 29, 1971).

510. Karr, Albert R. "Mr. Volpe's Surprising Achievements," Wall Street Journal, (May 25, 1971), 16.

511. Kelly, Howard J. "Group Auto Insurance – Is It For Real?" Proceedings – NAII 17th Annual Workshop, (April 19-21, 1971), 74-80.

512. Kemper, James S., Jr. "Automobile Insurance Regulation and Reparations Systems," Kemper Insurance Reports. Testimony before the Senate Commerce Committee, Washington, D.C., May 12, 1971.

513. "Kemper Predicts No-Fault by States; Asks Tax Deduction for Automobile Owners," The Weekly Underwriter, (June 5, 1971), 5.

514. "Lemmon Blasts No-Fault Concept Program of Automobile Claims Compensation," The Weekly Underwriter (November 2, 1968), 5.

515. Lemmon, Vestal. "Implications of the DOT Study and the Hart/Magnuson Proposal," Proceedings – NAII 17th Annual Workshop, (April 19-21, 1971), 1-6.

516. Lydon, Christopher. "Volpe to Bid States Adopt 'No-Fault' Auto Insurance," The New York Times, (March 15, 1971), 74.

517. Mair, Ian D. "Current Trends in Canadian Automobile Business Including the Facility," Proceedings – NAII 17th Annual Workshop, (April 19-21, 1971), 58-65.

518. "Massachusetts Adopts 'Limited' No-Fault Plan'," F.T.D. Newsletter, (September, 1970), 81.

519. "Mass. Auto Insurers Ask Court to Void 15% No-Fault Cut," The National Underwriter, (September 18, 1970), 1.

520. Maynes, E. Scott, and Williams, C. Arthur, Jr., Ed. Fault or No Fault? (University of Minnesota, March, 1971). Proceedings of the National Conference on Automobile Insurance Reform.

521. Mertz, Arthur C. "The Purpose and Role of the NAII Dual Protection Plan," Proceedings – NAII 17th Annual Workshop, (April 19-21, 1971), 18-30.

522. "Michigan, Illinois Reform Plans Win Strong Support from NAII," NAII News Memo, (June 11, 1971).

523. "Modified No-Fault is 'Not Enough', Nationwide Vice President Testifies," The Weekly Underwriter, (June 5, 1971), 10.

524. Montgomery, Jim. "Puerto Ricans Applaud No-Fault Car Insurance Initiated Last Year," The Wall Street Journal, (May 20, 1971), 1, 17.

525. Morris, John D. "Nixon Auto Insurance Plan Leaves Reform to States," The New York Times, (March 19, 1971).

526. Morris, John D. " 'No-Fault' System Gains in Congress," The New York Times, (May 16, 1971).

527. "NAMIA Head Says Mass. Gov. Hurting Auto Cover Reform," The National Underwriter, (May 14, 1971), 1, 46.

528. National Association of Independent Insurers. "Modified 'No-Fault' Insurance Passes," NAII Press Samplings, (July 6, 1971).

529. Nationwide Mutual Insurance Company. No-Fault Insurance – A Ready Reference, (Columbus, Ohio, April, 1971).

530. "No-Fault Bill Signed Into Law by Delaware's Governor Peterson," The Weekly Underwriter, (June 5, 1971), 5.

531. " 'No-Fault' Insurance Setting New Patterns," Omaha World Herald, (March 18, 1971).

532. "No-Fault Passed in Florida; Governor Expected to Sign Measure," The Weekly Underwriter, (June 12, 1971), 5.

533. "No-Fault Plans Hit More Potholes," Business Week, (May 15, 1971), 44.

534. "No Fault System Gains in Congress," New York Times, (May 16, 1971), 88.

535. "No Fault: Will It Work?" New York Times, (April 4, 1971), 34.

536. "Professor of Insurance, Fireman's Fund Executive in Exchange on No Fault," Insurance Adjuster, (July, 1971), 20.

537. Rokes, Willis Park. Automobile Physical Damage Insurance Affiliates of Sales Finance Companies, (Ann Arbor, Michigan: University Microfilms, Inc., The Ohio State University, December, 1959).

538. Rokes, Willis Park. "Climate for Successful Negotiations," Federated Claims Bulletin, Volume 14, No. 6, (June, 1968), 114.

539. Rokes, Willis Park. "Climate for Successful Negotiations," The Independent Adjuster, Volume 32, No. 3, (Spring, 1968), 6.

540. Rokes, Willis Park. "Consumerism and Insurance," The Journal of Risk and Insurance, Vol XXXVIII, No. 1, (March, 1971), 119.

541. Rokes, Willis Park. "Memory Taints Witness Credibility," Adjusters' Reference Guide, (Louisville, Kentucky: Insurance Field Publishing Co., fourth quarter, 1970-71), Technical Section reprint.

542. Rokes, Willis Park. "Memory Taints Witness Credibility," Trial, (Cambridge, Mass.: American Trial Lawyers Association, August/September, 1969), 46.

543. Rokes, Willis Park. "Psychological Factors Governing the Credibility of Witnesses, Part I," The Insurance Law Journal, No. 541, (February, 1968), 84.

544. Rokes, Willis Park. "Psychological Factors Governing the Credibility of Witnesses, Part II," The Insurance Law Journal, No. 542, (March, 1968), 150.

545. Rokes, Willis Park. "Psychological Factors Governing the Credibility of Witnesses, Part III," The Insurance Law Journal, No. 543, (April, 1968), 269.

546. Rokes, Willis Park. "Psychological Factors Governing the Credibility of Witnesses," Journal of the Beverly Hills Bar Association, Volume 2, No. 10, (November, 1968), 10-28.

547. "Sargent's Estimate of No-Fault 'Savings' Not Based on Insurance Dept. Evaluation," The Weekly Underwriter, (June 5, 1971), 11.

548. "Sargent's No-Fault Savings Estimate Not Based on Dept. Evaluation: Aide," The National Underwriter, (June 4, 1971), 1, 31.

549. Slattery, Thomas J. "AIA Exec. Scores Industry Critics of Auto Porposal," The National Underwriter, (December 27, 1968), 1, 4.

550. Saskatchewan Government Insurance Office. Saskatchewan Auto Insurance Guide, 1971.

551. "Soaring Repair Cost, 'Fragile' Cars Still Affecting Auto Claims: I.I.I.," The National Underwriter, (September 18, 1970), 1.

552. "Strong Opposition Voiced on Compulsory Auto Bill in Delaware," Insurance Advocate, Vol. 81, No. 10, (March 7, 1970), 5.

553. "Urge U.S. Force States to Adopt Uniform No-Fault," The National Underwriter, (May 14, 1971), 1, 8.

554. Webb, Bernard L. "Collective Merchandising of Automobile Insurance," The Journal of Risk and Insurance, Vol XXXVI, No. 4, (September, 1969), 465.

555. Webb, Bernard L. Mass (Collective) Merchandising of Automobile Insurance, (Santa Monica: Insurors Press, 1969).

556. Whiteman, Roy M. "Dual Protection and the Claimsman," Proceedings — NAII 17th Annual Workshop, (April 19-21, 1971), 92-97.

557. "Why the High Cost of Auto Insurance," The New York Times, (April 4, 1971), 34.

558. Wilson, Larry. "Omahan Supports Insurance Reform," Omaha World Herald, (June 29, 1971), 4.

INDEX

INDEX OF NAMES

INDEX OF NAMES

INDEX OF SUBJECTS

INDEX OF SUBJECTS

ABOUT THE AUTHOR

Dr. Willis Park Rokes is Professor of Business Administration and Chairman of the Dept. of Insurance, The University of Nebraska at Omaha. An attorney, a CPCU, CLU, and member of many professional and educational organizations, Dr. Rokes is author of numerous articles on insurance subjects, author of the well-known text "Human Relations in Handling Insurance Claims," editor of *Adjusters Reference Guide,* and monthly columnist in the *Insurance Field* magazine.